Adam in Seventeenth Century Political Writing in England and New England

Designed to contribute to a greater understanding of the religious foundations of seventeenth century political writing, this study offers a detailed exploration of the significance of the figure and story of Adam at that time. The book investigates seventeenth-century writings from England and New England, examining writings by Roger Williams and John Eliot, Gerrard Winstanley, John Milton, and John Locke, to explore the varying significance afforded to the Biblical figure of Adam in theories of the polity. In so doing, it counters over-simplified views of modern secular political thought breaking free from the confines of religion, by showing the diversity of political models and possibilities that Adamic theories supported. It provides contextual background for the appreciation of seventeenth-century culture and other cultural artefacts and feeds into current scholarly interest in the relationship between religion and the public sphere and in stories of origins and Creation.

Julia Ipgrave is Senior Research Fellow in the Department of Humanities at the University of Roehampton, UK.

Adam in Seventeenth Century Political Writing in England and New England

Julia Ipgrave

LONDON AND NEW YORK

First published 2017
by Routledge
2 Park Square, Milton Park, Abingdon, Oxon OX14 4RN

and by Routledge
711 Third Avenue, New York, NY 10017

Routledge is an imprint of the Taylor & Francis Group, an informa business

© 2017 Julia Ipgrave

The right of Julia Ipgrave to be identified as author of this work has been asserted by her in accordance with sections 77 and 78 of the Copyright, Designs and Patents Act 1988.

All rights reserved. No part of this book may be reprinted or reproduced or utilised in any form or by any electronic, mechanical, or other means, now known or hereafter invented, including photocopying and recording, or in any information storage or retrieval system, without permission in writing from the publishers.

Trademark notice: Product or corporate names may be trademarks or registered trademarks, and are used only for identification and explanation without intent to infringe.

Library of Congress Cataloging-in-Publication Data

Names: Ipgrave, Julia author.
Title: Adam in seventeenth century political writing in England and New England / by Julia Ipgrave.
Description: New York; London: Routledge, 2016. | Includes bibliographical references and index.
Identifiers: LCCN 2016017607
Subjects: LCSH: Political science—Great Britain—History—17th century. | Political science—New England—History—17th century. | Adam (Biblical figure) | Adam (Biblical figure)—In literature. | Bible and politics.
Classification: LCC JN191 .I64 2016 | DDC 320.01—dc23
LC record available at https://lccn.loc.gov/2016017607

ISBN: 978-1-472-46384-5 (hbk)
ISBN: 978-1-315-56558-3 (ebk)

Typeset in Sabon
by codeMantra

Printed and bound in Great Britain by
TJ International Ltd, Padstow, Cornwall

for Lawrence and Sylvia Bailey
my originals

Contents

Abbreviations used for key primary texts
and collected editions ix
Acknowledgements xiii

    Introduction: 'First the original' 1

1   Material, method and occasion 8

2   Conversations about Adam 42

3   Roger Williams and John Eliot's Indian writings and the story of Adam 85

4   Gerrard Winstanley and Adam for Millennium and Commonwealth 120

5   John Milton's Adam and the English nation 144

6   John Locke, Adam and the original of power 169

7   Eliot, Williams, Winstanley, Milton and Locke: Man's state and ongoing story 197

Bibliography 205
Index 219

Abbreviations used for key primary texts and collected editions

John Eliot

BN – *A Brief Narrative of the Progress of the Gospel amongst the Indians in New England, in the Year 1670* (London: John Allen, 1670).

ET – *The Eliot Tracts: with Letters from John Eliot to Thomas Thorowgood and Richard Baxter*, ed. Michael P. Clark (Westport, CT: Praeger Publishers, 2003).

    CSS – *The Clear Sun-shine of the Gospell breaking forth upon the Indians in New England* [Thomas Shepard].

    DB – *The Day Breaking if Not the Sun Rising of the Gospell with the Indians in New England.*

    FAP – *A Further Account of the Progress of the Gospel amongst the Indians of New England.*

    LAM – *The Light Appearing More and More towards the Perfect Day* [ed. Henry Whitfield].

    LC – *The Learned Conjectures of Mr John Eliot Touching the Americans, of New and Notable Consideration.*

    LFM – *A Late and Further Manifestation of the Progress of the Gospel amongst the Indians in New England.*

    SW – *Strength out of Weaknesse, Or a Glorious Manifestation of the Further Progresse of the Gospel among the Indians in New England.*

    TR – *Tears of Repentance: Or, a Further Narrative of the Progress of the Gospel amongst the Indians in New England.*

ID – *John Eliot's Indian Dialogues: A Study in Cultural Interaction*, ed. Henry W. Bowden and James P. Ronda (Westport, CT: Greenwood Press, 1980).

IG – *The Indian Grammar Begun.* (Cambridge: Marmaduke Johnson, 1666).

x *Abbreviations used for key primary texts and collected editions*

JEI – John Eliot and the Indians 1652–1657 Being Letters Addressed to Rev. John Hamner of Barnstable, England (New York: The Adams and Grace Press, 1915).

CC – The Christian Commonwealthor The Civil Policy or The Rising Kingdom of Jesus Christ (London: Livewell Chapman, 1659).

Robert Filmer

Sir Robert Filmer's Patriarcha and Other Writings, ed. Johann P. Somerville (Cambridge: Cambridge University Press, 1991).

> *ALMM – Anarchy of a Limited or Mixed Monarchy.*
>
> *OG – Original of Government.*
>
> *PA – Patriarcha.*

John Locke

ECHU – An Essay Concerning Human Understanding, 1690, ed. P. Nidditch (Oxford: Oxford University Press, 1975).

LCT – A Letter Concerning Toleration, ed. James Tully (Indianapolis: Hackett Publishing, 1983).

PN – A paraphrase and notes on the Epistles of St. Paul (London: Thomas Tegg, 1823).

Some Thoughts Concerning Education and *Of the Conduct of Understanding*, ed. Ruth W. Grant and Nathan Tarcov (Indianapolis: Hackett Publishing Company, 1996).

> *STCE – Some Thoughts Concerning Education.*
>
> *OCU – Of the Conduct of Understanding.*

TRC – The Reasonableness of Christianity (London: C and J Rivington, 1824).

Two Treatises of Government, ed. Peter Laslett (Cambridge: Cambridge University Press, 1960).

> *1TG – First Treatise of Government.*
>
> *2TG – Second Treatise of Government.*

John Milton

CPW – Complete Prose Works of John Milton, ed. Maurice Kelley, tr. John Carey (New Haven: Yale University Press, 1973).

> *DDC – De Doctrina Christiana (A Treatise on Christian Doctrine).*

Abbreviations used for key primary texts and collected editions xi

PTW – *Milton Poetical Works*, ed. Douglas Bush (Oxford: Oxford University Press, 1966).

    PL – *Paradise Lost.*

PW – *Prose Writings* (London: Dent, 1974).

    AR – *Areopagitica.*

    DDD – *The Doctrine and Discipline of Divorce.*

    RCG – *The Reason of Church Government.*

    RE – *Of Reformation in England.*

    REW – *The Ready and Easy Way to Establish a Free Commonwealth.*

    TKM – *The Tenure of Kings and Magistrates.*

TE – *Tractate on Education* Vol III, Part 4 The Harvard Classics (New York: P.F.Collier and Son 1909–14; Bartleby.com 2001).

Roger Williams

BT – *The Bloudy Tenent of Persecution, for Cause of Conscience discussed in a Conference between Truth and Peace* (London: J. Haddon, 1848).

CLE – 'Mr. Cotton's Letter Examined and Answered' in *The Bloudy Tenent of Persecution for Cause of Conscience Discussed and Mr. Cotton's Letter Examined and Answered* (1848 edition reprinted), ed. Edward Bean Underhill (Montana: Kessinger Publishing, 2004).

CWRW – *The Complete Writings of Roger Williams,* ed. Perry Miller *et al.* (New York: Russell and Russell, 1964).

    CNC – *Christenings Make Not Christians.*

    ED – *The Examiner Defended in a Fair and Sober Answer.*

    HM – *The Hireling Ministry None of Christ's.*

Key – *A Key into the Language of America* (London: Gregory, 1643).

LRW – *Letters of Roger Williams 1632–1682,* ed. John Russell Bartlett, (Providence: Narragansett Club, 1874).

Gerrard Winstanley

CW – *The Complete Works of Gerrard Winstanley*, ed. by Thomas N. Corns, Ann Hughes, David Loewenstein (Oxford, Oxford University Press, 2009).

    AHC – *An Appeal to the House of Commons, Desiring their Answer: Whether the Common-people Shall Have the Quiet*

Enjoyment of the Commons and Waste Land etc [Gerrard Winstanley, John Barker and Thomas Star].

BD – *The Breaking of the Day of God.*

DPO – *A Declaration from the Poor Oppressed People of England.*

FB – *Fire in the Bush* LFX – *A Letter to the Lord Fairfax, and his Councell of War.*

LFP – *The Law of Freedom in a Platform: Or True Magistracy Restored.*

MG – *The Mysterie of God, Concerning the Whole Creation.*

NLR – *The New Law of Righteousness.*

NYG – *A New-yeer's Gift for the Parliament and Armie.*

SP – *The Saints Paradice.*

TLH – *Truth Lifting up his head above Scandals.*

TLS – *The True Levellers Standard Advanced.*

Acknowledgements

For the completion of this book I am indebted to Tom Betteridge and Nicole Pohl (both at the time at Oxford Brookes University) whose stimulating conversations, searching questions and valuable insights greatly supported my study of Adam. I would also like to thank Bill Gibson and Brian Cummings for their detailed reading of my text and their helpful comments. My thanks are also due to the Colonial Dames of America in Rhode Island and Providence Plantations for their kindness in allowing me to spend three summers while I was working on this project, in George Berkeley's colonial home, Whitehall in Middletown, RI – a setting appropriate for and conducive to my thinking and writing. Finally, I would like to thank my husband Michael for his patient reading and commenting on this book at various stages and his interest and encouragement throughout.

Introduction
'First the original'

In 1642, just two miles distance from Say-Brook Fort on the mouth of Connecticut River, a Pequot sagamore[1] lay dying. His last thoughts were fixed on the story of Adam's creation and his fall, a tale that told him of 'the *Condition* of *all mankind*, & his *Own* in particular' and that, according to his deathbed claim, was *'never out of my heart'*.[2] In London in 1683, an English military colonel and knight ascended the scaffold to meet a traitor's death, the clinching second witness against him an anti-monarchist treatise based on the argument that Adam as created was a man like any other with no *natural* dominion over his fellows. About 20 years before, a blind poet had risen early in the half-light of winter mornings to dictate an epic poem which, through the telling of Adam's story, asserted Eternal Providence and justified the ways of God to men.[3] Wequash, Algernon Sidney and John Milton represent a diversity of seventeenth-century people for whom Adam was foundational in understandings of the human condition, controversial in politics and pivotal in the divine story of Redemption. In his person and his interactions Adam was the first pattern for man, for society and for man's relationship with his Creator. His character and story brought together those key ingredients for seventeenth-century political theory: man as he is, man in his dealings with others, God's purposes for man. This book investigates seventeenth-century writings, including detailed studies of five focus authors, to explore the varying significances afforded to Adam in the theorising of the polity through the turbulent times that characterised the century's middle years and the fluctuations of the later Stuart regimes. It was a time of experimentation in forms of government, whether in the various forms of monarchy or republic in old England, the forms of polity created in New England, or the divergent models of church governance that sparked controversies on both sides of the Atlantic.[4] In the discussions and debates that accompanied these experiments theology and politics were tightly interwoven.

The book has its focus on political thinking. In its approach it acknowledges J. G. A. Pocock's distinctions among the political scientist who studies the rise and role of an organised political language in a society's political activity, the political philosopher who extracts ideas worth using as the foundation of other abstract political propositions, and the political

2   Introduction

historian who studies the language used in a particular society to discuss political problems for the light it throws on the character of that society.[5] While not denying the value of the other two approaches, this study identifies most closely with the third of these reading the texts as texts-in-context. What relevance for modern politics might be found in these seventeenth-century writings is a subject for other studies. This book recognises that the language of politics is not that of a single disciplined mode of intellectual inquiry but 'the language which men speak for all purposes and in all the ways in which men may be found articulating and communicating as part of the activity and culture of politics'.[6] Care has thus been taken not to impose a false coherence on an author's writing – this will be particularly evident in the chapter on Gerrard Winstanley where the approach recognises the internal inconsistencies in the author's corpus and does not attempt to reconcile them – a contrast with the classic treatment of Winstanley by Christopher Hill and others who have read into Winstanley's writings a proto-Marxist ideology. Easy and anachronistic correlations of 'radical' thinking and 'radical' politics are avoided – Robert Filmer's arguments, for example, were innovative, but his political conclusions were essentially conservative. Care will also be taken not to isolate what appears to be a political thread and discard scriptural, theological content. Pocock offers the case of Thomas Hobbes's *Leviathan*, which has often been stripped by interpreters of its Biblical exegesis and eschatology; Locke's *Treatises of Government* have received similar treatment. A variety of genres of political commentary, in prose and verse, will be included. For this study I have selected a wide range of works that have direct relevance to the political thinking of the focus authors including genres not normally associated with political commentary today. John Milton's epic poem, *Paradise Lost,* is the most striking of these. Roger Williams's *A Key into the Language of America* includes verses, a phrasebook in the Narragansett language, ethnographic material, and autobiographical detail. John Locke's theological treatise, *The Reasonableness of Christianity,* is used in addition to his more obviously political writings. The interweaving of different threads of learning will be acknowledged with particular attention to the close interdependency of theological and political thought. The focus on various strands of learning in Chapter 2 demonstrates how a plurality of these (including reformed theology, travel writing, classical philosophy and humanism) were woven into interpretations of Adam and his relevance to the ordering of society.

The distinctive thrust of this book is its argument that, far from posing a restrictive frame, interest in Adam and his story in Genesis supplied foundations for a variety of political possibilities. Fundamental to this variety are the complexities of the Genesis text and the exegetical freedom that enabled Christian thinkers to find differing emphases and derive differing conclusions from their engagement with it. In an age of political uncertainty, novelty and strife, political thinkers brought to this fecund text the burning questions, 'who is man?' and 'where is he bound?' My analysis is informed by a categorisation (original to this study) of the different significances given to the figure of Adam in answer to these questions. The categories themselves are grouped into two clusters: Adam as state and Adam as story. In the first cluster, Adam signifies the state of mankind. The categories in this cluster are concerned with Adam as he is and build concepts and models of the polity on this. They are static understandings and fall into three interpretive groupings (nature, condition and decree) according to whether the emphasis is on what Adam possesses through his essential nature as man at Creation, on his condition subsequent to his fall or on the additional gifts and commands he has been given by God's will. Adam as man and Adam as patriarch both relate to this cluster of categories. The interpretation of Adam as man (his created nature or fallen condition) works with fixed understandings of man's state; it relates the Adam of Genesis to the observation and experience of humanity and to principles (such as equality and liberty) established through Biblical exegesis and the use of reason. The interpretation of Adam as patriarch also uses a combination of observation of human society (especially of the family) and Biblical exegesis but to draw different conclusions. It tends towards a more conservative politics that distinguishes between the Adamic patriarch and the rest of humankind subject to this patriarchal rule. In both cases there may also be a strand of political pragmatism, interested in what works given the nature of the human beings with whom we are dealing.

A second cluster of categories sees Adam less in terms of man's state and more as story. One story is genealogical, with an emphasis on the biological descent of humanity from the first ancestor; at a time of increasing encounters with other cultures in far off places, it provoked interesting discussions about the universal origins of mankind in its diverse forms. Another story presents the ordering of human society in the light of a continuing and progressive journey from Fall to Redemption. It is teleological with more interest in what will be than what is. It is dynamic, looks for signs of movement and transformation in current society and raises questions about the role of human political activity in bringing that end nearer. An understanding of human society as framed by the events of Fall and Redemption is Christian orthodoxy and shared by all the authors in the study, but in the conceptualisation and organisation of the polity there is a significant difference according to whether the dominant interest is in human society as it is now (in the meantime) or in human society as it is to be transformed at the end of time. The political turmoil of the seventeenth century, and the experiences of migration to a New World, as well as calculations giving millennial significance to particular dates, encouraged an interest in the latter and a sense that the time was now. At the same time a concern for stability in the face of political unrest and civil strife favoured the former. The dialogue between these two interests is evident in the writings of the authors being studied. One point of tension is that between a heightened expectation

4 *Introduction*

of the imminent resolution of the story that began with Adam and disappointment when the weight of man's fallen condition appears to hinder the hoped-for transformation.

The first chapter is concerned with the material, methods and occasions for this seventeenth- century exploration of Adam's significance. The first part of the chapter focuses on readings of the Biblical text and the second on the historical context. It begins with a brief introduction to the Biblical stories of Adam, as they appear in Genesis and as they are interpreted by Paul and embedded in the western Christian mainstream (Catholic and Protestant). It highlights the inconsistencies and tensions, in the original story and in its Christianisation, that make it such rich material. Categories that will be important through the book are drawn out of these distinctions. The chapter then proceeds to consider the different approaches to the text that the seventeenth-century authors had available to them in the context of reformed Christianity, suggesting that a combination of guidance and freedom in Biblical exegesis led to a commonalty of themes and diversity of interpretations. It shows how political readings of the Bible were encouraged in English Protestant thought alongside a close association of Biblical histories with contemporary events and indicates that an imitation of Biblical language and genres reinforced these influences. The second part of the chapter gives an overview of the times in which the authors were writing and to which they were applying Biblical readings. It considers both the political and religious order and the interrelations between them and identifies contemporary preoccupations – with legitimacy of sovereignty, with security and rights of person and property, with the direction of history, with expansion to new parts of the world and encounters with strange people, with freedom of religious conscience – that coloured interpretations and political applications of Adam's significance.

The second chapter introduces the contemporary conversations in which interpretations of Adam played a significant part, referring to prominent writings and thinkers of the time in addition to the authors discussed in this study. The presentation of the conversations is structured according to the categories of Adam as state (the pattern and condition of man and of polity) and Adam as story (Creation, Fall, Redemption, Restoration). Under a general heading of *Adam as state*, the conversations include discussions about patriarchalism, natural law and rights theories, covenant and conscience. Under *Adam as story*, they are concerned with millennial expectation, mystical discourses of the inner man and the incorporation of the American Indian into a shared narrative that begins in Eden.

The following four chapters form the bulk of the book. They take the writings of five selected authors for a more detailed study, trace the Adamic themes and consider how their interpretations of Adam informed or were informed by the authors' own political stances, noting both the internal logic and inconsistencies. The five authors selected for detailed attention are Roger Williams (c1603–1683), John Eliot (c1604–1690),

Gerrard Winstanley (1609–1676), John Milton (1608–1674) and John Locke (1632–1704). They have been chosen as exemplary rather than as representative of the writers and thinkers of the time. The inclusion of two New England authors alongside the English authors recognises a transatlantic community and the references made by authors on both sides of the Atlantic to happenings and experiences on the other side.[7] The New England experience has a particular pertinence to the Adamic theme because of the establishment of new political communities and the direct encounter with new peoples raising questions about shared ancestry and where these peoples fit within a universal story. Williams and Eliot both had close involvement with the Indians of New England. The five authors had in common with each other practical, as well as theoretical, involvement in politics. Milton and Locke both held government positions, and both found themselves at certain times in their careers in political opposition to the established order.[8] The other three authors were all involved in different ways in establishing their own political communities, Eliot with the foundation of his Indian praying towns, Williams with his settlement of Providence Plantations and the (particularly troublesome) settlement of Rhode Island, and Winstanley with his alternative digger community in Surrey. The authors were centrally placed within the politics of their time, and those of them who might appear as a challenge to, rather than part of, the dominant political order of their day, had not come adrift but were in direct dialogue with it and with key political figures within it. Williams's correspondence with the leaders of the Massachusetts Bay Colony and Winstanley's addresses to Fairfax and Cromwell are evidence of this. All the authors were writing in the context of points of change in political society and addressing these changes in their writings, and all drew on Biblical images and examples when doing so. The choice of authors often considered to be progressive in their political views counters the perception that Adamic doctrine tends towards political conservatism.[9] Their writings are positioned in relation to conservative positions, however, in particular through the prominence given to royalist Sir Robert Filmer's theories in Chapter 2.

Although there is not a strict chronological progression in the ordering of these four chapters, some concession to chronology has been made. The main political context of Chapter 4 (Winstanley) is the end of the Civil War and the years of the Commonwealth, that of Chapter 5 (Milton) is the time of transition back to monarchy with the Restoration, while the works of Locke that are the subject of Chapter 6 are written against the background of the 1689 Revolution and William III's reign. The writings of Williams and Eliot span much of this period, overlapping with the other authors. Positioning these New England authors and their Indian writings in Chapter 3, at the start of the detailed studies, means that the sequence commences with the broad canvas of Adam's significance across different nations before focusing in on his relevance to the English polity; it also reflects the movement of providential expectation to New England with the puritan migration and back to 'old' England with the political turmoil there and promised overthrow of the old order. More importantly for the book's structure, a comparison of the differing political theories of these New England writers has given an opportunity to present at the beginning contrasting interpretations of Adam, one that gives prominence to his state and one that gives prominence to his story, and the political implications of each. The chapter that follows both disturbs and throws new light on the distinctions between Adam as state and as story as it traces the interplay (and also disjunction) between different concepts of Adam employed by Winstanley to interpret the hopes and disappointments of the revolutionary years of the mid-seventeenth century. Chapter 5 follows Milton's project, through his epic poem *Paradise Lost* and his later political writing, to draw his countrymen into the story of Adam and urge them to work for the transformation of the English nation that it promises. The chapter on Locke takes us to the final years of the seventeenth century and a careful combination of scriptural exegesis and reason that interrogates the political significance of Adam establishes the will of God at the creation of man as the foundation for his natural state of liberty and of his political actions (establishment of the polity; resistance to tyranny) by which he exercises that liberty. Although the four detailed studies are alert to the playing out of the various categories of Adam as state and as story, care has been taken not to impose the categories as an interpretive framework, but to respect the integrity of the authors' writings and to structure each chapter in a way most suited to the readings that emerge. A final chapter draws together the Adamic themes as they emerge from the studies of the individual writers and takes their stories forward.

The focus is on Adam rather than on Eve, although there are occasional references to her when her presence affects understanding of Adam's role. She rarely held the central position frequently occupied by Adam in political discourse at the time, and her tale – though certainly worth telling and of particular interest to explorations of gender difference – is beyond the scope of the present study. There were some contemporary female voices that made themselves listened to, those of Mary Pocock and Anne Hutchinson for example, but the general masculine orientation of political and religious discourse is reflected in this study in the gender of the five selected authors and the adoption of the masculine language ('man', 'mankind' and so on) characteristic of the period. The application of inclusive language to this material would have distorted some of the meanings in the conversations and debates that are the content of the study. The seventeenth-century term 'Indian' will be used for the peoples variously known as 'American Indians', 'First Nation Americans', 'Native Americans', in order to maintain consistency between primary sources and the analysis.

Notes

1. A *sagamore* is the head of an Indian tribe.
2. As reported by his 'old friend' Roger Williams, in his Foreword to *Key*. Kristina Bross dedicates a chapter to the significance in American literature of the dying Indian's speech, in Kristina Bross, *Dry Bones and Indian Sermons* (Ithaca: Cornell University Press, 2004).
3. *PL* I, 25–6; For references to Milton's habits of composition see Barbara K. Lewalski, *The Life of John Milton: A Critical Biography* (Oxford: Blackwell, 2000), pp. 448–49.
4. Despite Scotland's close involvement in the political events of the century, Scottish authors have not been a focus. Scottish transatlantic migration really took off later than the period of study (the main destination before the Union being European) so the links that bound England to New England were stronger. T. M.Devine, *The Scottish Nation: A Modern History* (London: Penguin 2012), p. 25.
5. J. G. A. Pocock, *Politics, Language and Time: Essays on Political Thought and History* (New York: Atheneum, 1971), 'Machiavelli, Harrington and English Political Ideologies in the Eighteenth Century', p. 104.
6. Pocock, *op. cit*, 'Languages and their implications', p. 17.
7. The focus on England and New England (and lack of reference to Scottish activity, for example) reflects the strength of the relationship between these two parts of a transatlantic world. By comparison, Scottish migration before the middle of the seventeenth century had been directed towards Europe, and the shift from Europe to the Atlantic after this date was a slow one. T. M. Devine, *The Scottish Nation a Modern History,* London: Penguin, 2012, p. 25. Douglas Catterall has recorded the involvement of Scots in American ventures during the 1630–1660 period but as part of Dutch enterprises. Douglas Catterall, 'Interlopers in an Intercultural Zone? Early Scots Ventures in the Atlantic World 1630–1660' in *Bridging the Early Modern Atlantic World: People, Products and Practices on the Move,* edited by Caroline A. Williams (Farnham: Ashgate, 2009) pp. 75–96.
8. Milton was appointed Secretary for Foreign Tongues by the Council of State in March 1649; Locke was Secretary to the Council of Trade and Plantations (1673–74) and a member of the Board of Trade (1696–1700).
9. One example of this perception is found in Oren Levin-Walman's *Reconceiving Liberalism*, where he correlates Adamic doctrine with patriarchalism and portrays John Locke as a political progressive breaking free from the shackles of 'political Adamicism'. Oren M. Levin-Walman, *Reconceiving Liberalism: Dilemmas of Contemporary Liberal Public Policy* (Pittsburgh: Pittsburgh University Press, 1996), pp. 38–39. Another example is John Dunn's inability to give due credibility to Locke's political thinking because of the dependency of his thinking on belief in Adam and man's fallen state, a dependency he interprets as a 'harness' and 'ineluctable confinement'. John Dunn, *The Political Thought of John Locke: An Historical Account of the 'Two Treatises of Government'* (Cambridge: Cambridge University Press, 1969), pp. 263–64.

1 Material, method and occasion

The book

The original

'First for the original' are the opening words of Philip Hunton's discussion of political power (*A Treatise of Monarchy*, 1643).[1] They reflect a strong impulse in seventeenth-century political thinking to begin at the beginning, to go back to the original. This original could be understood in different ways corresponding to contemporary usage of the word. There was interest in origins as beginnings, not just as aetiological explanation (why we are as we are) but also in the narrative sense of setting something in motion, establishing a forward trajectory until we become what we were meant to be. There was also an interest in the other meaning of original as pattern, as model of what things should be. When the origins in question were traced right back to the beginnings of man's existence at Creation, the binding power of that pattern was particularly strong. If God is the prime mover, the way He fashioned humankind and human society is the way things should be. This study then follows the logic of seventeenth-century political thought by beginning as far back as it is possible to go with the first chapters of Genesis to identify what there is in these verses that helped to shape the theories and debates of that time.[2]

Chapters 1 to 3 of Genesis, chronicling the creation of the world and of mankind, Adam and Eve's paradisiacal existence in the garden, their fall and exile, are well-known for their inconsistencies (they present two variant stories of man's creation) and for theodical difficulties. Why did God create something that was good only to let it fall? What was the point of Adam and Eve's existence in Eden?[3] These tensions within the text give the passages the dynamism that makes them meet material for disputation and for formulation of a variety of conflicting political theories. In the seventeenth century a few bold scholars such as Hobbes and Spinoza went against accepted interpretations of the Bible by highlighting inconsistencies, contradictions and inaccuracies in the Pentateuch, and in the eighteenth century scholars were beginning to unpick the two accounts of Creation found in the first books of Genesis, the accounts that in the next century became known as P (Priestly) and J (Jahwist).[4] Most seventeenth-century readers of these texts worked from an understanding that the chapters somehow held together as a single work authored by Moses. Although it was not recognised at the time, the J and P distinction is employed here as a convenient shorthand for the variations between the Creation narratives that posed challenges for readings of Genesis in this period as in any other. One major inconsistency between the accounts is in the creation of Eve; this had implications for political thought. In P (Gen. 1:1 to 2:4a) the creation of Adam and Eve is simultaneous, and they appear to be given joint dominion over all:

> Furthermore God sayde Let us make man in one image according to our likenesses, and let them rule over the fish of the Sea, and over the foule of the heaven, and over the beastes, and over all the earth, and over everything that creepeth or moveth on the earth.
>
> (Gen, 1:26)[5]

> Thus God created man in his own image: In the image of God created he him; he created them male and female.
>
> (Gen. 1:27)

> And God blessed them and God said to them Bring foorth fruit and multiplie and fill the earth and subdue it.
>
> (Gen. 1:28)

In J (Gen. 2:4 to 3:24), on the other hand, Eve is not created until 11 verses after the Creation of Adam in 2:7, and then she is created from his rib and to be his 'helpe meet':

> Also the lord God sayde, It is not good that man should be himself alone: I will make him an helpe meet for him.
>
> (Gen. 2:18)

Both accounts in their explanations of how things began set out a pattern of how things should be. While the inclusive 'them' of P could be used to argue that mankind began as a society and so as a basis for more egalitarian political theories, the 'Adam first' account in J, especially when combined with God's gift of dominion in P, could be used as the foundation for patriarchal and absolutist conceptualisations of both family and polity.

Moving beyond these detailed points of difference, it has frequently been noted that P offers a more remote, heaven-centred perspective.[6] It is about order, establishing a hierarchy and man's (including woman's) place in it through the gift of dominion. It is setting out a pattern and has a fixity, a static quality, once all has been called into being: the sun will preside over the day, and the moon will preside over the night, and man will preside over all that moves on the face of the earth. The state of Adam is determined by decree and command: he is in God's image; he will rule; he must fill the earth and subdue it. J, on the other hand, is more earth-bound in outlook. It gives some indication of what life was like in that garden (eating freely, communicating directly with God, enjoying companionship); the story has characters with names whose words and actions are open to psychological interpretation.[7] There is reference in the text to social structures with which readers through the ages would be familiar; Genesis 2:24 speaks of a man leaving his father and mother and cleaving unto his wife. There is detail and drama, and above all there is the account (not present in P) of the temptation by the serpent, the eating of the apple and the Fall. There is aetiological interest in J at many levels, an explanation of the institution of marriage, for example, of the creeping movement of the snake and the enmity between that species and humanity, of the pains of childbirth, of mortality and of the less-than-perfect condition in which man lives out his lifespan. Later readings have been able to find origins for the whole burden of man's sinfulness and misery, the presence of evil and all that is wrong with the world in the happenings described in J. Genesis 6 offers an alternative explanation of the coming of evil with its tale of the corruption of humans by divine beings, understood by ancient rabbinical sources to be fallen angels, but in Christian understanding the Adamic Fall has dominated.[8] For political thinkers this story creates an interesting duality of pre-lapsarian and post-lapsarian man and the question of which state of man should be taken as the foundation of the polity: Adam in nature as he was created to be, or the condition of Adam after his fall. If J is taken together with P there is another state to consider: Adam as he is by God's decree gifted with dominion over all living things. The realism of the account of pre-lapsarian humanity in J describes things as they are (societies with mothers, fathers, wives and husbands) and confirms this state as what God intended, and therefore as good, by giving it scriptural endorsement: 'Therefore shall a man leave his father and his mother, and shall cleave to his wife'.[9] When, after the Fall, the man and woman are not in the state God originally created them, He dictates the terms of their new fallen condition: 'Thy desire shall be subject to thy husbande, and he shall rule over thee'; 'In the sweat of thy face shalt thou eate bread'.[10]

The J account also presents the origins of human history. It describes human actions that have consequences beyond the natural rhythms of existence established in the P account of Creation. It has movement (narrative as well as geographical) in the exile of the first parents that sets up the question of 'what next?' and raises the possibility of return. The place of these three chapters of Genesis within the Biblical canon makes them the commencement of a bigger story than is contained within their own verses. They are at the beginning of a book the rest of which is devoted to Ancient Hebrew history and the lives of the Patriarchs, and so they seem to set in motion a chronology and genealogy in which Christian writers over the centuries, and still in the seventeenth century, sought to position their own histories and those of the other peoples they encountered. It is a story that effectively has two beginnings: with Adam and Eve, first parents; and with Noah and his family, the sole human survivors of the destruction of the Flood. Then there is the location of these chapters at the start of the whole Christian canon in which the Old Testament is a precursor to the New, to Christ's birth, passion and resurrection and in which the account of Creation and Fall in Genesis is the beginning of a story that ends with the visions and eschatology of Revelation. The figure of the defeated dragon in this last book neatly balances the serpent in the first. Thus Adam is the starting point of two stories, a family history that embraces the whole human race and a history of the Fall and Redemption of mankind.

Any reference by seventeenth-century writers and thinkers to this story of origins is refracted through centuries of Christian exegesis of these texts, the recounting of which is beyond the scope of this study. Acknowledgement needs to be made, however, of the two giants in this tradition, of St Paul and of St Augustine, whose interpretations of the significance of the Fall, the imputation of Adam's sin to his descendants and the doctrine of 'original sin' had a profound impact on both Catholic and Reformed theology.[11] N. P. Williams suggested that Paul was influenced by theories of the origins of sin current in first century Judaism and that what he achieved was the crystallisation of the Adamic Fall doctrine within the Christian tradition.[12] In the Apostle's writing a flesh-spirit dualism can be detected, as in Gal. 5:16, yet he did not subscribe to a Manicheistic dualism of good and evil; rather, the roots of men's sinfulness and mortality in the disobedience of one man gave evil a contingent and temporal character.[13] More recent scholars recognise that Paul was interested in the universality of human sin but suggest that his concern was with the *present* plight of humankind rather than theories of how sin arose.[14] His theology was one of hope that in Christ the consequences of Adam's transgression are overturned.[15] He employed a parallel between Adam and Christ to establish this:

> For since by man came death, by man came also the resurrection of the dead. For as in Adam all die, even so in Christ shall all be made alive.
> (1 Cor. 15:21–22)

Augustine gave greater definition and a distinctive slant to the doctrine of the Fall with his view that Adam's sin was ingrained in human nature and transmitted by physical heredity as original sin (*originale peccatum*). He developed the idea of original guilt (*originalis reatus*) by which all men were deserving of punishment. Out of this lump of sinfulness (*massa peccati*) God's mercy fixed a number of souls who, through no merits of their own, would be saved.[16] The power of Augustine's influence on the western church gave a particular flavour to understandings of man's condition after the Fall. He also influenced understandings of the state of man at Creation. For Augustine the original state of man was glorious in health and youth, in intellect, and in moral character. The difference between pre- and post-lapsarian states was enormous; they were characterised by original righteousness and original guilt respectively. Later scholars, notably St Thomas Aquinas, tempered Augustine's description of the human condition with a clearer distinction between what was natural and what supernatural in Adam's attributes, between the *donum supernaturale* of 'original righteousness' and 'perfection', gifts of God's grace, and the *pura naturalia* or properties belonging simply to human nature as such.[17] According to these views, man by his fall had descended from the supernatural to the natural plane, though the loss of his original righteousness once possessed introduced a disorder and disharmony into the faculties of nature.[18] The question of what of these natural faculties persisted beyond the Fall had implications for the conceptualisation of post-lapsarian human society and whether it was based on a pessimistic or optimistic view of man.

Augustinian theologies of the Fall were given a new lease on life at the Reformation. Martin Luther, in particular, and John Calvin, less consistently, adopted the lowest possible view of the unredeemed human condition as one of 'total depravity' as a consequence of the Fall.[19] Both Reformers readily accepted Augustine's concept of original guilt and that of original righteousness to emphasise the gap between what man once was and what, through the Fall, he had become. Protestant opposition to institutional and hierarchical elements of the Church (the Mass, penance, the cultus of saints, pilgrimages, monasticism and other external works and forms) gave added significance to pre-destinarian elements of Augustine's thought that saw salvation as the direct work of God on the individual soul to which saved man contributes little or nothing.[20] The contrary views of Dutch theologian Jacobus Arminius, that God's election was conditioned on the believer's free act of faith in choosing Christ, met strong opposition from the Reformed establishment and led to the persecution of his followers.[21] Although there was agreement that the story begun by Adam would end in salvation through God's Grace and the sacrifice of Jesus Christ, there was bitter disagreement on the specifics of how and for whom that salvation would be effected.

Subsequent chapters will investigate in more detail, and with reference to the seventeenth-century context, the interplay between the Biblical accounts of Adam and political theory, but from this quick foray into the first chapters of Genesis it is possible to identify different significances for Adam that will appear again as themes and threads running through this study. There is an initial distinction to be made between Adam as state of being and Adam as story, or more precisely as an event that sets story in motion. The former is a point of stability; it explains the way things are or were established to be; it is about legitimacy and secure foundation for the polity. The latter is dynamic: it explains why things are changing or need to change; it is about direction, providence and political reform. Adam as state has three significances. There is Adam as decree, as God has ordained, gifts or commands that arise from God's will rather than belonging to Adam *qua* man; Adam as nature, possessing the faculties given by God at Creation that make him man; Adam as condition, his state of being after the Fall.[22] Adam as story has two significances. There is Adam as progenitor whose creation sets in motion a genealogical history of 'begat-begetting' that moves in time through the generations and in space across the world to include the whole human race in a common narrative, and there is a parallel story of cosmological dimension and eschatological character that proceeds according to a divine timetable, begins with the act of eating an apple and ends in Redemption and Restoration.

Political readings

Whatever else seventeenth-century men (and, less frequently, women) were reading to feed their political ideas, the Bible had a special status; the treatment of Adam within their political thought necessarily depended on their ways of reading this text. The mixture of guidance and freedom in their approaches to the Bible resulted both in identifiable trends and in diversity, a double direction evident in the understandings of Adam that are the subject of this study. The period covered by the study was one where the 1560 Geneva Bible was gradually supplanted by the 1611 King James Bible or Authorised Version as the one most widely read. The former, produced in Geneva by Marian exiles, was generally the dominant version until 1660. We know that Milton used both versions and that Locke, though he regularly used the King James when citing Biblical texts, was brought up with the Geneva Bible. It is highly likely that it was the version of the Bible with which Williams, Winstanley and Eliot were most familiar.[23] They would have been accustomed to its various editorial devices, its language, its detailed margin notes and glosses. The Geneva Bible is significant for it imposes a particular model of interpretation upon its readers, and its widespread use had a powerful influence on Biblical exegesis in this period.

The influence of the Geneva Bible was partly doctrinal. While Tyndale's idealistic aspiration for his earlier translation was an English Bible that every ploughboy might read, William Whittingham and his fellow exiles, translators and compilers of the Geneva Bible recognised that there were 'hard places', passages in the Bible that needed explanation. Accordingly, they provided detailed notes to guide the reader in accordance with their own Reformed theology. There was an emphasis on the Fall, on the link between Adam's transgression and a curse on all mankind; the correlation was made between the activity of the conscience, natural law and the law given to Moses; the Church was presented as the few, chosen by God. These themes will all be encountered and discussed later in the book. In the parts of the Bible attributed to him, the marginal notes stated, Moses declared those things 'which are in this booke chiefly to bee considered'. These entailed making of the Bible a whole story with its own internal logic of movement and completion, a logic that binds the Old Testament very closely to the New:

> Firstly that the world and all things therein were created by God, and that man being placed in this great Tabernacle of the world to behold Gods wonderfull works and to praise his Name for the infinite graces, wherewith he had endured him, fell willingly from God through disobedience: who yet for his owne mercies sake restored him to life, and confirmed him in the same promise of Christ to come, by whome he should overcome Satan, death and hell.

It also involved demonstration through the examples of the patriarchs that God's mercy never fails those whom 'he chuseth to be his church', and of others (Cain, Ishmael, Esau) to show that this Church does not depend on their reputation in the world but rather on God's faithfulness. In this way the Geneva Bible served to bring the present into the Biblical story, to make of the Bible a text wherein readers might trace their own lives and destinies, and one that has prime relevance to the place and the trials of God's people in the contemporary world.

The Geneva Bible encouraged a political reading of the Scriptures. It famously incorporated in its notes and its translation elements that were considered seditious by James I and that were deliberately excluded from the new Authorised Version of 1611. In particular there were margin notes that appeared to suggest the legitimacy of resistance to overweening rulers, and there was the frequent use of the language of tyrant (a word expressly disallowed in James' Bible) and slave. The royalist Sir Robert Filmer commented in 1648:

> The words [tyrant and slave] are frequent enough in every man's mouth, and our old English translation of the Bible useth sometimes the word tyrant. But the authors of our new translation have been so careful, as not once to use the word, but only for the proper name of a man – Acts xix, 9 – because they find no Hebrew word in the Scripture to signify a tyrant or a slave.[24]

As if to underline the revolutionary credentials of the Geneva Bible, in 1643 Edmund Carey used selections from the text to compile *The Souldiers Pocket Bible*, which was issued to soldiers in the Parliamentary Army and contained choice passages to assure them that God was on their side. Two of the quotes (number 5, from Dan. 3:17, and number 6, from 2 Chron. 32:7–8) drew on the Geneva Old Testament's support for revolutionary action against oppressive kings and so served to remove any lingering doubts the soldiers might have about going to war against the king.[25] The Geneva annotations do not consistently tend towards revolutionary politics, however; as Tom Furniss has highlighted in his study, there are others that recommend obedience or passive resistance. Given this ambiguity, it could be said that rather than influencing towards revolution, the commentary encourages a political reading of the text empowering readers to interpret contemporary events for themselves and apply what they read to their own particular circumstances, the actions of present day 'idolaters and tyrants' and their own sufferings.[26] In particular the Geneva Bible encourages its readers to identify with the experiences of the Israelites.[27]

Sola scriptura, spirit and reason

There is some tension discernible between the heavily annotated and commentated character of the Geneva Bible and the reformed *sola scriptura* – that emphasis on the sufficiency of the Bible as rule of doctrine and morals, and on the believer's direct, unmediated, access to that text. As an English translation intended for the common man (and produced for him in a handy portable size), it was designed to liberate the reader from the encouragement of ignorance and clericalism of which the Roman Church was accused. At the same time in the careful direction it provides the reader for the interpretation of Scripture, this Bible is an illustration of the magisterial nature of seventeenth-century orthodoxies in general, not just the Roman Church. It manifests an authority that several of the writers recorded in this study positioned themselves against. In his royalist treatise *De Patriarcha*, Filmer made it clear that the Bible is the only authority he will accept in the formulation of his thesis and pronounces against the 'schoolmen'; at the other end of the political spectrum, Gerrard Winstanley, in characteristically colourful language, described 'school learning' as the 'blacknesse of darknesse' and writes of the clergy and 'bitter professors' who take the Scriptures 'and flourish[…] their plaine language over with their dark interpretation and glosses … and thereby deceive the simple, and makes a prey of the poore'.[28] Winstanley's anticlericalism was echoed by Roger Williams in his treatise, *The Hireling Ministry None of Christ* (1652) and by John Milton in a number of works expressing his opposition to prelatical and ecclesial forms of Christianity. In *Of Prelatical Episcopacy* (1641), Milton wrote that only Scripture has divine authority, that it possesses 'brightness and perfection' supplying an 'all sufficiency' of spiritual knowledge.[29] An over-reliance on others' interpretation of the Scripture (the Fathers, the Church's tradition) is to do injury to 'the pure Evangelik manna' by 'seasoning our mouths with … tainted scraps and fragments'.

Although Scripture may be pure, its meaning is not always transparent, and so some aid is required in its exegesis. Brian Cummings has shown how this lack of transparency posed one of the major challenges of the Reformation, raising questions about the relationship of the letter of the written text to scholarly exegesis and the inspiration of spirit.[30] Milton, as a man of prodigious learning himself, did not deny that scholarship and secondary reading can have some part to play in Biblical interpretation – his *Areopagitica* presents an image of an industrious reading community ('many pens and heads') whose 'faith and knowledge' thrive by this exercise – but readers must be wary not to be in thrall to 'common doctrinal heads' crystallised in 'interlinearies, breviaries, synopses and other loitering gear'.[31] Ultimately illumination and re-illumination will be received from the openness of the actual Scriptures to which the reader turns and revisits in light of his reading. Reading the Bible is an individual quest for meaning with each believer entitled to interpret Scriptures for himself.[32] It is a dialogue with the Scriptures similar to the process Locke described in his own reading of Paul's epistles where, having studied various commentaries, he left these aside to read the text himself over and over again 'till I came to have a good general view of the Apostle's main Purpose in writing the Epistle, the chief Branches of his Discourse wherein he prosecuted it, the Arguments he used and the Disposition of the whole'.[33]

Locke described his coming to understanding in terms of receiving light. The illumination achieved during such reading is variously ascribed to the activity of the Spirit or of reason. Milton wrote of Spirit, conscience and reason ('that intellectual ray which God hath planted in us') as enabling that discernment of probability and truth in the Scripture.[34] Whatever term is used, the faculty for understanding is God-given, given by God to the individual to advance his own understanding. Milton afforded high status to the authority of the Spirit, acting within the individual reader in the activity of interpretation – it is 'the pre-eminent and supreme authority'; it is the action of the Spirit that makes us believe in the Scripture; but he did not step beyond the authority of Scripture (illumined by the Spirit) to suggest that the Spirit alone is the arbiter of moral living and right belief.[35] It was this move from the sufficiency of the Scripture to the sufficiency of the Spirit that the divine William Perkins feared when he wrote of those who 'condemn both human learning and the study of the scripture and trust wholly to revelations of the Spirit; but God's spirit worketh not but upon the foundation of the word'.[36] This spiritualist trend was discernible in the preachers of the parliamentary army, William Dell and John Saltmarsh, when they proclaimed that the Holy Spirit freed men from all bonds of the law and among the Quakers with their emphasis on direct experience of God.[37]

The Scriptures are very present in the writings of Winstanley, in his language and imagery; nevertheless there are also indications of the kind of subordination of Scripture to in-dwelling Spirit of which Perkins warned. Winstanley encouraged his readers to 'rest no longer upon words without knowledge' but 'look after that spirituall power; and know what it is that rules them, and which doth rule in and over all, and which they call their God and Governor or preserver'.[38] He described the writings of the evangelists as the 'report or declaration' of the Gospel rather than the Gospel itself; they were just the words of men with similar experience to himself rather than the authority that should determine his own understanding.[39] Winstanley did not deny the truth of Scripture but argued that its truth was perceived through its accordance with the activity of the Spirit within the reader: 'When I look into that record of experimentall testimony, and finde a suitable agreement betweene them, and the feeling of light within my own soule, now my joy is fulfilled'.[40] As will be seen in a later chapter, Winstanley's reliance on internal spiritual insight and visions led to a predilection for apocalyptic imagery and to esoteric and mystical interpretations of the story of Adam.

Although, like Winstanley, Locke emphasised the freedom of the individual in Biblical interpretation, his scriptural exegesis could hardly be more different in style; he adopted a much more literal approach. Locke and Milton, both men of considerable education and learning, shared the view that God had made his Book accessible to all, so that all might benefit from its guidance. Milton remarked that the Bible is 'translated into every vulgar toungue, as being held in main matters of belife and salvation, plane and easie to the poorest'.[41] Milton's 'main matters' perhaps corresponded to the 'plain propositions' that Locke understood the ordinary working man to be capable of extracting from the Biblical text, for such men, he suggested, are disinclined to consider 'sublime notions' or to be 'exercised in mysterious reasoning'.[42] As the majority of men are not able to engage in complicated thought, the Bible that supplies all that is needed for their guidance must present that guidance in a way accessible to them; thus the most important tenets of the Bible become those easiest to understand:

> The all merciful God seems herein to have consulted the poor of this world, and the bulk of mankind; these are articles that the labouring and illiterate man can comprehend.[43]

The result was a reductionist view of the Bible that distilled its doctrine into the central belief that Jesus is the Messiah and was presented above all as a moral code for living. The focus in Locke's Biblical writings is the New Testament, with emphasis on Christ's teaching. *The Reasonableness of Christianity* begins with a discussion of Adam but this serves to place him within a New Testament framework as Locke interrogates the Pauline exegesis of the Genesis story. Locke's perspectives on the Bible had much in common with those of William Chillingworth, whose 1637 book, *The Religion of Protestants A Safe Way to Salvation,* he greatly admired, recommending it as part of his programme for the education of young gentlemen. Chillingworth both claimed that the Bible alone is the religion of the Protestants, and gave those Protestants considerable leeway in how they interpret that Bible. There is scope for difference of interpretation as long as the fundamentals, expressed as they are in plain and unambiguous terms ('only to believe in Christ and call no man master but him only') are adhered to.[44] Above all the emphasis is on right living, and interest in the source and knowledge of that morality is another influential strand in seventeenth-century interpretations of Adam and his significance to the contemporary world.

18 *Material, method and occasion*

Allegory and typology

It has already been observed how the commentators of the Geneva Bible presented the examples of the patriarchs, Abraham, Isaac, Jacob and others as proof that His mercy will never fail those whom He chooses to be His Church, and the examples of Cain, Ishmael and Esau as a reminder and assurance to that Church that God's ways and God's favourites are not those of the world. In these and other examples characters and events of the Bible were taken to signify something other than their historical selves. In the chapters that follow, this book will investigate what that 'something other' was in the case of the Biblical character and story of Adam in particular and seventeenth-century interpretations of their significance.

The allegorical interpretation of scriptural figures has a long tradition in Biblical exegesis, the early chapters of Genesis having provided particularly fertile material for such treatment. Indeed, in the third century Origen dismissed the idea that the story of Creation and Adam could be understood in any way other than allegorically:

> And if God is said to walk in the paradise in the evening, and Adam to hide himself under a tree I do not suppose that anyone doubts that these things figuratively indicate certain mysteries, the history having taken place in appearance and not literally.[45]

By the time the Geneva annotations were produced, the climate for Biblical scholarship had changed. The sixteenth-century reformers were placing increased emphasis on the literal sense of the Bible, and the tradition of allegorising Biblical material had been criticised by leading figures. Calvin himself accused Origen of 'torturing Scripture ... away from the true sense', and William Tyndale pronounced that the allegorising exegetes of the Roman Church had replaced God's literal promises with mysteries so that 'the faith was lost thorow allegories'.[46] The Reformers' opposition to allegory was not absolute, however. Tyndale allowed allegories as illustrations of points made in homilies but not for their authentication, and the distinction was made between Scripture that had been intended as allegory and the allegorisation of Scripture that had not, for example in James Durham's comment in his 1668 *Exposition of the Song of Solomon* about the great difference 'betwixt an Allegorick Exposition of Scripture, and an Exposition of Allegorick Scripture'.[47] Another distinction was made that has direct bearing on the interpretation of Adam. Calvin claimed that Moses did not intend the story he told to be read allegorically, but the history he records is nevertheless an allegory because 'God's continual government of the world' is an allegory.[48] The events reported in the Bible can signify both themselves as actual happenings and something else that is or has happened subsequently, that is to be or is still to happen. It is a move from the fiction often involved in allegory to typology – what Barbara Lewalski calls the 'Protestant Symbolic Mode' – that retains the historicity of the signifier as well as of the thing signified.[49] As both type and anti-type are historically real, so Adam can (*pace* Origen) be both an actual character who existed in time and a figure for something or someone else. Possible tensions between reformist concern for the literal sense of Scripture and a symbolic mode of thought were resolved by William Perkins when he declared the literal sense as that intended by the author and so, in the case of the Bible, that intended by the Holy Spirit.[50] In his discussion of Paul's Christian interpretation of the history of Abraham's family in Galatians, Perkins wrote:

> They are not two senses but two parts of one full and intire sense for not onely the bare historie, but also that which is thereby signified is the full sense of the h[oly] G[host].[51]

This reconciliation of historic and symbolic mode, of Old Testament and New Testament senses, is important for Adam as well as Abraham, not least because Paul himself set up a typological relationship between Adam and Christ in 1 Corinthians.

As will be seen, different authors in the period of study had different interpretations of Biblical typology. One distinction was between external and internal types, those that interpret meaning in terms of the history of a people, a link between the people of Israel and the English nation for example, and those that draw parallels between Biblical narratives and their own inward journey, such as the self-reflective writing of John Bunyan. Milton employed both forms when he related the transition of the English state from monarchy to commonwealth to the liberation of the Israelites from the tyranny of Egypt and when he interpreted his own mission as a poet in terms of the parable of the talents.[52] Another, more significant, distinction is made by Henning Graf Reventlow in his classic study of Biblical authority in the early modern era.[53] Reventlow traces two typologies back to Eusebius's *Ecclesiastical History*, where he sees the events of Exodus 15 replicated in Constantine's victory at the Milvian Bridge. The first is a spiritual typology, which is a Christocentric finding in the Old Testament of earthly models of Christ's heavenly rule. The second typology is historical; it sees Biblical events repeated in the visible course of ongoing history – the link between the Exodus and the English nation's escape from tyranny would be an example. While Augustine's theology limited typology to the spiritual, the second found a home in the development of medieval historiography and gained strength in the seventeenth century, particularly, Reventlow suggests, through the experiences of the settlers of New England whose journeys, struggles and aspirations could find ready parallels in the Old Testament. The experiences of civil war and political upheaval in England and her immediate neighbours were also fertile ground for such typologies.

Locke's concern that the Scriptures should be 'plain and intelligible' for the ordinary man meant he avoided typological interpretations. The other authors discussed in this study did employ typologies. The typologies adopted are not always consistent, however, being contingent on political and personal circumstances. Some of Winstanley's writings will be found to be influenced by a spiritual typology where all types merge into a mystical coming of Christ. The Pauline Adam and Christ typology is central to this. Between the two New England authors we find divergence: Eliot adopted an historical typology when he likened his mission to the Indians to Ezekiel's raising of the dry bones or advocated as God's will, for his Indian converts as well as for the English nation, a political organisation that mirrored Moses's ordering of the Israelites in Exodus. Williams adopted a spiritual understanding when he argued that all types have ended with the coming of Christ and, against common readings of contemporary events, denied the validity of any claims that England might be seen as a new Israel. This was spelled out in *The Bloudy Tenent*, where Williams declared that Christ (and those that are Christ's) is the only antitype of the former figurative and typical'.[54] Allegorical and typological interpretations of Adam are not the only ways of linking his history to later conditions and events, however; his status as the first father of all men means there are genetic and hereditary links not present in the cases of Ezekiel or Moses or the nation of Israel. The significance of these for contemporary man and political society was the subject of Robert Filmer's treatise *Patriarcha* and of Locke's refutation of Filmer's ideas in the *First Treatise of Government*.

Biblical genres

However much they held the Bible to be a unity in inspiration and story, seventeenth-century readers were well aware of the variety of genres it contained. Milton as master of poetry and prose was well positioned to appreciate this richness and complexity in Biblical text. In his *Reason of Church Government Urged against Prelatry*, Milton described the Song of Solomon as 'a divine pastoral Drama' and Revelation as 'the majestic image of a High and stately Tragedy'; he wrote of the 'frequent songs' in the law and prophets as 'over all kinds of Lyrick poetry ... incomparable'.[55] He used all of these forms in his own telling of the story of Adam's Creation and Fall. Amy Bizik has also identified in *Paradise Lost* the complex narrative and edifying import of a parabolic form.[56] Lewalski observes how the Protestant poets of the sixteenth and seventeenth centuries looked to the Bible and its commentators for genre theory and genetic models; the writings of the authors selected for this study demonstrate clearly that not only poets but other writers too followed these models.[57] Scriptural influences are evident in the frequent direct Biblical quotations and in the interweaving of Biblical language into their comments on the times and their political writings. The language was part of the interpretation endowing the internal life of the individual, the history of the nation or the ordering of the polity with the mystical spiritualism of Revelation and Daniel or the divine imperative of prophetical writings. Winstanley's works were rich with apocalyptic imagery, and Milton employed the devices of Old Testament prophets in his prose addresses to his compatriots.[58] Locke's style was less prophetic, more reasoned and didactic; his greater ease with New Testament genres is apparent in his focus on the Gospels in *The Reasonableness of Christianity* and on Paul's writings in his *Paraphrase and notes on the Epistles of St Paul*. The mixture of Biblical genres gave license to authors to adapt a variety of styles in the presentation of their message, as in Williams's mingling of verse and prose, in *A Key into the Language of America,* his factual observation and metaphorical figures, moral pronouncements, autobiographical references and detailing of customs by which the Indians' public and domestic affairs were regulated. The concise moral statements embedded in Williams's verses are reminiscent of Biblical proverbs; his use of the deer as the image of God's persecuted saints recalls the panting hart of Psalm 42.[59] Eliot's accounts of his own missionary activities among the Indians echo those of the Apostles and Paul in Acts and the Epistles; his detailed proposals for *The Christian Commonwealth* borrow directly from the constitutionalism of Deuteronomy.

The Biblical text also presents problems, and attempts to overcome them become part of the interpretive activity and colour the meanings that emerge. Most striking of these are Milton's blending and ornamentations of elements of the Biblical story of Adam in order to present a coherent and universally applicable story of man and his relationship with God. In this he was supported by his own knowledge of Jewish traditions of commentary and midrash. Eric Auerbach noted that the Hebrew Bible is characterised by 'parataxis', a juxtaposition of events often without the logical subordination to narrative.[60] Jewish scholars have used midrash to fill in the narrative gaps and make the Scripture more attractive and relevant to contemporary concerns. In *Milton and Midrash*, Golda Werman has demonstrated how Milton used this device to fill in the various lacunae created by the parataxis of the Old Testament style and also to re-write the Biblical narrative with a distinctively Christian flavour, so that for example, the sound of God walking can become Jesus and the Spirit of God moving over the waters, the Holy Spirit.[61] He was able to insert the midrashic invention that turns the serpent into Satan and brings the Biblical tale into the Christian narrative of Fall and Restoration with which the Geneva Bible commentary began and which links Adam's story to the temptations and trials of the inner man and of the society to which he belongs.

The times

Political order

Philip Almond's book, *Adam and Eve in Seventeenth Century Thought*, presents the seventeenth as 'the century par excellence' of the literal reading of the Genesis story.[62] Mark Kishlansky affords it another distinction when he characterises the period as a time when 'the writing of political theory reached heights unattained since the Golden Age of Athens' and cites in support of his hyperbole Robert Filmer's *Patriarcha*, Thomas Hobbes' *Leviathan*, James Harrington's *Oceana*, John Locke's *Two Treatises of Government*, James I's republication of *The True Law of Free Monarchies*, Henry Parker's articulation of the first theory of parliamentary sovereignty and the Levellers' *Agreement of the People* and Henry Ireton's *Heads of the Proposals*.[63] He could have included in his list, among many others, John Eliot's *The Christian Commonwealth*, Gerrard Winstanley's *The Law of Freedom in a Platform* and John Milton's *The Ready and Easy Way to Establish a Free Commonwealth*. Some of these texts have become classics of political theory, and others are viewed more as historical curiosities. Indeed, the discomfort of later ages with theological framing and Biblical reference (particularly when literally understood) has meant that sections or elements of even the accepted classics among them have often been viewed in the same way or neglected altogether.[64] This has for long been the fate of Locke's *First Treatise* and of the third and fourth books of Hobbes's *Leviathan*. Concerns with demonstrating the proto-Marxist credentials of Winstanley's writings meant that not just their religious imagery, but their overarching theology has been read as metaphor.[65] The current intellectual climate is perhaps more open than that of three or four decades ago to acknowledging the importance of religion in these seminal texts, the work of Jeremy Waldron on Locke being one example of a contemporary political scholar taking the religious foundations of classical political theory seriously.[66] In this vein the present study, through detailed study of selected texts, brings together the two characteristics of the period mentioned above: attention to Biblical text and a flourishing of political thought.

The relationship of political ideology to religious belief may be one point of difference in modern interpretations of seventeenth-century thought; another is the relationship of political ideology to events. Among the political writings cited above, and alongside those that argue for monarchical and authoritarian governance, there are works that speak of sovereignty of the people, justify resistance against tyrannical rulers, advocate republicanism and demand common rights for all to the use of land and property. The list includes some that are viewed as the foundational texts of liberalism and others that have been described as precursors of socialism or communism. These have in the past been incorporated into teleological understandings of history (Whig or Marxist) as part of that great march towards liberty and equality progressing through the seventeenth century in social, economic and political as well as intellectual developments. The traumas of the middle years (the 1640s and 1650s) in particular were seen as part of an inexorable movement towards these desirable ends. It was this kind of thinking that led Christopher Hill, riding on the tide of Marxism in British intellectual life, to popularise the term 'the English Revolution' for what had previously been known as the Civil War and Interregnum.[67] In his small book of this name, he argued that the Civil War manifested the criteria needed for a

Marxist bourgeois revolution. The student movement of the 1960s pushed the seventeenth-century Marxist revolution a stage further, so that the more radical elements of the period (among them the Levellers, Ranters and Diggers), viewed as promise of a different kind of revolution, were moved to central stage in historical writing, in particular in Hill's later book *The World Turned Upside Down*.[68]

Characterisations of this period as one of revolution have been discredited by revisionist historians. Ironically, the multiple and detailed biographical studies of local gentry prompted by a desire to track this bourgeois revolution provided the strongest arguments against it. They showed that rather than being part of a class movement, the gentry were divided among themselves in the great crisis.[69] There have been conflicting views (among 'revisionists' and 'counter-revisionists') on the degree to which the provincial gentry caught up in the war were influenced by political ideology at all.[70] John Morrill found allegiance owed little to principle but more to family loyalty, local quarrels or the proximity of either army, while Richard Cust and Ann Hughes concluded from their local studies that provincial action *was* ideologically led.[71] However principled or otherwise they may have been, it seems that there was among these 'middling sort' of men not so much revolutionary fervour as resistance to change.[72] Contemporaries were more likely to use the word 'innovation' for what might now be described as revolution.[73] The terms 'innovation' or 'invention' had negative connotations, as in the Calvinist parliamentarians' fears about the liturgical 'innovations' of Archbishop Laud and the complaints of the Somerset Grand Jury about 'the great and heavy taxations by new invented ways upon the county'.[74]

This opposition to 'innovation' had deeper roots than concern about the immediate impact of a particular change. J. G. A. Pocock's studies of seventeenth- and eighteenth-century political thinkers position his subjects against the background of late medieval European political thought with its very strong bias towards stability. The condition of the world, natural and social, was divinely ordained, and the sense of it could be accessed through man's God-given reason, a reason based on experience: as things have been so they are and so will they be. Only the universal, the unchanging, the timeless was truly rational.[75] This conceptualisation of the world and society was reflected in the legalism of the period. Common law was understood to be a reflection of natural law, that light given by God to men, and many of the complaints heard locally or centrally at this time were appeals to the law that changes were threatening to overthrow.[76] Magna Carta was used by both sides in the Civil War to support their cause and show that they stood for the right and proper order of things. Those who were concerned not just about recent contraventions of the law but about deep-seated wrongs might go back further in time to find the point – the Norman Conquest for example, or the rise of papal power – at which the edifice had been destabilised or overthrown and seek again the stability of the state of things as they were and ought to be.[77] In this journey through history in the search for originals (as pattern and beginning), the dawn of human society and settlement with our first ancestor in the book of Genesis was the ultimate reference point.

The interest in the past and in states of being of this view of the world are far removed from the progressive, future orientation of Hill's 'English Revolution', yet the recognition of these ways of thinking as characteristic of seventeenth-century political theory and a twenty-first-century dismissal of Whiggish and Marxist teleologies as anachronisms do not mean that there were no seventeenth-century teleological interpretations of the unfolding of events. One of the challenges of the unchanging, timeless view of the world described by Pocock is 'the problem of the intelligibility of the particular, the local and the transitory'.[78] One way of dealing with the very real experience of change was to view it as an aberration and defend, or seek to return to, the *status quo ante*. Another response was to see in these changes God's activity in the world, to have faith in this activity as working towards the fulfilment of His prophecies of old and the achievement of His purpose for His creation. Pocock writes that: 'The language of apocalyptic was ... widely employed because only a dramatized providence seemed capable of explaining secular and particular happenings when their particularity was so marked as to assume the character of sudden change'.[79] As a process it involves something similar to an Aristotelean 'emplotment' whereby events are more than singular discordant occurrences but acquire definition from their contribution to the development of a plot leading to resolution.[80] Adam as man's original state of being and Adam as the one who set history in motion through the Fall are both brought into the interpretation of the seventeenth-century experience, and events, political ideology and Biblical exegesis come together.

Roger Williams described the age in which he lived as 'wonderful, searching, disputing and dissenting times'.[81] Other, less forthright, souls found them fearful and disturbing times, but whatever their inclination seventeenth-century men and women had recourse to the familiar verses and stories of the Bible to explain the trends, happenings and uncertainties of the age. The nature of those same trends, happenings and uncertainties gave prominence to certain elements within those explanations. Cold statistics tell the story of the Civil War years. A sizeable proportion of the male population took up arms in the 1640s, probably 150,000 in the summers of 1643, 1644 and 1645, perhaps 11% of males between the ages of 16 and 50 in a population of 4.3 million.[82] One in 20 males died as a direct consequence of battle and as many again of the diseases of war and military life. There were tens of thousands of widows and orphans and war invalids; others had to face troops trampling their crops, with soldiers quartered in their homes, their goods requisitioned, and, in the suburbs of some cities, their homes pulled down to strengthen defences. It was a context in which discussion of natural rights to the preservation of the person and of property was particularly pertinent, and the roots of such rights were sought in the original state of mankind.

The character of the times, full of signs and portents, leant itself to apocalyptic interpretation found not just in the writings of radical hotheads such as Winstanley, but in those of the more respectable and mainstream writers such as John Eliot – who, it will be seen, was momentarily caught up in millennial expectation of the immanent ending of the story.[83] Responses to the events of war could lead to divergent political models. Hobbes set out rational grounds for obedience to an autocratic ruler as an end to that war, one against another, which he argued was mankind's condition in the state of nature. For Milton, the depredations and sufferings of war gave added urgency to the cause of liberty, for to give up on the struggle would be to disrespect the sacrifices of so many, 'making vain and viler than dirt the blood of so many thousand faithful and valiant Englishmen'.[84] One of these authors found in the turmoil of the age evidence of what man is and the other signs of where he is bound.

The drama of the seventeenth century was not only found in battle and military campaign. There were contemporary reports of other forms of unrest, though the intensity of this drama has been disputed by modern historians. Revisionists see exaggeration in accounts of massive social upheaval found in the parliamentarian and royalist propaganda alike, in the words of Sir John Oglander, for example, who declared that 'such times were never before seen in England when the gentry were made slaves to the commonalty and in their power, not only to abuse but plunder any gentleman'.[85] Troubles there were, but they conformed to traditional patterns of collective unrest, attacks on unpopular landlords, riots about enclosures, grain shortages and taxes. David Underdown challenged those revisionists who separated the high politics of the period from the interests of the localities, but his studies have emphasised the conservative rather than radical character of much popular action at the time. He argues it was driven by concerns about encroachment on traditional rights to land and to its use, especially encroachment by outsiders and new forces, in the western counties the crown's sale of the royal forests to courtiers and entrepreneurs, for example, and grants for drainage schemes in the fens of the eastern counties and of Somerset.[86] In public discourse these changes were attributed not so much to economic market forces as to moral categories. Sermons and government pronouncements reiterated the commonly held view that shortages and economic hardship were the results of greed and sin; Underdown writes of a 'moral economy'.[87] Given these concerns, it is not surprising that interest in property, in rights to the ownership and use of land, is evident in the writings of several of the focus authors of this study. To cite two contrasting positions: Winstanley called for the abolition of property, while Locke made property-ownership the foundation of civil society, and both made reference to the first chapters of Genesis to justify their schemes. In this Biblically literate era, questions of ownership and use found various answers in differing interpretations of Adam's dominion and of Adam as cultivator of land.

26 Material, method and occasion

Changes in the local economy and the growth in population in the early decades of the seventeenth century meant that it was a time of increased mobility as young men in particular travelled in search of betterment or simply livelihood. Alison Games, an historian from the transatlantic school of history, has traced an escalation in migration and the movement of migrants to neighbouring districts, to the cities, to further away destinations and abroad to many countries particularly to Ireland and the New World.[88] Approximately 300,000 English migrated to America in the seventeenth century, half to the Caribbean and the rest to North America. As the land they settled was not rich in minerals any wealth and prosperity was to be found in cultivation and so the theorising of land ownership continued, particularly as the English claimed ownership of land that other nations had already inhabited for generations.[89] This movement gave an added dynamism to the motif of Adam the cultivator as the settlers spread the God-given task of cultivation across new territories and far flung corners of the earth. God's command to Adam and Eve in Genesis 1:28, 'increase and multiply, replenish the earth and subdue it' was included as a powerful impetus for migration to New England in John Winthrop's papers giving reasons for leaving England.[90] At the same time, there was a need to explain the differences and divergent histories (and also the similarities) of the new peoples they encountered, as well as an interest in incorporating them within the Biblical story that begins with a common ancestor. Roger Williams and John Eliot both engaged in this task, though with different conclusions.

In the 1970s and 1980s, attempts to find explanation for seventeenth-century upheavals in terms of long-term social and economic change took the history of the period into the provinces, but the later years of the last century saw a revival of interest in happenings in the (till then under-researched) political centre of Westminster and Whitehall, in the work of Clive Holmes for example, who argued that the leading men of the counties were not limited by provincial concerns but were keenly interested in metropolitan political life.[91] There was certainly much to interest in the centre in a century when long-standing structures of the state were abolished (or disbanded) and later restored. It saw the trial and execution of one king and later the deposition and exile of another, 11 years of personal rule (from 1629 to 1640) by the king, the purging and dissolution of parliament by military coup in 1648 and 1653, the abolition of the House of Lords (1649) and that of the bishops (1646) and the restoration of both with the return of the monarchy. The middle years of Charles I's rule, of the Commonwealth and Cromwell's Protectorate were particularly fraught but Tim Harris's study of Charles II shows the continuing influence of this political unrest into his reign in response to attempts to return the polity to the *status ante bellum*.[92] That political theorists of the 1680s (notably Algernon Sidney, James Tyrell and John Locke) should base their arguments on refutations of Robert Filmer's political writings from the 1620s and 1630s aimed to bolster support for the authority of the early Stuart monarchs, shows how debates were kept alive during the period of study.[93]

Historians such as David Wootton and Philip Baker have identified an 'elite radicalism' among the governing classes, country squires and wealthy grandees who argued for a reapportioning of the king's and parliament's powers in order to constrain the authority of the former and among parliamentarians who during the early years of the conflict readily used the language of contractual government and people's right to resist an unjust ruler and discussed these concepts in print.[94] There is disagreement over the degree to which such ideologies were generated in response to events and by the need to justify political positions taken, or were themselves the drivers of political change. The revisionist argument held that 'Civil War gave rise to modernization not modernization to Civil War'.[95] Employment of the concept of 'modernization' by revisionists or by the old-school historians whose work they critique, should not discount another strand in political theory at the time, a different teleology that interprets the sweeping away of existing structures of government as signs of a new dispensation, the heralding of the reign of King Jesus. John Eliot and Gerrard Winstanley were both at some stage infected by such millennial hope and sensed that the ending of the story was nigh.

For those who see the Civil War as driven by events rather than ideology, the role of the king is very important. Morrill finds very little evidence before 1640 even of 'a polity crumbling into civil war'; for him it was Charles I, the 'problem king', with his poor judgement of men and situations and his authoritarian approaches to government, who created the situation and polarised the nation.[96] Conrad Russell identified 'long term causes of instability' established before Charles's accession (the problem of multiple kingdoms; religious divisions; the breakdown of a financial and political system in the face of inflation and costly war), but the 'fortuitous element' that triggered the descent into Civil War and constitutional crisis was the personality of the king.[97] Whether the ideology prompted or proceeded from the political positioning of these years, there was an existing wealth of allusion and theory available to support different sides in the argument, conversations that form the content of the next chapter. What is indisputable is that the character and actions of Charles I (and fears that his style of kingship might be replicated by his descendants) made questions about sovereignty, its origins, location and rightful exercise, particularly salient. Charles's style of governance meant that the theme of the tyrant ruler gained prominence in political debate. It was not a new theme; indeed, the motif of tyranny and legitimacy of disobedience was present in the annotations of the Geneva version of the Bible that would have been the familiar Biblical text for much of the century, but events of this reign, and, 40 years later, nervousness about the direction of the policies in that of James II, gave it an added vitality.[98] Justification of people's resistance to tyranny is the basis of Locke's *Two Treatises of Government*. Morrill notes another feature of

Charles I's monarchy that has relevance for the development of political theory. Charles's succession was undisputed; there was no other contender for the throne and no disaffected younger brother who could focus the opposition by presenting himself as an alternative king, no William of Orange in the wings.[99] Resistance to Charles entailed not just the replacement of him as monarch but the reconfiguration or replacement of the monarchy itself. The political crisis of the middle years of this century was thus fertile ground for the development of the republican ideals that thinkers such as James Harrington and John Milton espoused; between the kind of absolutist monarchy Charles appeared to favour and outright republicanism was the limited or mixed monarchy found in Philip Hunton's treatise but deplored by Filmer and Hobbes as tending to anarchy.[100]

As political thinking swung between fears of tyranny and fears of anarchy the period became one of experimentation in practice as well as theory. Any government set up to replace the personal rule of Charles was subject to close scrutiny. Fears that the tyranny of the king was being supplanted by a new authoritarianism under the Long Parliament fuelled unrest in the Army in 1647; it enabled the brief prominence attained by the Levellers, with their demands for radical franchise reform, in the Putney Debates of 1647 and 1648.[101] Failure to agree to a viable alternative to monarchy during the years of Interregnum ultimately led to the recall of the Stuarts. Both the exercise and legitimacy of sovereignty were in question. As, in seventeenth-century thinking, God was the source of all authority, it was to be expected that the political theorists of the day should return to the story of His creation of Adam and of mankind in general to discern God's intentions for the governance of this new race and find the original for the sovereignty of the monarch (as in the writings of Filmer) or of the people (as in those of Locke).[102]

Religious order

The influence of religion on the seventeenth-century political scene has been variously understood by modern historians. The dominant historiography in the mid-twentieth century that viewed the changes of the period in terms of trends over time was able to emphasise the emancipatory logic of the Protestant reformation. More orthodox Calvinist clergy might support the parliamentary cause in the Civil War as a means of completing the English Reformation, and the religious radicals of the age, the separatists and 'mechanical preachers' of the interregnum years, took the struggle for freedom and equality further still. This was the flavour of Hill's account of the spread of mid-century radical opinions in *The World Turned Upside Down*.[103] In the face of this movement, the Protestant, largely Presbyterian, mainstream was becoming increasingly conservative and embattled.[104] Evidence of the spread of religious radicals was found in the lists of 'heresies' and expressions of alarm in a number of anti-tolerationist pamphlets and protests at this time notably Thomas Edwards's 1646 *Gangræna*, in which he warned of the 'errors, heresies, blasphemies and insolent proceedings' of the sectaries.[105] Two of this study's selected authors, Roger Williams and John Milton, were named for their radical opinions by Ephraim Pagitt in his list of notorious 'atheists' who 'print, and practise their heretical opinions openly'.[106] By contrast, Morrill argues that such fears of religious radicalism were exaggerated at the time, citing as evidence the mere 5% of the populace that attended religious assemblies outside the parochial structure between 1643 and 1654. For him the 'silent majority' of the population was content with a comfortable and readily accessible Anglicanism of ritual and straightforward morality. According to Morrill, they rejected the demanding Calvinism of the mainstream clergy; in religion, he identified a divide between the popular and the elite.[107] Different from both of these, Hughes emphasises the interpenetration of popular and elite culture, of mainstream and radical in public discourse both printed and oral.[108] She describes a religious context that is dynamic and fluid, characterised by heated oral disputation and printed polemic fuelled by an imperative to defend truth and confute error. It was a time for lively debate about the meaning and import of Biblical texts. Religious debate was present not just in the provinces but at the very heart of the political establishment. Indeed, and by way of illustration, before the 11 years of Charles I's personal rule (1629–1640), the last speech made in Parliament as the king's serjeant advanced to seize the mace was a passionate attack on innovations in religion and on those who would counsel the king to collect revenues not granted by Parliament.[109] The final act of the Parliament before its disbanding was the assembly's agreement to the three resolutions against tonnage and poundage and Arminianism.[110] Alongside the theological and liturgical questions of grace and practices of worship debated in this first half of the century were questions about who (if anyone) had the right to impose religious uniformity – what were the roles of crown, parliament and Church.[111] Far from being confined to the turbulent years of Charles I's reign and the Civil War period, this intermingling of religious and political affairs characterised the century as a whole so that in 1678 Edward Stillingfleet was able to declare in his Fast-Day sermon to Parliament; 'that which ... hath been the great Occasion of our Trouble, and is still of our Fears ... is *Religion*'.[112] This continuing prominence of religious questions in politics was, Jacqueline Rose has argued, a product of the 'ambiguous Reformation' of the Tudor era, which had entrenched the idea of godly kingship in a complex constitutional and legal framework and given debates about political legitimacy and resistance a peculiarly English form.[113]

There were a number of religious fissures that had an impact on the politics of this century. The Protestant–Catholic divide remained strong, Protestantism being closely aligned with Englishness and Roman Catholicism (or 'Papacy') with conspiracy and foreign infiltration. Anti-Catholicism was rife; it appeared in standard Protestant bombast against the 'Anti-Christ' and 'Whore of Babylon'.[114] Even the religiously tolerant (such as

Milton and Locke) often drew the line at tolerance of Roman Catholics.[115] A number of plots, real and imagined, reminded the English at various points in the century that the influence of Rome was to be feared, from the Gunpowder Plot of 1605, claims that the Jesuits were behind the Irish rebellion of 1641, the fabricated Popish Plot of 1678, and, working in the opposite direction, the Rye House Plot, an assassination attempt on the king and his Roman Catholic brother in 1683 in which Locke's patron Shaftesbury was implicated and which led to the exile of both men. Test Acts (1673 and 1678), targeting Roman Catholics by requiring conformity to the Church of England from holders of public office, encouraged debates about religious toleration and the power of the magistrate to decide in religious matters. The overt Roman Catholicism of James, Duke of York and heir to the throne, led to the Exclusion Crisis of 1679 and 1680, where the political elite was torn between those who favoured James's exclusion from the throne and those who supported the king in his resolute resistance. Again the powers of the king relative to Parliament were being tested, and debates and arguments employed in the reign of the first King Charles were resurrected in the reigns of his sons. It was the period that saw the publication of Filmer's *Patriarcha* half a century after it was written, with its Adamic justification for the absolute rights of hereditary monarchy, prompting in response the *Treatises of Government* (also based on interpretations of Adam) of Locke who returned from exile in the train of the Protestant William of Orange when James's unfortunate reign ended in his flight abroad.[116]

John Morrill noted a significant shift in anti-Roman Catholic sentiment in the seventeenth century when the old Elizabethan and Jacobean fear of the enemy without was, by the later 1630s, replaced by a fear of conspiracy at the heart of the state with the king himself, married to a Roman Catholic, entertaining the presence of Roman Catholics in his Privy Council and introducing continental, Roman Catholic, models into the regulation and ceremony of his court.[117] This background is helpful for understanding the stir caused by the 'innovations' to church order and liturgy that Charles I and his archbishop, William Laud, were responsible for pushing forward in parishes across the country. The enforcement of precise forms of church furnishing, worship and ritual, and the emphasis on episcopal adjudication rather than parochial self-determination, had a more Catholic than Reformed flavour. These changes and Charles's appointments favoured clergymen whose theology was Arminian in character. Nicholas Tyacke identified the king's promotion of Arminianism (and introduction of 'popish' ceremonies) as the prime cause of the Civil War.[118] It is, in fact, a conclusion that accords with Thomas Hobbes's contemporary analysis of the historical course of events.[119] Tyacke writes of a Calvinist consensus in the Elizabethan and Jacobean church and argues that only with the ascendancy of Laud did conflict emerge as it pitted radical anti-Calvinist theology against traditional reformed predestinarianism; the Arminians and Charles were the religious revolutionaries.[120] As a complaint against the king in the 1629 parliament worded it, 'some prelates near the King, having gotten the chief administration of ecclesiastical affairs under His Majesty, have discountenanced and hindered the preferment of those that are orthodox [i.e. Calvinist] and favoured such as are contrary'.[121] Peter Lake argues that talk of a Calvinist consensus is an exaggeration, that there were variations in degree of commitment to a strict predestinarian line before the 1620s; for him the question was rather which opinions dominated and at whose expense.[122] The anti-Calvinist writings of James I's chaplain, Richard Montagu, proved something of a test case when they were bitterly debated in parliament and eventually banned in 1628. Charles saw fit to promote Montagu in the face of this action by his parliament, a sign not only of his theological preference but of his independence of action. The events of the 1620s indicate that at this time questions about the fallen condition of man, the extent of his free will to accept or reject God's saving grace, were political issues, the cause of friction between the king and Parliament.

The king's determination to impose his preferred patterns of worship on his people and promote his preferred theologies in England, and particularly in the largely Presbyterian Kingdom of Scotland, raised the issue of the rights of the monarch or magistrate to determine the religious practices and beliefs of his subjects. It was an issue bound up with questions of religious toleration and freedom of conscience. That the monarch should have a decisive influence on religious matters in his kingdom was widely accepted orthodoxy at the beginning of the Stuart century. Indeed on his very journey south to take up his English throne James I was met in Northamptonshire by a group of clergymen who presented him with a petition (the Millenary Petition) said to be supported by a thousand ministers asking him to move forward reforms in the ceremony and doctrine of the Church. The Hampton Court Conference that resulted from this petition was a showcase for the new king's erudition and famously resulted in the production of the new Authorised Bible but did not achieve many lasting reforms to convince the movers of the petition that the king was keen to support the furtherance of the Reformation. Nevertheless, James was wiser in his religious policy and appointments than his son and so did not force the issue. Charles's most spectacular display of lack of wisdom in this respect was his attempt to impose episcopacy and Laudian forms of service on the Scottish Church, leading to riots, rebellion and ultimately war with serious consequences in English politics and the slide into the Civil War.

Religion and the influence of the state on religious practice and belief proved to be a point of division not only between king and Parliament but between the Parliamentary leaders themselves. As in the 1640s Parliament gained control of events it put forward its own programme for church reform. A sermon of 1641, *A Glimpse of Sion's Glory,* suggested that because the reformation by congregations of ordinary people had proved 'mixed with much confusion and a great deale of disorder', God is stirring up 'the Great ones of the Land', especially the Parliament, to organise and advance the Reformation.[123] However, these 'Great ones' were themselves in disagreement with each other as they included in their number reforming Episcopalians, Presbyterians and Independents.[124]

The Westminster Assembly was convened in 1643 as an assembly of divines to advise lawmakers on ecclesiastical change. It included a formidable array of Scottish Commissioners, giving weight to its demand for Parliament to establish a national Presbyterian Church.[125] Without some form of control, it was argued, the religious life of the nation might fall into anarchy and error; this was the period of the already mentioned polemic against sectaries and heresies. A handful of clergymen within the assembly, influenced by examples from the Netherlands and New England, advocated Congregational forms of church government and opposed the Presbyterian hierarchical organisation and insistence on doctrinal uniformity; for them 'New Presbyter is but old Priest writ large'.[126] In their struggle against the dominant Presbyterians, the Congregationalists increasingly combined with the sects to form a coalition that came to be known as 'independency'. The erosion of the Presbyterian ascendancy as the Civil War wore on and the increasing dominance of Cromwell, himself favourable to the Independents, meant that the shift to the Presbyterian system was not enforced. Williams, who was visiting England in the heyday of the Assembly, was caught up in the debate publishing works (notably *The Bloudy Tenent*) arguing against the state control of religion and limitation of religious freedom inherent in the Presbyterian demands. In his tracts Williams argued for the freedom of the individual and his conscience in matters religious, but also for the purity of God's Church. The many changes in the religious order in recent English history were held up as proof of the inevitability of inconsistency and error when the Church is subjected to the regulation of 'natural, sinful, inconstant men'.[127] Milton set out a forceful argument for religious liberty from both magistrate and presbyter in *Of Civil Power in Ecclesiastical Causes*, when the death of Oliver Cromwell in 1658 revived hopes of the settlement of a national Presbyterian Church and establishment of doctrinal norms.[128] He held firmly to what he believed to be a basic tenet of Protestantism, that 'the scripture only, can be the final judge or rule in matters of religion, and that only in the conscience of every Christian to himself'.[129]

The configuration of churches in New England differed from that in the home country, Congregationalism being the established orthodoxy. This system was founded on the principle of covenant, people forming churches by covenanting themselves to each other and promising to obey the word of God. There was a concern to maintain the churches' purity by limiting congregations to God's elect; this meant that acceptance as a new member came to depend on proof of one's election through the delivery of individual testimonies recounting personal experiences of God.[130] Membership of these churches was a prior condition to full political participation in the civic community in Massachusetts Bay, for it was the male church members who elected 'selectmen' to run the towns. The churches themselves had been set up as self-sufficient and self-regulating; nevertheless, in the 1640s they too were caught up in struggles to contain what were seen as Presbyterian threats to congregational autonomy, notably in the examples of 'deviant' church practice discussed at the Cambridge Assembly of 1643 and in the Remonstrance of 1646, a petition demanding the adoption of a Presbyterian parish-type concept of church membership. Key issues were qualification for church membership (whether proof of regeneration was needed), a subject of vital importance in a society where exclusion from churches effectively meant political disenfranchisement and the broader but closely related question of the relationship between civil and ecclesiastical authority.[131] At the same time, similar concerns about the growth of sectaries were evident in New England, in particular the anti-nomianism of Anne Hutchinson and her followers in the 1630s and later the Baptists and Quakers being singled out for attention by Massachusetts clergy as in John Norton's *The Heart of New England rent at the Blasphemies of the Present Generation*.[132]

The debates around the magistrate's authority in matters religious, about religious tolerance, religious liberty or conformity and about who should or should not be included within the Church are of particular interest to the focus of this study because underlying the discussions are not only concerns about relationships between politics and religion but fundamental questions about the nature of man, about the extent of his natural knowledge and his accountability for his beliefs. The ideas of Francis Rous, one-time parliamentary campaigner against Arminianism who came to support the Independents' cause, are a case in point. He wrote of man as both a natural and a spiritual character and argued that since men are men before they are Christians, 'for faultinesse in Christianity, you must not destroy the *man*'.[133] His separation of man as a political person and as a spiritual person has echoes in Williams's writing. In a 1648 debate with the Leveller John Wildman about 'whether the magistrate have, or ought to have, any compulsive and restrictive power in matters of religion', Henry Ireton insisted that the first four Commandments can be known by man through the light of nature and therefore may be held accountable by other men for any actions contrary to these.[134] But Wildman replied with a minimalist account of what can be known by nature; the light of nature can do little more than determine that there is a God but gives no notion of who or what that God might be, 'and therefore the magistrate cannot easily determine what sins are against the light of nature and what not'.[135]

This necessarily brief overview of the seventeenth-century background to this study has provided the contexts and occasions for the engagement of political ideology and Adamic theory being explored. It has shown points at which understandings of Adam (as state or as story) are relevant to contemporary efforts to interpret the character and happenings of the period and has identified some of the elements that the experiences described make particularly important to these discussions. These include questions about the preservation of person and property, about land ownership, about man's inclination to war or to liberty, about natural knowledge, freedom of conscience, about the location and legitimacy of sovereignty, the rights of resistance to tyranny. It was a time when the conditions being experienced and questions being asked provoked a flourishing of political thinking. The next chapter will examine the intellectual climate for this thinking by introducing the varied conversations about Adam – about lordship, about man's nature, about kinship, about providence – in which our selected seventeenth-century authors engaged and a number of the key thinkers (among them Robert Filmer, Thomas Hobbes, William Ames) who influenced their writing. This exploration will be structured according to the categories identified in the introduction of Adam as state – as he is in his natural created state or fallen condition – and Adam as story – the narrative of Fall and Redemption that structures the history of mankind.

Notes

1. Philip Hunton, *Treatise of Monarchy* (London: E. Smith, 1689), 2. This clergyman and political writer wrote his anti-absolutist work in 1643 advocating a mixed monarchy with checks and balances. The treatise was banned at the Restoration but reprinted in 1689.
2. Another political origin myth from the seventeenth century that had a specifically English application was that of the 'Norman Yoke' that enslaved the English. Winstanley uses it in a number of places including *An Appeal to the House of Commons* where he likens Charles I to William the Conqueror.
3. This last question, J. M. Evans argues, was answered by Milton in *Paradise Lost* by presenting humans' existence as a kind of spiritual apprenticeship – J. M. Evans, *Paradise Lost and the Genesis Tradition* (Oxford: Clarendon Press, 1968).
4. One such scholar was Jean Astruc, who in 1753 published anonymously *Conjectures sur les mémoires originauz don't il paroit que Moyse s'est servi pour composer le livre de la Génèse. Avec des remarques qui appuient ou qui éclaircissent ces conjectures*. He was keen to insist, pace Hobbes and Spinoza, that Moses was still the author. The J and P distinction follows the Documentary Theory of German Biblical scholars Graf and Wellhausen. In all, four narrative sources were identified in the Pentateuch – J, E, D and P ('Jahwist', 'Elohist', 'Deuteronomist' and 'Priestly').
5. The Geneva Bible is used in this book for direct Biblical quotes.
6. Ana M. Acosta, *Reading Genesis in the Long Eighteenth Century: from Milton to Mary Shelley* (Aldershot: Ashgate, 2006), 13f.
7. This is particularly the case in translation where the association between the names 'Adam' and 'Eve' and their Hebrew meanings of 'man' and 'living' is weakened.
8. Genesis 6 may be behind the reference to fallen angels in 2 Pet. 2:4 and Jude 6. In his classic work *The Ideas of the Fall and of Original Sin: A Historical and Critical Study* (London: Longmans, Green and Co, 1929), N. P. Williams argued that it was Paul's favouring of Adamic origins of sin that led to a decline in influence of the Fallen Angels thesis – Williams, *Ideas of the Fall*, 112.
9. Gen. 2:24.

10. Gen. 3:16; Gen. 3:19.
11. Paul is the sole New Testament authority for the Adamic Fall doctrine.
12. Williams, *Ideas of the Fall*, 113.
13. 'Live by the Spirit, I say, and do not gratify the desires of the flesh. For what the flesh desires is opposed to the Spirit, and what the Spirit desires is opposed to the flesh; for they are opposed to each other to prevent you from doing what you want'. Gal. 5:16.
14. Anthony C. Thiselton, *The Hermeneutics of Doctrine* (Grand Rapids, MI: Wm. B. Eerdmans Publishing Co., 2006), 281.
15. Rom. 5:18–19: 'Likewise then, as by the offence of one the fault came on all men to condemnation, so by the iustifying of one, the benefite aboundeth towarde all men to the iustification of life. For as by one mans disobedience, many were made sinners: so by the obedience of one, shall many also bee made righteous'.
16. Augustine, *Ad Simplicianum* 1.1.10; 1.2.20.
17. Franciscan writers were more hesitant than Dominican writers about the concept of original righteousness – Thiselton, *Hermeneutics*, 290.
18. Williams, *Ideas of the Fall*, 401–402.
19. Ibid., 425f.
20. Ibid., 425f.
21. Arminius's followers were known as Remonstrants.
22. 'Nature' here refers to Adam at his first Creation, not to Calvin's inclusion in the natural of 'depraved habit' (Thiselton, *Hermeneutics*, 291).
23. See James P. Byrd, *The Challenges of Roger Williams: Religious Liberty, Violent Persecution and the Bible* (Georgia: Mercer University Press, 2002), 3 n. 3.
24. Sir Robert Filmer, 'Anarchy of a Limited or Mixed Monarchy', in *Sir Robert Filmer's Patriarcha and Other Writings*, edited by Johann P. Somerville (Cambridge: Cambridge University Press, 1991), 147–48.
25. Tom Furniss, 'Reading the Geneva Bible: Notes toward an English Revolution?' *Prose Studies: History, Theory, Criticism* 31 (1) (2009), 1–21.
26. Ibid., 27.
27. A point emphasised by John R. Knott in *The Sword of the Spirit: Puritan Responses to the Bible* (Chicago and London: University of Chicago Press, 1980), 29.
28. *FB*, 202; *FB*, 200.
29. Lewalski, *Life*, 130–31.
30. Brian Cummings, *The Literary Culture of the Reformation: Grammar and Grace* (Oxford: Oxford University Press, 2002); Luther stated that while Scripture itself was clear there are two kinds of clarity, one (*externa*) requires rigorous critical exegesis; the other (*interna*) is dependent on the working of Grace, for the Spirit is required for understanding any part of Scripture – Cummings, Ibid., 173.
31. Don Marion Wolf, ed., 1980 *Complete Prose Works of John Milton* (Yale: Yale University Press, 2.584; see James Dougal Fleming, *Milton's Secrecy: and Philosophical Hermeneutics* (Burlington, VT: Ashgate, 2008), 164f.
32. *Complete Prose Works* 6, 583–84.
33. Locke's 'Preface' to his paraphrases of St Paul's epistles – PN, xiii–xiv, in *The Works of John Locke in Nine Volumes (the Twelfth Edition)*, Vol. 7 (London: C&J Rivington, 1824).

34. Henning Graf Reventlow, *The Authority of the Bible and the Rise of the Modern World*, tr. John Bowden (London: SCM, 1984), 164. In the first chapter of his theological thesis, (DDC, Ch. 1), Milton establishes his principle that the Scriptures are to be interpreted through the illuminating light of the Holy Spirit rather than reliance on commentators. His treatise on *The Doctrine and Discipline of Divorce* argues against 'the extreme literalist' (DDD, 307) approach to the Scriptures and presents a model of the application of reason and conscience to Biblical text (DDD, 309f). In *Areopagitica* he argues that the individual's reason and conscience rather than government censorship are the safeguards against erroneous doctrines and teachings (AR, 150, 156); for reason as 'that intellectual ray' see *RE*, 23.
35. DDC, 587, 590.
36. William Perkins, *Workes, Vol. III*, edited by J. Legate and C. Legge III (London, 1618), 413.; Perkins was writing with reference to anabaptists and antinomians.
37. Reventlow, *Authority*, 12.
38. TLH (CW, I), 414.
39. TLH, 429.
40. TLH 435. Cf. also TLH, 429: 'The declaration or report of words out of the mouth or pen of men shall cease; but the spirit endures for ever; from whence those words were breathed: as when I have the thing promised, the word of the promise ceases'.
41. CPW vol. 1, 498.
42. TRC, 157.
43. TRC, 157.
44. *The Works of William Chillingworth M.A. of the University of Oxford, Tenth Edition* (London: D. Midwinter et al., 1742) Vol. IV, 204.
45. Origen, *De Principiis* IV, 15.
46. John Calvin, *Commentaries on Galatians*, cited in Thomas Luxon, *Literal Figures: Puritan Allegory and the Reformation Crisis in Representation* (Chicago: University of Chicago Press, 1995), 81; William Tyndale, *The Obedience of a Christian Man* (1528) cited in Luxon, *Literal Figures*, 80.
47. Ibid., 81.
48. Ibid., 94.
49. Barbara K. Lewalski, *Protestant Poetics and the Seventeenth Century Religious Lyric* (Princeton, NJ; Princeton UP, 1979).
50. In this Perkins employs a Thomist syllogism: 'Since then that is the sense of the scripture, and the literal sense, which the Holy Spirit intends, however it may be gathered, certainly if the holy Spirit intended the tropologic, anagogic or allegoric sense of any place, these senses are not different from the literal' – Luxon, *Literal Figures*, 98.
51. Luxon, *Literal Figures*, 99; Paul himself refers to Abraham's story as an allegory (Gal. 4:24).
52. Lewalski, *Life*, 306.
53. Reventlow, *Authority*, 140.
54. BT, 278.
55. RCG, CPW vol. 1, 813–16.
56. Amy Stewart Bizik '*Sufficient to Have Stood though Free to Fall': The Parabolic Narrative of Free Will in Paradise Lost*, (Dissertation, University of Arizona, 2008).
57. Lewalski, *Protestant Poetics*, 31.

58. For example the jeremiad at the conclusion of *REW*, 243–44.
59. *Key,* 105–106.
60. Eric Auerbach, *Mimesis: The Representation of Reality in Western Literature* (Princeton, NJ: Princeton University Press, 1973).
61. Golda Werman, *Milton and Midrash* (Washington, DC: Catholic University of America Press, 1995).
62. Philip C. Almond, *Adam and Eve in Seventeenth Century Thought* (Cambridge: Cambridge University Press, 1999), 213.
63. Mark Kishlansky, *A Monarchy Transformed: Britain 1603–1714* (Harmondsworth: Penguin, 1996), 4.
64. Pocock, *Politics, Language.*
65. See 'Introduction' in Christopher Hill, ed., *Winstanley: The Law of Freedom and Other Writings,* (Harmondsworth: Penguin, 1973), 42–59.
66. Jeremy Waldron, *God, Locke and Equality: Christian Foundations in Locke's Political Thought* (Cambridge: Cambridge University Press, 2002).
67. Christopher Hill, *The English Revolution 1640* (London: Lawrence & Wishart, 1940). More recently the descriptors 'English Revolution', or 'English Civil War' have fallen out of favour for not giving due recognition to the significant roles played by Scotland and Ireland in the events of the period.
68. Christopher Hill, *The World Turned Upside Down: Radical Ideas During the English Revolution* (Harmondsworth: Penguin, 1972); John Adamson writes dismissively of this interest in seventeenth-century radicals, 'For a moment, Flower Power peered into the murky waters of Civil War sectarianism and, Narcissus-like, fell in love with its own reflection' – John Adamson, ed., *The English Civil War: Conflicts and Contexts 1640–49* (Basingstoke: Palgrave Macmillan, 2009), 21.
69. Discussed in John Adamson 'Introduction: High Roads and Blind Alleys. The English Civil War and its Historiography', in Adamson, *English Civil War.*
70. See Margot Todd's 'Introduction' for the 'high road', revisionist and counter-revisionist categorisation of historians of the Civil War in *Reformation to Revolution: Politics and Religion in Early Modern England,* edited by Margot Todd (London: Routledge, 1995).
71. John Morrill, *Revolt in the Provinces: the People of England and the Tragedies of War 1630–1648* (New York: Longman, 1999); Richard Cust and Anne Hughes, ed., *The English Civil War* (London: Arnold, 1997); Richard Cust and Anne Hughes, *Conflict in Early Stuart England: Studies in Religion and Politics, 1603–1642* (London: Longman, 1989).
72. The word 'revolution' was not used of contemporary events in the seventeenth century. At that time it denoted a cycle or rotation rather than abrupt change – N. H. Keeble, ed., *The Cambridge Companion to Writing of the English Revolution* (Cambridge: Cambridge University Press, 2001), 8 n. 26.
73. Noted by Michael Wilding, *Dragon's Teeth: Literature in the English Revolution* (Oxford: Clarendon Press, 1987).
74. John Morrill, 'The Causes and Course of the British Civil Wars' in Keeble, *Cambridge Companion,* 13; Cited by David Underdown, 'Popular Politics before the Civil War', in Todd, *Reformation,* 218.
75. Pocock, *Politics, Language,* 81.
76. The common lawyer Sir Edward Coke argued that common law was a reflection of natural law and so inherently equitable, and that understanding common law was dependent on an artificial process of reasoning that required trained

lawyers rather than something any reasonable person could understand – Kishlansky, *Monarchy Transformed*, 37.
77. Examples include Winstanley on the Norman Conquest *TLS* and Matthew Poole on Papal Power, *Commentary on the Holy Bible: Vol. III, Matthew to Revelation* (McLean, VA: MacDonald, 1985).
78. Pocock, *Politics, Language*, 81.
79. Ibid., 84.
80. Paul Ricoeur, *Time and Narrative: Volume 1* (Chicago and London: University of Chicago Press, 1984), 65.
81. Roger Williams, *The Complete Writings of Roger Williams, Vol. 6*, edited by Perry Miller (New York: Russell and Russell, 1964), 228.
82. Morrill, 'Causes and Course', 23.
83. Thomas N. Corns, 'Radical Pamphleteering' in Keeble, *Cambridge Companion*, 71–86; The respect in which Eliot was held by his contemporaries in the Massachusetts Bay colony is evident in Cotton Mather's biography, *The Life and Death of the Reverend John Eliot* (London: John Dunton, 1694).
84. *REW*, 224.
85. Francis Bamford, ed., *A Royalist's Notebook: The Commonplace Book of Sir John Oglander, Kt., of Nunwell, Born 1585, Died 1655* (London: Constable & Co., 1936), 104.
86. David Underdown, *Revel, Riot and Rebellion: Popular Politics and Culture in England 1603–1660* (Oxford: Oxford University Press, 1987) and Underdown, *Popular Politics*, 208–31.
87. Underdown, *Popular Politics*, 215.
88. Alison Games, 'Migration', in *The British Atlantic World 1500–1800*, edited by David Armitage and Michael J. Braddick (Basingstoke: Palgrave MacMillan, 2002), 31–50.
89. Nuala Zahedieh 'Economy' in Armitage and Braddick, *British Atlantic*, 51–68.
90. Alden T. Vaughan, ed., *The Puritan Tradition in America, 1620–1730*, revised edition (Hanover and London: University Press of New England, 1972), 26.
91. Clive Holmes, *Seventeenth Century Lincolnshire (History of Lincolnshire)* (Lincs Local Hist. Soc, Hist. of Lin., November 1980).
92. Tim Harris, *Restoration: Charles II and His Kingdom 1660–85* (London: Allen Lane, 2005).
93. I have accepted Peter Laslett's dating of Locke's *Two Treatises of Government* to the period from 1679 and 1683 with later revisions in his introduction to John Locke, *Two Treatises of Government*, edited by Peter Laslett (Cambridge: Cambridge University Press, 1960).
94. David Wootton, 'From Rebellion to Revolution', in *English Civil War*, edited by Richard Cust and Anne Hughes, 340–56; Philip Baker, 'Rhetoric, Reality and the Varieties of Civil War Radicalism' in Adamson, *English Civil War*, 202–21; Ibid., 209–10. The leading parliamentarian theorist was Henry Parker.
95. Adamson, 'Introduction'.
96. Morrill, 'Causes and Course', 13.
97. Conrad Russell, *The Causes of the Civil War: The Ford Lectures Delivered in the University of Oxford 1987–1988* (Oxford: Clarendon Press, 1990); See also Kevin Sharpe, *The Personal Rule of Charles I* (New Haven: Yale University Press, 1992), which focuses on the character of the king and his actions and presents the mid-century crisis as something of a fluke.

98. Examples exploring tyranny and disobedience include comments on the Hebrew wives disobeying Pharaoh's order to kill all male babies (Ex 1), 'their disobedience herein was lawful, but their dissembling evil'; on God threatening to abandon Israel because of the sins of Jeroboam (1 Kgs 14.16) 'the people shall not be excused, when they do evil at commandment of their governors', and on Jezebel's death (2 Kgs 9) presented as an 'example of God's judgements to all tyrants'. James I ensured that his new, authorised version was free of 'seditious' notes and any mention of the word 'tyrant'. Morrill notes, however, that though historical treatises, play-texts and ballads of the early years of the century might ponder the evils of tyrannical government in the remote past and in places geographically distant, there was very little evidence of the application of these examples to the Stuart realms, or of suppression of such political writing – Morrill, 'Causes and Consequences', 13–14.
99. Morrill, 'Causes and Consequences', 14–15.
100. In Robert Filmer's 1648 *The Anarchy of a Limited or Mixed Monarchy* and Thomas Hobbes's *Behemoth or the Long Parliament* (written c1638 and published 1682) where he claims 'the whole nation' is 'in love with *mixarchy*, which they used to praise by the name of mixed monarchy, though it were indeed nothing else but pure anarchy' – Thomas Hobbes, *Behemoth or the Long Parliament*, edited by Ferdinand Tönnies (Chicago: University of Chicago Press, 1990), 116–17.
101. The Army's declaration of 14 June 1647 stated: 'We were not a mere mercenary army hired to serve any arbitrary power of a state' – Kishlansky, *Monarchy Transformed*, 175.
102. Here both senses of the term 'original' are intended: original as beginnings, and original as pattern. Filmer's *Patriarcha* was written in the 1620s and 1630s but published in several editions in the 1680s.
103. Christopher Hill, *The World Turned Upside Down: Radical Ideas During the English Revolution* (Harmondsworth: Penguin Books, 1973).
104. For this use of 'mainstream' to denote those clergy who supported the parliamentary cause in the Civil War as a means of completing the reformation of the English church, see Ann Hughes, 'The Meanings of Religious Polemic' in *Puritanism: Transatlantic Perspectives on a Seventeenth-Century Anglo-American Faith*, edited by Francis J. Bremer (Boston: Massachusetts Historical Society, 1993), 204.
105. Thomas Edwards, *The Third Part of Gangræna or a Catalogue and Discovery of Many of the Errours, Heresies, Blasphemies and Pernicious Practices of the Sectaries of the Time* (London, 1646).
106. E[phraim] P[agitt], *Heresiography*, 2nd edn (London, 1645) cited in Lewalski (2000), 202 and 604, n. 24. Milton was cited for his writing on divorce and Williams for *The Bloudy Tenent*, a publication that was banned by Parliament.
107. John Morrill, 'The Church in England 1642–1649', in *Reactions to the English Civil War*, edited by John Morrill (London: Macmillan, 1982).
108. Hughes, 'Meanings'.
109. The mace is the symbol of the monarch's presence in the chamber.
110. For a dramatic account of this final session, see Kishlansky, *Monarchy Transformed*, 115.
111. Jacqueline Rose, *Godly Kingship in Restoration England: The Politics of Royal Supremacy 1660–1688*, (Cambridge: Cambridge University Press, 2011).

40 Material, method and occasion

112. *A Sermon Preached on the Fat-Day at St Margaret's Westminster, November 13 1678*, cited in Jacqueline Rose, *Godly Kingship*.
113. Rose, *Godly Kingship*, 3.
114. See Thomas Scanlan's thesis on the association of Protestantism and Englishness in Thomas Scanlan, *Colonial Writings and the New World 1583–1671: Allegories of Desire* (Cambridge: Cambridge University Press, 1999). There are numerous examples of the use of this imagery in seventeenth century religious polemic, among them Joseph Salmon's *Anti-Christ in Man* (1647) and Edward Burrough's *The Epistle to the Reader*, an introduction to George Fox, *The Great Mystery of the Great Whore of Babylon Unfolded* (London the 9. Mo. 1658).
115. Milton's *Areopagitica*, and Locke's *Letter Concerning Toleration* excluded Roman Catholicism (or 'Popery') from the general toleration being advocated.
116. Perhaps not brave enough to accompany William when he arrived in Devon with his invasion fleet, Locke came later with Queen Mary when the success of William's mission had been secured. For details of Locke's political involvement (and his political caution), see Roger Woolhouse, *Locke: A Biography* (Cambridge: Cambridge University Press, 2007).
117. Morrill, 'Causes and Course', 16.
118. Nicholas Tyacke, 'Puritanism, Arminianism and Counter-Revolution', in Todd, *Reformation*. Arminianism in England differed from continental forms in that, as promoted by Charles and Laud, it had an additional sacramental dimension building on the survivals of the English Reformation, the episcopacy and the elements of the pre-reformation mass preserved in the Prayer Book.
119. Martin Dzelzainis, 'Ideas in Conflict: Political and Religious Thought during the English Revolution', in Keeble, *Cambridge Companion*, 32.
120. The association of Arminianism with the king's party does not mean a necessary correlation of royalist politics and Arminian doctrine, as the move towards Arminianism in Milton's theology proves. His opposition to Calvinist determinism and predestination was linked to his commitment to liberty and human responsibility – Lewalski, *Life*, 420f.
121. Cited in Tyacke, 'Puritanism, Arminianism', 65.
122. Peter Lake, 'Calvinism and the English Church 1570–1653', in Todd, *Reformation*.
123. This sermon was possibly delivered by Thomas Goodwin; see W. Clark Gilpin, *The Millenarian Piety of Roger Williams* (Chicago: University of Chicago Press, 1979), 75.
124. The influence of the Episcopalians was seriously impaired by the refusal of Calvinist bishops to take part.
125. Among the Scottish Commissioners were Samuel Rutherford, Alexander Henderson, Robert Baillie and George Gillespie.
126. To use Milton's phrase – Kishlansky, *Monarchy Transformed*, 169. The 'Congregational Way' proposed by Thomas Goodwin and his colleagues was often advertised by them as 'the New England Way', the success of the colonies being cited as proof that God favoured this system; see Francis J. Bremer (2nd edn), *The Puritan Experiment: New England Society from Bradford to Edwards* (Hanover and London: University Press of New England, 1995).
127. *BT*, 215.
128. Lewalski, *Life*, 361.

129. John Milton, *A Treatise of Civil Power in Ecclesiastical Causes* (London: J. Johnson, 1790), 4.
130. John Cotton, apologist of the 'New England way', set out the basic principles of the congregational system in a 1636 sermon at Salem. For an account of the system, see the first chapter of Harry S. Stout, *The New England Soul: Preaching and Religious Culture in Colonial New England* (Oxford: Oxford University Press, 1986).
131. The deviant practices in question were those of Thomas Parker and James Noyse, respectively pastor and teacher of the Newbury, Massachusetts, congregation who opened baptism and the Lord's Supper to all but notorious sinners. See the 1631 decision by John Winthrop and his associates that 'noe man shal be admitted to the freedom of this body polliticke, but such as are members of some of the churches within the lymitts of the same' – Bremer, *Puritan Experiment*, 60.
132. Cited in Bremer, *Puritan Experiment*, 139.
133. *The Ancient Bounds, or Liberty of Conscience, Tenderly Stated, Modestly Asserted, and Mildly Vindicated* (1645) – Dzelzainis, 'Ideas in Conflict', 42.
134. *Army Debates*, 125, 149, 154 – cited in Dzelzainis, 'Ideas in Conflict', 44.
135. *Army Debates*, 161– cited in Dzelzainis, 'Ideas in Conflict', 44.

2 Conversations about Adam

Adam as state

Adam the patriarch

Among seventeenth-century exponents of patriarchalism the name of Sir Robert Filmer stands out.[1] His various works, *Patriarcha, The Anarchy of a Limited or Mixed Monarchy* and *Observations concerning the Original of Government,* used the Genesis story of Adam's creation to argue that an absolutist monarchy is the only legitimate form of government.[2] Filmer is famously the theorist against whom Locke constructed the arguments of his *First Treatise of Government* and so established the basis for his better-known *Second Treatise,* that platform for so much subsequent liberal thought. Another liberal hero (and martyr), Algernon Sidney, penned a refutation of Filmer in his *Discourses concerning Government,* which was used as evidence against him in his trial at the time of the Rye House plot.[3] His speech on the scaffold kept Filmer's theories to the fore.[4] In it he described the royalist's model of absolutism as 'by all intelligent men ... thought to be grounded upon wicked principles equally pernicious to magistrates and people'. Sidney's speech in turn prompted a number of responses defending Filmer, including that by Tory publicist Edmund Bohun, *A Defence of Sir Robert Filmer, against the Mistakes and Misrepresentations of Algernon Sidney.*[5] In their studies of Filmer and of seventeenth-century patriarchalism, James Daly and Gordon Schochet suggest that his significance was largely given to him posthumously by the Whigs, who set him up as a straw man (almost a caricature) against which to argue their own case for the legitimacy of resistance to a tyrannical monarch.[6] They demonstrate that he was not representative of royalist thinking as a whole. On the other hand, the publication of numerous editions of his works between 1679 and 1688 suggest that royalist supporters of the Duke of York's hereditary rights to the throne, and of his autocratic rule once king, found his writing useful.[7] Whatever Filmer's impact on royalist thinking, it is clear he had a significant influence on those who refuted his ideas: on the thinking of Sidney in his *Discourses,* on that of James Tyrell in his *Patriarcha non Monarchia* (1681) and also of Locke in his *Treatises of Government.* His influence has continued beyond these times to colour modern interpretations of the impact of Biblically grounded, Adamic theory on political thought. As the theory in response to which Locke (frequently hailed as the founding father of modern liberalism) wrote his *Treatises* (frequently hailed as its founding document), Filmer's patriarchalism came to represent in the liberal tradition, the shackles of 'political Adamicism' from which political progressive, Locke, broke free.[8] The distinction given to Filmer in his era and in traditional interpretations of political thought at this time make his theory an appropriate point of departure for this chapter. Positioning his work in relation to that of his critics and those he criticises, and to a broader range of contemporary conversations about Adam, will demonstrate that, contrary to a ready association of Adamic doctrine with political conservatism, for seventeenth-century men and women engagement with the first chapters of Genesis opened up a variety of interpretations and political possibilities.

Filmer's royalist theory was grounded in his interpretation of the Creation narratives in Genesis. He argued from the fatherhood of Adam for royal absolutism: sovereignty was given by God directly to Adam, transmitted genealogically (and by primogeniture) to his heirs and exercised by all who possessed it without any accountability to their subjects. This understanding of the origins of sovereignty in Adam encouraged the foregrounding of Adam and Adamic themes in the works of his critics. As Peter Laslett wrote of Locke, he was arguing in his *Treatises* with terms of reference chosen by Filmer.[9] So Locke began with patriarchalism and sought arguments to undermine its logic.[10] In his rebuttal of Filmer he engaged with historical understandings of society and explored family relations as part of his discussion. Filmer's heavy emphasis on Adam's ownership of the goods of the world provided a lead-in for Locke's disquisition on the rights of property. In this Whig conversation with patriarchalism, Filmer influenced not just the content but also the terms. He was diligent in his use of scriptural sources to inform his political theory. Indeed, as Daly notes, few Puritans demonstrated clearer commitment than Filmer to *sola scriptura* or the dismissal of merely human intellectual tradition.[11] The scriptural basis of Filmer's theory was also its weakness. Biblical passages are open to a variety of interpretations, and so Scripture could be used against Scripture. Sidney countered Filmer with another understanding of the Biblical history of kings and used the authority of St Paul and of Calvin's exegesis in his support.[12] Tyrell and Locke were able to unpick Filmer's argument through different interpretations of the same texts, for example arguing that the words of the Genesis account gave no more dominion to Adam than to Eve.[13] When Locke delivered the crushing criticism, 'God must not be believed, though he speaks it himself, when he says he does anything, which will not consist with Sir Robert's hypothesis', he signalled the dependence of his own argument on God's Word 'correctly' understood.[14]

Filmer's politics were based on his reading of Adam's state in Genesis. This state he understood to be different from the state of man in general, a difference that had been determined even before men other than Adam existed. Filmer explained that at Creation even before he had any subjects to rule, Adam was 'Monarch of the World' and by right Governor of his posterity.[15] This difference, Adam's sovereignty, was passed down genealogically and through primogeniture to his heirs, two moments of pluralisation of this heirship being noted, the several kingships of the sons of Noah after the Flood, and those of the fathers of the 72 families divided at Babel.[16]

The sovereignty that Adam received at Creation and that his heirs inherited from him was an unlimited supremacy where the sovereign's arbitrary will determined the law by which all should be governed:

> It was God's ordinance that Supremacy should be unlimited in Adam, and as large as all the acts of his will: and as in him, so in all others that have supream power.[17]

Filmer did not deny that there were higher laws (God's laws) and conceded that the king should rule in accordance with them. A father is bound by the 'law of nature' to preserve his children, he wrote in *Patriarcha*, 'but much more is a king always tied by the same law to keep this general ground, that the safety of his kingdom be his chief law'.[18] But this concession does not invalidate the legal voluntarism of the sovereign, for the king's will is law. It is not for subjects to pass judgement on the right or wrong of what he does but to obey. The sovereign is not answerable to the people though ultimately he will be answerable to God.[19] This principle Filmer used to defend the Stuarts against those who claimed a right to resistance on account of the monarch's mistreatment of his subjects. He used it to reject any but an absolute sovereignty; there was no place in his scheme for a mixed constitution such as that advocated by Hunton.

Filmer was uncompromising in his dismissal of any concept of man's natural liberty, a position that pitted him against prominent natural law theorists of his day. Although he used the terminology of 'nature' and 'natural law', his use emphasised what is decreed by God's will – as when he wrote of 'the natural institution of regal authority' – rather than what is part of the essential nature of man.[20] He employed it for a divinely ordained order, for the state of the world and of human society, not for the state of being of the individual man. When he declares in *The Original of Government* that there is no need for war 'in the pure state of nature' because God at Creation provided for every man's needs, it is an argument from divine economics rather than human psychology.[21] Indeed, Filmer was less interested in the essential nature of man than in that which separates some men (the ruling sort) from the others. Adam as the original of political order is of more interest than Adam as the original of man. For Filmer 'every man is either a king or a subject'.[22] As no one is king or subject by dint of being a man, so Adam is not sovereign by his nature as a man but by God's decree. The legal voluntarism with which Filmer credited the monarch was an echo of his doctrine of divine voluntarism. Filmer's whole political theory depended on God's will, its exercise unhampered by even self-imposed limits; in fact, Filmer conceded, God's will is even free to override the inherited right to sovereignty of the heir to Adam should he see fit, for ultimately sovereignty depends on God's will alone.[23] God's will determines every aspect of the political order, the power, form of power, and person who exercises that power:

> Not only the power or right of government but the form of the power of governing and the person having that power are all the ordinance of God, the first father had not onely simply power, but power Monarchicall as he was a father immediately from God.[24]

In this passage Filmer argued that the fatherhood of Adam and that of his successors over their subjects was a particular kind of fatherhood unlike others as it came directly from God. Again Adam is distinguished from the rest of mankind.

Recognition of some connection between Adam's sovereignty over his descendants and the political authority of the current monarch was mainstream thinking for much of the century. Chapter 2 of Bishop John Overall's *Convocation Book* (sanctioned at the 1610 Convocation) started with Adam and the patriarchs, their God-given power and authority and their children's divinely ordained obligation to fear, revere and obey, and proceeded to argue that *potestas regia* may justly be called *potestas patria* with the same legitimacy, rights and requirements of its subjects. It was a correlation supported by the Church of England Catechism at the time, which linked the Fifth Commandment to obedience to the king. That such patriarchalism was not an exclusively royalist position is demonstrated by the fact that during the 1650s the word 'king' was changed to 'magistrate' in many catechism books.[25]

Filmer went further than mainstream thinking, however, in the genealogical basis of his claims and in the exclusive legitimation of sovereignty in God's gift to Adam. There were several examples where royalists explicitly dismissed the claim of lineal succession from Adam to the current monarch as untenable and unnecessary for a patriarchal legitimation of sovereignty. In 1643, in his *The Unlawfulnesse of Subjects Taking up Armes*, Dudley Digges treated as obvious the fact that kings are no more closely related to Adam than anyone else, and 40 years later Thomas Goddard acknowledged in *Plato's Demon* that rulers cannot trace their pedigrees back to Adam as 'we know very well, that all the Kingdoms upon the Earth have often times changed their Masters and Families.'[26]

Many royalists were also prepared to accept (*pace* Filmer) that while the king's power ultimately comes from God, it could be conveyed to the king through the agency of men. Sir Philip Warwick, for example, made a distinction between power 'in the abstract' and 'in the concrete' to explain this dual procession: God gives all power 'in the abstract and sustenance of it' but it can come from man 'in the concrete or specification'.[27] Many royalists were also influenced by classical, Aristotelian and medieval, state-of-nature and natural law political theories, which give a degree of consent to the people. Since nature wills the good of the community, majority consent is based on natural law and so is a valid form of legitimation of sovereignty. For Richard Hooker, political society is both natural and divine; it combines a divine origin of monarchical rule requiring obedience from subjects with political power belonging to people and transferred by contract and consent.[28] Adam Blackwood, John Hayward and William Barclay were all defenders of monarchy, yet all incorporated the concept of original natural liberty of man into their schemes.[29] Thus royalist patriarchal theories of sovereignty presented a variety of forms other than the genealogical model of Filmer, forms that were perhaps less readily unpicked and dismissed by critics of royal absolutism.

In recognition of this variety, Schochet identified three different models of patriarchalism current in the seventeenth century: anthropological patriarchalism, moral patriarchalism and ideological patriarchalism.[30] Anthropological patriarchalism entails recognising patriarchy as part of the natural order on the basis of observation and description of societies and their histories. Classical theory can support this empiricism, in particular Aristotle's political naturalism that spoke of the organic and necessary growth of the family into perfected political order. This naturalism, adopted by Aquinas, was generally accepted as standard in the Middle Ages. Moral patriarchalism places obligation on subjects on account of the authority given to fathers and political title given to Adam by God. Only absolute government is divinely sanctioned. Overall's derivation of *potestas patria* from God's grant of authority and dominion to Adam belongs here.[31] Filmer added to this a strict legalism that links authority with the genealogical succession of Adam's heirs. Both of these categories, as used by Schochet, are genetic models in that the way sovereignty began explains its essence. In both there appears to be a necessary link between origin and continued patterns of authority and obligation, that combination of beginnings and pattern included in earlier meanings of the word 'original'. The second is dependent on scriptural exegesis and vulnerable to different interpretations of the same texts; Tyrell's and Locke's sharp rebuttals of Filmer are evidence of this. The anthropological model with its empirical base may seem more secure. Indeed, contract theorists like Hobbes and Locke both found it hard to escape the fact that the authority of the father has been a decisive influence in the formation of political societies, a weakness in Hobbes's theory that Filmer was happy to exploit.[32] However, what is generally observed to be the case (the development of political societies from patriarchal family units) is not inevitably the case, and the question to be asked here is whether patriarchal political arrangements are conventional or necessary.

The third model, ideological patriarchalism, treats fathers as symbols for all persons vested with authority. It derives political obligation from the duty of children to their parents. This category works with correlations, and Schochet associates it in particular with the seventeenth-century Church's interpretation of the Fifth Commandment, by which the parents to whom honour is due can be taken to represent the king or magistrate, and the children those who honour them as his subjects.[33] Rather than identifying the rightful possessor of sovereignty or conveying legitimacy to a sovereign, this model requires the obligation of the subject once that relationship has been legitimised, and this holds good for the monarchist and the parliamentarian. As Edward Gee stated in *The Divine Right and Originall of the Civill Magistrate* (1658), derivation of authority imports two things: God's institution of authority in general and his conveying that power to particular persons:

> Gods ordaining at the first the conjugal, parental, herile, and political power, that is, his appointing that husband, parent, master, or prince shall have authority over their respective correlatives (suppose by those words of the commandment, *Honour thy Father, &c*) doth not of itself put any of those authorities in being, or one person more than another; or it makes no man a husband, father, master, or Prince.[34]

An ideological model also enables the incorporation of other correspondences between different planes of existence, so we can relate head and body, father and children, king and subjects in the kind of chain of being familiar from E.M.W. Tillyard's Elizabethan world picture.[35] The head and body image was used alongside that of father and child in James I's *The True Law of Free Monarchies* (1598) and famously appeared in graphic form on the title page of the first edition of Thomas Hobbes's *Leviathan*. This use of correspondences differs however from Filmer's literal and legalistic view of the inheritance of sovereignty through the genealogical fatherhood of Adam.

Adam the man: natural law and natural rights

It has been observed that Filmer is probably more often viewed through the eyes of his critics – most particularly those of John Locke – than through his own writing. The value of his writing and the notion of patriarchalism it promotes appear outmoded to modern eyes, while his critics and those he criticised have often been seen as precursors of the dominant strand of modern liberal political thought, in particular through their interrogation of the principles of natural law and natural rights or experimentation with social contract theories. It is for this reason that the latter's work is often considered in conversation with those who came after, whether Thomas Jefferson or John Rawls, rather than with the varied political theories of their day, and key elements of their thinking that are not part of this liberal genealogy are often played down.[36] In this section the conversations about natural rights and law are essentially seventeenth century, with the occasional reference to earlier seminal works that influenced seventeenth-century critics; they focus on the very un-'modern' theme of Adam – his presence or absence, the character of his role and its implications – in explorations of the relationship between man's nature as man and the origins of political society. Filmer again is given a prominent role both to ensure the study is grounded in conversations of the day and because his antipathy to state-of-nature political theories, to the notions of natural liberty and natural rights throws into relief contemporary investigations of the themes.

In the opening lines of his *Patriarcha*, Filmer clearly identified the opposition:

> Since the time that school divinity began to flourish there hath been a common opinion maintained as well by the divines as by divers other learned men which affirms: 'Mankind is naturally endowed and born with freedom from all subjection, and at liberty to choose what form of government it please, and that the power which any one man hath over others was at first bestowed according to the discretion of the multitude. This tenet was first hatched in the schools, and hath been fostered by all succeeding Papists for good divinity.[37]

That first flourishing of school divinity was the flourishing of the medieval scholasticism and the 'common opinion maintained' is the natural law theory that developed from Aquinas's melding of Christian and ancient philosophies. It subscribes to the concept of natural law imprinted by God in man at his creation. The law's basic tenet is 'good is to be done and pursued, and evil avoided'.[38] It is knowable by human reason and so gives a moral guidance independent of (though in accordance with) the positive moral law of Scriptures. It is teleological, in the Aristotelian tradition, for by this theory man is not created in his perfect state, like Filmer's Adam, but rather the law *inclines* him towards his proper acts and ends.[39] Aquinas, like Aristotle and Cicero, finds those ends within the context of communal living 'since man is naturally a civic and social animal', and the political state is perceived as an institution oriented towards the happiness of its subjects.[40] In Filmer's *sola scriptura* perspective the dependence of the schoolmen's theory on classical models is already a disqualification for, without the benefits of the Creation story in Genesis, they are bound to err, an idea articulated more forcefully by the Anglican divine Robert South: 'an Aristotle was but the rubbish of an Adam, and Athens but the rudiments of Paradise.'[41] It was not just the roots of natural law theories but their conclusions that were an issue. The particular 'succeeding Papist' Filmer targets in *Patriarcha* is the Spanish Jesuit, Francesco Suarez, his opening paragraph being a rather crude summary of the Spaniard's application of natural law theory to the origins of the state. In Suarez's view political power first began when several families came together in one perfected community and the assembled heads of those families chose what government they judged to accord best with their needs.[42] This could hardly be more different from Filmer's starting point as it entails man's choosing rather than God's decree and an origin in an egalitarian society of many rather than the sovereignty of one.

In his quarrel with Suarez, Filmer was participating in a wider European conversation in what has been termed the 'heroic' period of modern natural law theory, a time of Protestant experimentation with scholastic natural law ideas.[43] The prime targets of Filmer's 1652 *Observations concerning the Originall of Government* were two of the most influential contributions to this experiment; Hugo Grotius's *De Jure Belli ac Pacis* (1625) and Thomas Hobbes's *Leviathan* (1651). In England the genealogy of natural law thinkers included Richard Hooker, John Selden, Hobbes, Richard Cumberland, Tyrell and Locke, whose ideas were not only in dispute with Filmer's but also in dialogue with each other and with continental writers, in particular Dutch Grotius and German Samuel von Pufendorf.[44] The terms of the debate are encapsulated in the question put to the *justice* by the *freeholder* in Tyrell's dialogical tract, *A Brief Enquiry into the Ancient Constitution and Government of England*: 'were men at first born Subjects, or did they become so by some Human means?'[45] For those of Filmer's persuasion there was no time when human beings were not subject to another man's authority.[46] What was at issue here was more than a theory of the original formation of human society; it was a question of the relations between divine decree and human agency in the event, as Philip Hunton explains in his *Treatise of Monarchy* (1643):

> There seem to be two extremes of Opinion: while some amplifie the Divinity, thereof, others speak so slightly of it as if there were little else but Humane Institution in it.[47]

As might be expected from this comment, Hunton's own mixed monarchy charts a course between the two.

To focus on human institution is not to deny God any role in the origins of the polity, but the 'extreme opinion' places the divinity at a remove from the direct relationship between God and Adam entailed in Filmer's model from Genesis, a first cause (with overtones of deism) rather than continuing positive command. In the exercise of earthly power man acts not by direct decree from God but by the resources, the inclination and reason 'written on his heart' at Creation.[48] Although that strength may have been given him by God, he is acting in his own strength from his own knowledge; he is not responding to the arbitrary will of the Creator but according to fixed principles in nature applicable to all, whether – to quote Tyrell – 'he be a single man in the state of Nature, or the Supream Powers in the Commonwealth'.[49] Where an autonomous access to God's law is allowed there is a danger of God himself becoming redundant. Certainly Filmer is jealous of God's reputation for omnipotence and goodness and quick to pick up on any passages that imply any diminution of His authority and providence. He objects to Hobbes's description of the state of nature as one of war, on the grounds that God in his goodness has provided sufficient for all and so there is no reason for conflict.

> God was no such niggard in the creation, and there being plenty of sustenance and room for all men, there is no cause or use of war till men be hindered in the preservation of life, so that there is no absolute necessity of war in the state of pure nature.[50]

Suggestions in the writings of Selden and of Grotius that the nature of human society and of the polity changed decisively after the Flood were criticised by Filmer as derogation from the providence of the Almighty who would not ordain a community that would not last.[51] This emphasis on the immutability of providence is not entirely consistent with his voluntarist God, but the example reinforces his basic concern that God should be recognised to be in control. Another example where Filmer finds confusion among natural, human and divine law is Grotius's theory of property. Grotius begins with the 'natural common', the use of all things in common by the law of nature. He identifies a primitive state that lasts until the invention of arts to improve and farm leads to inequality, which in turn necessitates a coming together to establish, by human compact, a propriety in goods recognising the claims of each to his own. For Filmer an origin of property in human institution would mean that the duties in the second table of the Decalogue, relating as they do to property, are themselves of human origin, and the divine foundation of the moral law is called into question:

> But if property be brought in by human law as Grotius teacheth then the moral law depends upon the will of man.[52]

What is at issue is more than the extent of God's role in mankind's scheme; it is the character of his role. Filmer's political theory begins with a clear understanding of what the relationship should be based on the accounts of that between Adam and God in Eden. His ordering of society depends on an *ab initio* granting of authority to one man and the subsequent direction of the rest of mankind by that one man's will. It is essentially hierarchical founded in unequal relationships – God and Adam, patriarch and family, sovereign and subject. As has been seen, the exercise of authority within these relationships is voluntaristic, the behaviour of the inferior in each relationship being subject to the will (freely exercised) of the superior; God's relationship with Adam parallels Adam's with his own subject. It does not necessarily follow that a voluntarist conception of God requires a voluntarist monarch – Augustine contrasts mankind's 'fellowship of equality under God' with the pride that 'seeks to impose its own dominion on fellow men, in place of God's rule' – but it establishes a pattern of rule or a metaphor.[53] Thus Hobbes's God in Eden is one who 'required utterly simple obedience to his precepts, without argument as to whether the precept was Good or

Bad' and his civil sovereign – 'that *Mortall god*, to which we owe under the *Immortal God*, our peace and defence' – likewise has the power to demand unquestioning obedience and to make things good or evil by his command.[54] Hobbes used the story of the forbidden fruit in Eden to illustrate the nature of God's arbitrary rule over man that makes things good or bad by His positive law; 'without the command, the fruit of the tree has nothing in its nature by which its eating could be morally bad i.e. a sin'.[55]

The forbidden fruit is a potent image of God's authority and was commonly used by Protestant commentators for interrogating the concepts of a natural law outside God's positive law. While Filmer all but excludes such a concept from his scheme, others prefer not to deny it but to explore its limitations, to restore the direct relationship and emphasise the importance of obedience to God's positive law. Among these Henry Ainsworth contrasted this command with the law of nature 'graven on Adam's hart', describing it as 'a significative Law' concerning a thing that in itself is indifferent but is made unlawful and evil at the pleasure of God.[56] William Whaleley combined natural law theory and positive law when he argued that though Adam by nature had the ability and 'moral liberty' to eat or not eat the apple, God actually abridged his liberty in order to establish Adam's subjection to Him and His own absolute power over all:

> God did take away from him the moral liberty of eating it, and by his authority saw good to abridge his liberty, and this alone to make it appear to Adam, that he was an absolute and a soveraigne lord over him and had full power and authority to forbid him what he saw good to forbid, and to command what he saw good to command. So the Lord did here call Adam to a profession of his absolute subjection to God his maker, and of God's absolute right to himself and all other creatures.[57]

Similarly, John Salkeld declared the law of nature insufficient as a trial of Adam's obedience 'because it is not altogether manifest by the law of nature that God is sole and supreme Lord over all mankinde: for some doe imagine that the law of nature is a propertie onely due unto a reasonable creature, as every species, or kind of living creatures hath their particular properties agreeing to their nature'.[58] It is a temptation for man to hold himself to be self-sufficient and dependent on his own properties. Without a positive law, the nature of the creature usurps the decree of the Creator as supreme Lord.

That reliance on natural law tends to a marginalisation of God or his relegation to a 'first cause' sideline, is suggested in the writings of Grotius. He himself confessed to belief in God as the 'last source that the law of nature is derived' but suggested that God did not have the power to alter that law of which He was the source: 'The Law of Nature is so unalterable, that God himself cannot change it'.[59] If the law is so unchanging, is implanted in man's essential nature from Creation and is identifiable independently of divine positive law through human reason and experience, then it is possible to proceed without reference to God. Grotius's famous *etiamsi daremus* is an expression of this conclusion. Of natural law, Grotius tells us, 'all we have now said would take place, though we should even grant, what without the greatest Wickedness cannot be granted, that there is no God, or that he takes no Care of human Affairs'.[60] This same double track – law established by God, but accessible without God – is also observable in Locke's *Essays on the Law of Nature* (c1663), where he both shows that God is the ultimate source of morality *and* gives rational foundation to morality; it is something that can be discovered by the use of reason and experience and as suited to man's essential nature.[61] A. P. d'Entreves wrote that the secularisation evident in the work of Grotius and his successors sharply divided what the Schoolmen had taken such pains to reconcile, and though the trend may not characterise the faith of either Grotius or Locke, it led towards the Nature's God of Jefferson and the Supreme Being of the French Revolution, who are 'not more akin to the Supreme God of the creed than Deism is to Christianity'; 'what Grotius had set forth as a hypothesis has become a thesis'.[62] These are the conversations with modern liberalism mentioned above. Although it will be shown that they are but a partial understanding of the movement of political thought, Filmer's fears suggest that there was a contemporary concern that the logic of natural law theory tended towards atheism.

In his introduction to Locke's *Essays*, A. John Simmons posits a shift in thinking about moral relations in the seventeenth century, which he explains in the contrast between two pictures.[63] To summarise briefly, in the first picture God occupies the centre; His Creation of the universe and plan for humankind allow him to give binding laws to us. Our moral duties are owed to Him as Creator, moral Lawgiver and Sovereign. Each of us has duties not to harm others, but these are duties owed to God – others are to be respected as part of God's property and plan. The emphasis is less on rights, more on duty and worship. In the second picture, God is still important, but although He is still Creator, Lawgiver and Planner, the ends promoted by his law are now seen as 'detachable'. The law is now *for* us and less *over* us, and its facilitation of human ends is as prominent as its facilitation of God's ends. Fellow humans are not just God's creatures but are our equals in other ways, as rational and purposive beings and in their similarity to us; they are to be taken seriously in themselves. This provides the foundation for civil society and principles for the establishment of the polity. Duties are *owed* to others not just *with respect* to others. Simmons writes of a change between the two pictures from the language of duty to the language of rights:

> Duty's primacy in the first picture stems from the gross inequality of the parties concerned (God and humankind). Once the relevant parties are conceived of as equals, rights take a more prominent place.

An illustration of this second picture is found in Robert South's exposition of 'that great Rule, of doing, as a Man would be done by'. This rule he claims,

> is as old as Adam, and bears date with humane Nature itself; as springing from that Primitive Relation of Equality, which all men as *fellow Creatures* and *fellow Subjects* to the same Supreme Lord, bear to one another in respect of that common Right which every man has *equally* to his life and to the proper Comforts of life; and consequently to all things actually necessary to the support of both'.[64]

The focus is on men's natural equality and fellowship with one another, on the rights they possess to the fulfilment of human ends, life and its comforts. South combines natural law (that great Rule) with rights. Both Hobbes and royalist Dudley Digges found the terms 'law' and 'rights' to be confused in contemporary usage and drew the same distinction between them: Law was 'obligation that binds' and Right 'consists in liberty to do or forbear'.[65] The language of rights opens up new lines of division. While there seems to have been a wide consensus that the right to self-preservation is a basic right there were variations of opinion beyond this; for Locke, for example, the right to property was fundamental, for Winstanley property was a violation of a natural right to use of the common. Natural rights theories were influenced by both positive and negative views of human nature. In his *Second Treatise* Locke quoted at length Hooker's view that we are naturally inclined to seek fellowship with one another because on our own we lack the resources to secure a life fit for 'the Dignity of Man', while others conceive of natural rights as something secured against one another in a world prone to violence.[66] According to Hobbes, man has a natural right to all means necessary for self-preservation from the aggression of other men. There were differing views on whether or not one's natural rights can be foregone or transferred, whether one right might be forfeited to secure another. Grotius, Digges, Selden and Hobbes all countenanced the surrender of individual rights to a sovereign in exchange for security of life.[67] For Locke, on the other hand, all the basic rights of life, liberty and property were inalienable. His model includes the establishment of a polity where these rights are best secured but also retains the people's right of resistance should the sovereign become tyrant and his actions pose to them a threat.

Natural man, reality and fiction

Simmons's two-picture model cannot be read as a simple binary model of positive law and moral law; theocentric and anthropocentric, duties and rights; the thinking it seeks to characterise is (by the author's admission) fluid and complex.[68] However, it does help to identify different emphases interwoven in the literature of the period. The two pictures can be related to contrasting interpretations of Adam and the Genesis story, to one that emphasises decree, God's positive command and direct authorisation establishing Adam's subjection to Him and Adam's lordship over others – not just 'thou shalt not eat of it' but also 'till the earth and subdue it and rule over it' – and to another that interrogates the figure of Adam (as first but also as fellow man) for what he tells us about ourselves and our essential nature as humans, what we are and what we were created to be. This interrogation Locke undertook in response to Filmer through detailed exegesis of scriptural verses and Milton did very differently, but again with great attention to detail, in his fictional elaboration of the scriptural story in *Paradise Lost*. But the focus of the second picture is not just man but man in relation to man, a focus to which it is difficult to do justice by concentrating on Adam in the garden where he is initially alone or where his only human relationship is with Eve; her physical generation from Adam's side, gender differences, and contemporary conventions about the relationship between man and wife made it difficult (though it was sometimes attempted) to extrapolate from this Edenic society to human society more generally.[69] Writers whose understandings of political society were built upon the natural rights that men exercise in relation to each other (equality with the other, freedom from subjection to the other's will) were often led to look to other models of pre-civil man for their explanations of origins. Filmer went so far as to suggest that a focus on natural rights, in particular the right of liberty, is a denial of Adam's Creation. In his *Observations of Aristotle's Politics* he declares that 'A Natural Freedom of Mankind cannot be supposed without the denial of the Creation of Adam', a conclusion Locke set out to refute in his *First Treatise of Government*.[70] Filmer's critique of 'right of nature' theorists includes the warning, 'we must not deny the truth of Creation'.[71] His problems were the (to him) unBiblical suggestions that there might be an original state of being when man was not a subject and that that state was one of a plurality of humans:

> I cannot understand how this 'right of nature' can be conceived without imagining a company of men at the very first to have been all created together without any dependency one of another, or as *'mushrooms (fungorum more) they all on a sudden were sprung out of the earth without any obligation one to another'*, as Mr Hobbes' words are in his book De Cive, chapter 8, section 1; when the Scripture teaches us otherwise, that all men came by succession and generation from one man.[72]

The logic of plurality led some natural law and natural rights theorists to propose an alternative origin of political society from the Adam–God relationship by waiting till there was a condition of plurality to work with. Pufendorf, for example, deferred the establishment of government until Adam's sons were setting up their own households. Selden proposed an interruption in the donation of dominion over all to man first initiated in

Eden and has God acting again to set up a general community between Noah and his sons after the Flood. Suarez made a distinction between economic and political power and characterised Adam's authority over his family as the former; political power emerged later through consent between the heads of a number of households. In this model Suarez was making use of Aristotelian teleology and the philosopher's differentiation of things according to ends and purposes. The end of household is generation, that of the state is preservation, so, as their purposes are different, familial and political rule are different in essence.[73] In his significance to the polity Adam is thus reduced to the level of other men each with their own families; he is first man rather than first among men. Although his historicity is not doubted, his relevance to history is reduced.

These versions of the emergence of political power are all contained within the bounds of the Biblical story; even Filmer is prepared to acknowledge that Selden's determination 'is consonant to the history of the Bible'. However, there was a powerful counter-narrative to Adamic Creation that had come down from the ancients and could tempt men away from the chronology of Scripture. The narrative was particularly evident in humanist readings of Cicero's *De Inventione* and the alternative model of human beginnings presented there. Louis Le Roy, an author widely read in this period, reinterpreted Cicero for his audience.[74] The tale he tells is as follows: at the beginning men were 'very simple and rude in all thinges, little differeing from beastes', they subsisted by gathering herbs, fruits, roots and flesh of raw animals, were clothed in animal skins, lived in ditches, caves and wooden lodges. After a while Le Roy's primitive men grew dissatisfied with their raw meat and nakedness and sought to 'soften the wild and savage manner' by cultivating crops, gathering together in companies so that 'in such a manner were they reduced, from the brutish life which they had led to this sweetnes and civilitie'. Like Cicero, he posits a low 'brutish' starting point for human beings and has them raised to civility by their own efforts; it is a story of human betterment. Cicero, and the Christian humanists whom he influenced, had an interest in a civilising process effected through communication, deliberation and reason and in the laws which human societies imposed upon themselves in *ius gentium* (laws between nations) and *ius civile* (laws of the state). Such images of natural man, though they are rather less stark, have some resonances with the famous 'nasty, brutish and short' descriptors employed to effect in Hobbes's *Leviathan*.[75] In the same chapter of his treatise, Hobbes used America as an illustration of a place where men still live in this state. The pre-civilisation, wild man was a standard figure in writings about America in the sixteenth and seventeenth centuries from various sources, found, for example in literature associated with the activities of the Virginia Company. Company promoter Robert Johnson writes of naked 'wild and savage people' who live like herds of deer in the forest and 'have no law but nature' and Robert Gray of 'savages' who have no property but only general residence 'as wild beasts have in a forest'.[76]

Such accounts of natural man met criticism other than Filmer's. The challenge to theological and political orthodoxy of Ciceronian conceptions of man's beginnings was not lost on Bishop Overall. They contradicted the scriptural account of man's creation and, to the bishop's thinking, gave far too much political agency to men in general and too little to God. So in Canon II of his *Convocation Book* he decried the theory 'that men at the first, without all good education, or civility, ran up and down in woods and fields as wild creatures, resting themselves in caves and dens, and acknowledging no superiority one over another'. To assent to this view would be to 'greatly err'.[77] Such criticisms could be answered if it were recognised that the savage and brutish conditions described were not the original state of man but the consequences of the Fall. In relation to the Indians of America, the theological problem of encounter with such different lifestyles could be addressed by interpreting this wild condition not as their original but as their fallen condition. This interpretation can be found in the language of the same corpus of Virginia literature already referred to, for example when Christopher Carleill spoke of the merit of *'reducing* [leading back] the savage people to Christianitie and civilitie, and Richard Hakluyt advised Sir Walter Ralegh 'to *recall* the savage and the pagan to civility, to draw the ignorant within the orbit of reason and to fill with reverence for divinity the godless and the ungodly'.[78] Contemporary outrage at the libertinism of Hobbes's state of nature would have been considerably lessened had critics taken his description as a post-lapsarian rather than Edenic condition.[79] Confusion was engendered by loose usage of the term 'natural' to mean both the original and the pre-civil state.[80] A consistent distinction between the language of nature and of condition would have increased clarity.

The idea that it was the fallen condition of man that necessitated governance – different both from Filmer's Adamic patriarchalism and from the classical image of the fullness of human flourishing in the *polis* – was a common one traceable to Augustine.[81] As man, by this understanding, fell into the need of governance rather than into the state of governance, the point of the origination of government is again deferred. This is not to deny the direct pre-lapsarian relationship of power and command between God and Adam with which Filmer's model begins, or that this is the ideal state of being to which we should seek return, but it does mean that the institution of political society is not to be found in Eden but elsewhere. This was Milton's understanding as explained in *The Tenure of Kings and Magistrates*. Hobbes adopted a view of Adam's relationship with God and of the political order with results very similar to those of Filmer, but for him this arrangement was bound to a particular time and particular people. Adam's polity is a 'reall' not 'metaphoricall' kingdom of God, with direct rule from the Almighty.[82] This direct Godly rule, he claimed, was renewed in respect to God's own people in the covenant with Abraham – an arrangement that ended with the appointing of Saul as king on the Israelites' request – however, the particularity of this arrangement, with the holy nation of Israel, meant that for

Hobbes it was not relevant to the condition that his countrymen now find themselves in or to the political society of his day. Although he stood by the belief that Christ's Kingdom would bring eternal life and a new order at the end of time, it held no current political concern.[83]

Another trend in political thought, discernible in Hobbes's writing in particular, entailed the dissociation of political theory from human history. Filmer was quick to pick up on Hobbes's admission that political society historically began with families: 'the beginning of all Dominion amongst men was in families in which, first, the Father was absolute Lord of his Wife and Children'.[84] Filmer correctly observed that this contradicts Hobbes's 'state of nature' theory as an account of the origins of the state. In his enthusiasm for origins, however, he possibly did not register that for Hobbes the historicity of his 'state of nature' is not important, that actually origins do not account for much. Hobbes's account of the historical origins of the state is descriptive – it starts with families and then progresses to territorial wars between families – but, by Hobbes's thinking, it does not end in anything useful for the present. He did not view the inheritance through generations of a family of land that has been conquered by ancestors in the past as a good basis for loyalty and peace. Hobbes admitted that his *Leviathan* had a particular message for royalists who had done as much as they could in support of such a hereditary monarch and who now had the right to seek the safety of their lives and livelihood under the new regime.[85] In such a context Hobbes's words are very pertinent: 'the present aught always to be preferred, maintained and accounted best'.[86]

Hobbes's *Leviathan* has a normative force. In his 'review and conclusion' he places it in the context of university learning intending that from thence, through preaching, it might instruct the people so that they become good citizens, not swayed by malcontents and enemies of the state but willing to contribute to the peace and defence of the realm.[87] His lawless state of nature is neither an historical nor a current state of affairs – he admits 'it is very likely that since creation there never was a time in which mankind was totally without society' – but is an imaginary state of horror to persuade men to obedience by showing in stark terms 'what manner of life there would be where there were no common power to feare'.[88] His institution of sovereignty is hypothetical – 'as if every man should say to every man I Authorise and give up my Right of Governing myself'.[89] Influenced by Hobbes, Pufendorf uses a similar device, to convince his readers of the value and necessity of the *civitas*:

> Even though the human race as a whole has never at one and the same time been in such a state, certainly not at an extreme degree thereof, it is hardly irrelevant for us to delineate it so. For not only may we come to understand how many good things humans owe one another, becoming disposed thereby to philanthropy and sociality, but also, in a special instance someone or other may in fact fall into such a state either deeply or to some degree.[90]

There are other examples of the didactic use of imagination or exaggeration to present an alternative against which the current political, civil and economic order can be measured. The Indians of America are often presented as the significant other, visually so in the frontispiece of Hobbes's *De Cive* where the graceful, crowned figure of European Imperium stands on one side against a backdrop of agricultural order and urban splendour while on the other stands Libertas, a sour-faced semi-naked Indian, with a hinterland of wilderness through which Indians chase or flee from each other with bows and arrows and, no doubt, evil intent. Hobbes's descriptions of America and its people are ambiguous in their relation to any reality. In *Leviathan* he writes:

> For the savage people in many places of *America*, except the government of small Families, the concord whereof dependeth on naturall lust, have no government at all; and live at this day in that brutish manner, as I said before.[91]

Here he claims for them the brutish lawlessness of his imaginary state of nature, admits to an exception in the existence of families in this society (the historical origins of the state) and then disqualifies those same families with the accusation that they are regulated by lust. Not surprisingly this very sentence with its internal contradictions is seized upon by Filmer to discredit Hobbes's whole scheme.[92] In like manner Locke presents as fact this imagined America whose people 'have not one hundredth part of the Conveniences we enjoy'. He uses it to give a fictive history to the whole human race, 'in the beginning all the world was America', and explain at length the link between labour and the right of property.[93] Hobbes wrote of 'no government', Locke of a lack of comforts. This principle of subtraction, frequently employed for the Indians, was used by English writers to underline the benefits of civil society to their fellow countrymen. In her study of sixteenth- and seventeenth-century anthropologies, Margaret Hodgen noted this common negative trope: 'no letters, no laws, no kings, magistrate, government, commonwealth, rule, commandes; no arts (or occupation); no traffic (shipping); no husbandry, no money, no weapons, no clothes, no marrying, no bourne or bound'.[94] William Alexander summed it up with the neat tag, '*sine fide, sine lege* and *sine rege*'.[95] At the same time counter-narratives such as Roger Williams's *A Key to the Language of America,* claiming that the Indians possessed the very things they were deemed to lack, were used to critique English society, a lesson reinforced in the simple verses with which he punctuated his work. The exaggerated claims of the Indians to former lives of depravity, as ventriloquised by John Eliot in his Indian narratives, could be seen as further examples of fictionalised states of being, used in this case to highlight by contrast the benefits of civility and faith acquired by these Indians through conversion in Eliot's praying towns. These will be discussed further in Chapter 3.

That falseness of these depictions of the wild men of America is suggested by the accounts of closer observers, with an interest in the Indians' culture, who often painted very different pictures of the societies they encountered. Williams's *Key* is one such example. In her study of encounters between the English and native Americans, Karen Ordahl Kupperman found that no one who actually came to America and described personal experience of Indians ever projected the 'wild man' image described by Robert Johnson.[96] In his critique of Hobbes, Richard Cumberland (as translated and expanded by Tyrell) makes this very point, referring the author to the 'true and exact relations of those places in *America*' where he himself has found contrary evidence of the Indians' lively concern and care for each other, of their exercise of their own system of justice but also of the 'Natural Peaceable Temper of the People', all of which provides evidence for his own theories of natural law and of man's natural inclination to right action.[97] Cumberland's comments signal another shift of focus away from consideration of Adam to a study of our fellow man as the site of our understanding of our essential nature and of the natural laws by which we should direct our lives. His is not just an ethnographic interest in far-flung people but also a scientific one that links 'the sweeter passions of love, hope and joy' to motions of the blood and heart, emphasises the physiological benefits ensued when doing good to others and obstructions to the blood caused by envy and hatred and uses these to reinforce his principle of natural sociability.

Cognitio dei, conscience and covenant

Some of these trends in the theorising of human society and governance – reference to post-lapsarian communities, hypothetical or semi-fictionalised states of nature, observations of the present whether of other cultures or of their own behaviours, psychological and physiological make-up – represent a shift away from that direct relationship between God and Adam in the garden.[98] They are in keeping with d'Entreves's claims about the secularisation of natural law theory and his conclusion that 'God is increasingly withdrawn from immediate contact with men'.[99] J. Budziszewski reached a similar conclusion in reference to Reformed responses to natural law, in particular in relation to the accent they gave to the consequences of the Fall in their political theology.[100] The contrast is between natural law theories of the Schoolmen that (to use Aquinas) the 'natural gifts remained after sin' or 'the light of natural reason, since it pertains to the species of the rational soul is never forfeit from the soul', and those of the Reformed theologians (Budziszewski includes William Ames in his list) who held human nature and human reason post Fall to be so corrupted that it was no longer possible to grasp God's purposes or participate in the Eternal Law.[101] It is an epistemological problem, for how can corrupted humanity know God's purposes or partake in His eternal law except through the revelation of the Scriptures (and the positive law they contain) and the gift of Grace?

Related to this is the question of those who have not heard or accepted His Word or His Grace. Are they excluded from all such knowledge, and what implications does this have for their participation in a civic society if they are ignorant of the laws (natural or positive) that God has ordained for men to follow? The possibility of knowing God's law outside the promulgation of Scripture and knowledge of Christ was not an invention of the Schoolmen but firmly grounded in St Paul, who in the second chapter of Romans wrote of the Gentiles that, though they 'have not the Law, doe by nature do the things conteined in the law' (Rom. 2:13), they 'shew the effect of the Lawe written in their hearts' (2:14), and in the first that God might be known by the things He has made (Rom. 1:19–20). In addition, those of the Reformed tradition were likely to be well schooled in the writings of classical authors, familiar not just with the natural law theories of Cicero and others but with the social and political ethic of the Roman Stoics, for example, that might appear as proofs of such a law.[102] On the other hand, John's Gospel affirms that God can only be known as revealed in Christ, a paradox noted by Luther himself.[103] The problem was more than a clash of scriptural meaning. There was what Torrance Kirby identifies as 'a genuine dialectical difficulty in reconciling the authority of the natural law with the core assumptions of Reformation soteriology and scriptural hermeneutics', leading to heated debate.[104]

The conflict between Filmer's *sola scriptura* and natural law has already been noted. In the previous century Richard Hooker's appeal to the light of reason in support of the Elizabethan Church led to a tirade of outraged criticism. In his attempts to maintain intellectual continuity with the natural law tradition, Hooker was accused of promoting 'Romishe doctrine' and 'the darkenesse of schoole learning'.[105] Budziszewski goes on to suggest that there were two responses to the dilemma. One was to reject natural law theory and rely on Scripture alone. He terms such thinkers 'rejectionists'; Hooker's critics were of this mould, as indeed was Filmer. The other response is to reinterpret natural law, not seeking clues to divine design that might have survived from the Fall but working with that which follows from the fact that it is corrupt, and so not man's natural created state but his present condition, a position closer to Hobbes. Set out in this way the duality is too simple. In fact, as Torrance Kirby has shown, Hooker was not out of keeping with much Reformed theology when he sought to combine reason and Scripture. In a passage of his *Lawes of Ecclesiastical Politie* (quoted at length in Locke's *Second Treatise*), Hooker distinguishes between two higher rules, the Law of God and the Law of Nature, and argues that human laws should be consistent with both: 'Laws Humane must be made according to the general Laws of Nature, and without contradiction to any positive Law of Scripture, otherwise they are ill made'.[106] This plurality of streams of the eternal law is in line with the thinking of several of the Magisterial reformers, in particular with Calvin's *duplex cognitio dei*. Both natural reason and positive divine law have a role in man's knowledge of God; by the first, he can know God as Creator, but as Redeemer by divine law alone. To have some knowledge of God is not necessarily a comfort for those who do not have Scripture. What Calvin takes from Paul's letter is the argument that the ungodly's knowledge of God's law outside the Scripture or Christ's revelation renders actions that contravene this law inexcusable; they cannot plead ignorance of the law.[107] That such ideas were firmly established within the English Reformed tradition is evident in their inclusion in the *Westminster Confession of Faith* generated by the Westminster Assembly:

> Although the light of nature, and the works of creation and providence do so far manifest the goodness, wisdom, and power of God as to leave men inexcuseable; yet they are not sufficient to give that knowledge of God, and of his will, which is necessary unto salvation.[108]

Contrary to Budziszewski's thesis, pre-lapsarian theology held a firm place in Reformed theological and political thought in England, New England and Scotland.[109] The law of nature was part of the theology of such influential Puritan divines as William Perkins and (despite Budziszewski's claim) of his pupil William Ames, 'the spiritual father of the New England churches'.[110] Ames taught that in his innocent state man had no need for proclamation of the law that he received internally at Creation, but after the Fall there were only some relics of the law left that needed to be renewed 'as with a fresh pencil'[111] in the moral law given to Moses on Sinai. That Ames believed there were some remnants in man despite his corruption is evident in his discussion of the law of nations where he acknowledges the existence of natural law that is received everywhere and earns universal censure if broken. The question of how men might come to know that law and apply it to their lives is answered by Ames (and other Reformed theologians) with the concept of conscience.[112] He put particular stress on conscience being not just a source of knowledge but a guide to right action:

> [Conscience] is not a *contemplative judgement,* whereby truth is simply discerned from falsehood; but a *practicall judgement,* by which that which a man knoweth is particularly applied to that which is either good or evil to him to the end that it may be a rule within him and direct his will.[113]

Conscience played an important part in the controversial theology of preparation that developed in the early seventeenth century. The degree to which fallen man could play an active role in his own regeneration was much disputed, indeed the *Westminster Confession* expressly pronounced against it declaring 'natural man, being altogether averse from that good, and dead in sin, is not able, by his own strength to convert, himself, or to prepare himself thereunto'.[114] However Perkins and Ames helped to popularise an alternative position that retained God's monergism but nevertheless made room for some human activity. They suggested that men and women had some part to play in their preparation for regeneration, in particular through the examination of their consciences, which would reveal both the depth of their sinfulness and the way to direct their life aright, though it could not determine their eventual salvation. Eliot's whole missionary enterprise to the Indians was founded on this idea. It had relevance beyond the individual, contributing to a Reformed political theology whereby the right ordering of civil society depended on the constituent members' examination of their consciences.[115]

The emphasis on conscience had profound political consequences not just in the moral improvement of the citizenry, but because it set up a measure – knowable to each man in union with his God – against which that individual could assess the rightness or wrongness of a sovereign's commands, particularly pertinent to the troubled times of the seventeenth century. As Philip Hunton observed in his 1643 treatise, 'when king and subject are in conflict, then everyman is to use his own conscience to guide him'.[116] Feelings intensified when those disagreements related to matters of religion. The subject of the liberty of conscience vis-à-vis the state became a hotly debated issue not least in the writings of John Milton and Roger Williams, and questions of liberty of religious conscience and resistance to the monarch were intimately bound up with the conflicts of Charles I's reign. In *The Ready and Easy Way* Milton writes of the Stuart monarchs that 'their hard measure to liberty of conscience' was 'the rock whereon they shipwreck themselves'.[117] That a man's conscience was subject to error was recognised and so the Scriptures might be consulted to check its accuracy; nevertheless, the role of conscience takes political theory back to the Edenic direct relationship between God and Adam.[118] Protestant writers emphasised the etymological root of *conscire*, 'knowing together', to highlight this closeness, and Perkins described a man's conscience as 'a little God sitting in the middle of men's hearts', so it might be seen as a remnant of that intimacy once found between Adam and God talking together in the garden.[119] Ames links conscience to a 'covenant' between God and Adam, a term that gained increasing significance over the sixteenth and seventeenth centuries.

In the seventeenth century, Biblical covenants were commonly used as types for civil and political society. Covenants in this sense were understood to set up a threefold relationship (not just man with man, people and magistrate, but God, people and magistrate) that has implications for the authority of the ruler. In Samuel Rutherford's *Lex, Rex* (1644), for example, the threefold formulation of the magistrate's authority is subject to limits interpreted from the Scripture, and it is also answerable to the people – the means by which God's authority is legitimately transferred to the magistrate in the first place.[120] It was the model used for the founding of new political communities in New England and for Eliot's Indian towns. A more aggressive version, which uses covenant to justify political resistance or even require it as a religious duty, can be traced from the Marian exiles in Geneva through to the famous dictum of Charles I's judge, John Bradshaw, *'rebellion to tyrants is obedience to God'*.[121] That Mary's and Charles's forms of 'tyranny' were both ecclesiastical and political strengthened their opponents' cause and their resolve. God's interests and those of the people were deemed to be the same, and their collective consciences supported by the Scripture were the instruments for discerning what these might be and how one might act upon them. This understanding was manifested in the oaths of personal loyalty, which every Englishman above 18 was called upon by parliament to make with the 1644 Solemn League and Covenant and its Scottish forerunner the National Covenant. As Margaret Steele has written, 'with all of society bound by a covenant in subordination to God, conventional social and political allegiance thus took a back seat to faith and the 'Politick Christian' was created'.[122] As just such a 'Politick Christian', Winstanley used the covenant 'which both Parliament and people have taken jointly together to endeavour a Reformation' to justify his and his followers' political action in digging upon common land and to hold to account Parliament, the courts and those who initiated proceedings against them.[123] Milton, as another, argued in his *Ready and Easy Way* that Charles I himself broke the terms of the covenant between himself and his people because he usurped the role of God within that covenant by putting himself above God's supreme law of nature.[124]

The interplay of conscience, conscience-prompted disobedience, covenant and Reformed soteriology proved divisive. Different understandings of ecclesiology threatened the unity of the covenant (whether that of the nation or of New England colonies), for men's consciences were leading them in different directions towards Presbyterian or Episcopal forms of national Church or towards Independent congregations. The fact that in Reformed theology the Covenant of Works had been superseded by the Covenant of Grace for those destined for Redemption raised another problem: if the covenant by which the people are to be bound to God within civil society is the latter, then it should only engage the Saints (the recipients of Grace) to whom that covenant applies.[125] This was the argument of the Congregationalists and Independents and a subject for fierce debate among the new, covenanted communities of New England.[126] In the religiously and politically divided society of Old England and the young and vulnerable communities in New England there needed to be a broader conception of governance and some way of regulating behaviour and conscience across the population. A Covenant of Works was required for those not included in the Covenant of Grace, and it was this practical need, addressed through systematic theology rather than scriptural exegesis, that reinforced the importance of Adam in Reformed political theory in Scotland, England and New England.

Michael McGiffert and Glen Moots have shown how, from the end of the sixteenth century, Covenant of Works theology moved from an emphasis on the Biblical covenant given to Moses at Sinai, to an Adamic covenant that, although it has little Biblical support, is of more universal application.[127]

It was given through the father of the human race to all of mankind while the Mosaic covenant was only made with God's people, the Jews. The first full formulation of this covenant was found in Robert Rollock's 1597 *Treatise of God's Effectuall Calling* in which he makes the Covenant of Works 'a legal and natural covenant ... [which] at the first creation was engraven in man's heart'. Formulations of this covenant often conflated moral and natural law by explaining the Decalogue as a restipulation of the Adamic covenant of works presented to Moses. The *Westminster Confession* restated this and gave it catechetical weight, professing that God bound Adam at Creation in a Covenant of Works that required strict obedience, that it continued after the Fall as a perfect rule of righteousness, that it was delivered on Mount Sinai in the Ten Commandments (alongside other laws specific to the Jews), that 'the moral law doth for ever bind all, as well justified persons as others, to the obedience thereof; and that not only in regard of the matter contained in it, but also in respect of the authority of God, the Creator, who gave it'.[128] 'What Covenant did God make with Adam?' was one of the questions devised to test Eliot's Indians on their knowledge of the fundamentals of Christianity; the answer they gave was 'A Covenant of Works, *Doe this and live,* thou and thy Children, *Sin and dye,* thou and thy Children'.[129] Francis Turretin named this Adamic covenant the Covenant of Nature, thereby emphasising its pre-lapsarian origin. The combination of preparation theology and pre-lapsarian theology acknowledged the potential for moral seriousness and personal probity outside the gathered church of the elect and widened the body of covenanting people to include both wheat and tares – a national settlement was possible.[130] The universality of the Adamic covenant had implications for the scope of civil involvement with things religious. It could be the basis for civil regulation not of religion itself but of opportunities to fulfil the moral law to which all were subject. David Weir sees the civil guarantees of Sabbath observance as the example of this.[131]

Moots commends the sixteenth- and seventeenth-century innovations of pre-lapsarian and preparation theology for having 'opened the door for a gracious accommodation of natural law into Reformed political theology'.[132] This was not a wholesale incorporation, however; the tensions referred to above remained in place between natural law theory, with the greater human autonomy it seems to afford, and belief in the absolute supremacy of God's will. The notion of covenant places emphasis on the latter; it involves God's condescension towards his people, His direct communication and their continuing obligation. Carl Trueman writes – in his study of the divine John Owen – that the notion 'facilitates articulation of the basically relational nature of theology, as something which is to be considered in terms of God's relation with his creation'.[133] It does give emphasis to the legal aspects of that relationship. According to John Owen, God gave Adam an internal light so he could know him as Creator, Lawgiver, Ruler and Rewarder and could reflect upon His ongoing commands and actions in the wider world. This was in addition to the direct command to obedience in relation to the fruit of the Tree. The relationship goes beyond legal obligation, however, for God's reward for obedience, 'eternal life', is far greater than any keeping to the law by Adam could deserve. This is also an emphasis in Turretin's theology; God's relationship with man moves beyond proportionate rewards to superabundant blessings, and so he deals graciously with his creature. In this covenant God's decree is not a strict legalism but also entails divine Grace.[134]

Owen was keen to emphasise that this light by which Adam knew God was internal but not innate. The word 'natural' is used for what Adam had from Creation, not just for what was essential to man's nature, for God had given to man beyond the essential. Elsewhere Owen proposed a twofold distinction in Adam's qualities: those essential elements that constitute man's nature (the natural in the narrower understanding of the word) and the principles of obedience to the law given to him and the ends proposed (the moral).[135] His moral qualities are linked to specific capacities given to him by the Holy Spirit: an ability to discern God's will; a free disposition to legal duties; a psychological disposition to do good and avoid sin.[136] Adam's capacities from Creation are directed God-ward, and their ultimate purpose is obedience to God's law, though the rewards God proposes for him in this original covenant are greater than any that might proceed from legal obligation alone. In this understanding, nature is subservient to decree, and both ultimately pale in the light of God's grace. The force of the decree is not, as with Filmer, to give Adam dominion over his fellows but rather that he and his descendants should be alert to the workings of God's will in the world and act when they are being transgressed. Such alertness was evident in Owen's own readiness to speak out and criticise in political and ecclesial affairs throughout much of the history of the century.

The Adamic covenant has post-lapsarian implications for its binding force on subsequent generations. For Turretin this representative relationship between Adam and the rest of mankind was both natural (biologically connected as father of the human race) and forensic, rooted in the covenant relationship that makes Adam the legal representative of humanity, a combination of nature and decree.[137] It has a negative force, too, for its corollary is that in Adam's act of disobedience, we are all made covenant breakers, as Winstanley spelled out in *The Mysterie of God*; 'all flesh broke the Covenant in Adam, and all flesh died'.[138] Adam's sin is not just transmitted through natural generation. Owen wrote that 'Adam is the sin of us all, not only by propagation and communication ... but also by imputation of his actual transgression unto us all'.[139] However, the gracious and benevolent nature of the first covenant links the relationship of God with Adam in the garden to the superabundance of God's grace in Christ's redemptive work in fulfilment of all the righteousness, so the Adamic covenant is brought into relationship with the eschatological conclusion of the story that begins with the eating of the apple.[140]

Adam as story

The end of the story

While patriarchal and state-of-nature models of the polity may accept and even trace their legitimacy to the historicity of Adam, there is a fixedness about them that makes them ahistorical. They deal with continuation (one legitimate model of sovereignty) and constancy (essential nature and eternal law). They are resistant to forces that upset the natural or decreed state of being, whether the political action of the people or the tyranny of the sovereign. An alternative interpretation of the significance of Adam, one that focuses on the story set in motion by his act of disobedience, embraces change. This sense of the unfolding of history from its beginning in Adam to an anticipated end is illustrated in the vision the Archangel Michael presents to Milton's Adam in Book XII of *Paradise Lost*. There, as in a range of contemporary writing and preaching, the events and prophesies of the Bible, the tribulations of current times and hopes of future restoration are drawn together into a universal narrative. The completion of that story begun in first book of the Bible could be predicted through the dramatic imagery of the last, offering as it did a rich confusion of types and prophesies to be mined. In literature and sermons of the time there was a widespread perception that people were living in a decisive age of history – perhaps the final days – a perception that in some cases contributed a sense of urgency to societal and political as well as individual reform. For some, the millennium was very near at hand. In his aptly named 1641 sermon, *A Glimpse of Sion's Glory*, Thomas Goodwin announced it would begin in 1650 and reach perfection about 45 years later. Thomas Brightman, in *Apocalypsis Apocalypseos* 1609, traced the sounding of the seventh trumpet of the Apocalypse to the 1558 accession of the Protestant Elizabeth I, and so 'the time is at hand; the event of things immediately to be done'.[141] Calculations on numbers from Revelation backed up these predictions. Dispensational interpreters, as Matthew Poole explained in his *Biblical Commentary*, saw the time, times and half a time' of revelation as 3 ½ years, each of 360 'prophetic days' or ordinary years, and so if the fixed rise of the beast is viewed as 400, 1660 was to be the end of the beast's rule.[142] Other calculations came out differently, but the middle years of the century were generally a time of heightened expectation.

It was, as has been noted, a time of profound change in society, in established orders and hierarchies, including the break with Rome and later the overthrow of monarchy, and explanation of these evident changes were sought in a dramatised Providence. There was a growing sense of England's role in Providence. Alexandra Walsham describes how providentialism played a pivotal role in forging a collective Protestant consciousness by fusing anti-Catholicism with patriotism.[143] This consciousness was cemented in the later sixteenth century at a time when Queen Elizabeth (Governor of an English Protestant Church) was leading the English nation in wars against

Roman Catholic Spain. Joseph Mede, for example, gives a heightened role to Elizabeth in his eschatological tract *Clavis Apocalyptica* (1627); he views the Spanish foe of 1588 as 'champions of the cause of the beast' and explains how, in the resounding defeat of the Armada and subsequent campaigns the English and their allies in the Low Countries were 'pouring out copiously the cup from the powerful hand of God'.[144] Less interested in the activity of monarchs, Milton gives John Wycliffe a prominent place in his interpretation of England's providential role as 'first evangelic trumpet' of the Reformation.[145] Such nation-based providentialism worked against Augustinian two-cities dualism. It sought instead the expression of heavenly Jerusalem on Earth, so Brightman says of Revelation: 'Heaven doth everywhere in this Book signify the universal Church ... because it can have no other expresse image than on this earth.'[146] The apocalyptic battles between heaven and earth became battles between different forces on earth. The whole provided a strong narrative and interpretive framework for contemporary social, political and ecclesiastical events.

Through the first half of the seventeenth century the narrative became more radical. This shift is partly explained by the disenchantment of Puritan elements in the Church with the Elizabethan settlement and the subsequent handling of church affairs by James I and Charles I. The hoped-for transformation of the Church of England had not been achieved, and they were concerned by their increasing marginalisation. Rather than England's being the elected instrument for God's work of Redemption, the nation was itself seen to be in need of reform. There was a growing idea of the saints, or chosen few, who would forward the cause of the Kingdom, often in opposition to the authorities. Brightman signalled this shift in interpretation when, in *Apocalypsis* he associated England, not with Philadelphia, the church that will be saved at the time of general destruction, but with Laodicea, the sinful church that rejected God's Word and was warned by God: 'I will spue thee out of my mouth'.[147] As Walsham has recorded in her study of English providentialism, England's sinfulness became a common theme, with jeremiads popular in Puritan sermons.[148] This is evident in titles given to the printed versions of some of these: Thomas Adam's *England's Sicknes, Comparatively Conferred with Israels* (1615); John Fosbroke's *England's Warning by Israel and Judah* (1617); John Jones's *Londons Looking back to Jerusalem* (1630).[149]

In the light of this reinterpretation of England's role in providence it is not surprising that some should have looked elsewhere both for security from destruction and for freedom to work for the furtherance of the Kingdom. As John Winthrop travelled to the New World in 1629 with the group of Puritans who would found the Massachusetts Colony, he wrote his famous Arabella Sermon in which he declared that they were acting 'through a special overruleing providence' in order to establish 'a due form of government both civill and ecclesiasticall', 'to laye but one stone in the foundation of this new Syon' and seek a place for the refuge of those whom God meant to save in the general destruction.[150] There was a sense not only that the migrants were leaving England but that God was going with them. As Thomas Hooker preached, 'as sure as God is God, God is going from England'.[151]

In spite of the definiteness of such pronouncements there was still uncertainty as to whether New England was to be a new Israel itself or an experimental model for a new Israel that would one day break out in the old country. Indeed changes in the political situation in England, the experience of civil war and commonwealth and high millennial hopes that accompanied these events strengthened the position of old England as a focus of providential expectation once more. While Winthrop and his colonists had intended to raise up a 'City on a Hill' in the New World for the gaze of their fellow men, eyes turned again to the old. This raised expectation of England, combined with economic hardship, meant that by the mid-1640s New England was experiencing what Andrew Delbamco termed a 'reverse migration', so were the narratives of the two Englands and that of the redemption of the world bound together.[152]

Winthrop's approach to the final days was similar to that of many Puritans of his time. He had a sense of practical responsibility for establishing the right conditions. It was his concern to 'lay a stone' for the building of the New Jerusalem. This was not the only understanding common at this time, however. John Wilson has made a useful distinction between 'prophetic' and 'apocalyptic' eschatologies.[153] *Prophetic* eschatologies, he argued, characterised the views of many Presbyterians who (like Winthrop) saw man as God's instrument in preparing the kingdom. God's providence is working through mundane purposes. Current political circumstances formed an opportunity for God's faithful stewards to reform religion and civil practice in conjunction with divine purposes.[154] *Apocalyptic* eschatologies involved God's 'intrusion upon the present'.[155] The future intended by God was not to be the mundane and direct outgrowth of political and civil strife. It was something God would achieve by his own efforts without the help of his faithful servants. There are different time frames to these eschatologies, being gradual or instantaneous transformations respectively. Those with political interest who adopted *apocalyptic* eschatologies were free to turn their attention to a politics for the meantime – a mode of organising human affairs suited to the time of suspended expectation that, at some unforeseeable date, will be abruptly overturned by the advent of Christ's Kingdom. The state of man (natural and fallen), rather than his role in the overarching narrative of God's redemption of the world, becomes the principle for the organisation of the polity. Thus Hobbes acknowledges separate time frames and frames of interpretation in the structuring of *Leviathan* when he makes a clear distinction between 'the Propheticall' and 'the Naturall Word of God'.[156] The former shapes the content of Part III of his book, with its eschatological reference and interest in the 'Supernaturall Revelations' of God's will, but it is from the latter, known by experience from the principles of nature, that (in Parts I and II) he develops his political scheme for the present. As will be seen in Chapter 3, Wilson's category of *apocalyptic* eschatology has more in common with Roger Williams's understanding and implications for his political theory, while *prophetic* eschatologies underlie much of John Eliot's writing and practical work in his Indian towns.

The inner story

Eschatological reference, heightened language and typologies of beasts or dragons are found in another conversation, that which concerns the inner man and the struggle between good and evil within each individual's soul. This language flourished in the 1640s and 1650s when changes in the political order gave rein to radical religious expression, not just in discreet sectarian corners but in more public settings. To take two examples, John Saltmarsh and William Dell, both of a radical and mystical bent in their theologies, were the most influential preachers in Cromwell's army, favoured by the general for their strong support for religious toleration and their preferring of inward experience over the outward forms and ordinances of religion.[157] The preaching and writing of such men (and women) moved the story from a cosmic scale to the most intimate workings of man's soul.[158] In the typologies that were employed, Adam was afforded a prominent role.

The influences behind these trends can be found in the works of continental mystics, often available in Latin but several being translated into English at around this time. Jakob Boehme, the 'Teutonic master' (Teutonicus) to his English admirers, was one of the most prominent of these. His works attracted a number of translators and champions politically conservative/royalist and politically radical; his central ideas, that the visible is a parable of the invisible and that God manifests himself within men, deeply impressed.[159] In his 1648 introduction to Boehme, *The Ground of What Hath Ever Been Lieth in Man*, John Sparrow emphasised that all that is in the Scriptures has come out of man's experience and therefore can now be grasped by us and all that was in Adam lies in the ground and depth of any man. Indeed this inner experience was to be preferred to scriptural knowledge and Sparrow was so bold as to write:

> The ground, of all that was in Adam is in us; for whatever Ground lay in God, the same lieth in Christ and through Him it lieth in us, for He is in us all. And he that knoweth God in himself ... may well be able to speak the word of God infallibly as the holy men that penned the Scriptures. And he that can understand these things in himself may well know who speaketh by the Spirit of God and who speaketh his own fancies and delusions.[160]

Sparrow writes 'he is in us all' and so signals a universalism typical of much mystical thought by which God manifests himself in the individual man or woman but also manifests himself within *every* man and woman in multiple, parallel tellings of the same story. This meant that the mystical writers and preachers could include in their number those who, like Saltmarsh, Richard Coppin, Jane Leade and also Winstanley, held the (at the time most unorthodox) doctrine of universalism by which, because of God's love and mercy, all mortal souls would ultimately be reconciled with God.[161]

St Paul's identification of Christ with the second Adam was used to set up an internal duality of two Adams, within each man (of flesh and spirit, evil and good) and to make this inner struggle the focus.[162] So we have the following in John Saltmarsh's 1647 tract *Sparkles of Glory*:

> These two creatures are two distinct natures, from whence all things of flesh and spirit came forth; the two Adams are the two seeds, roots, or principles, of these two natures or creations, the old and the new; so in the knowledge of these two there opens a prospect both of heaven and earth, of the first man and the second who are the womb of all things, carnal and spiritual, and into whom are gathered up all the mystery of Christ and antichrist, Ephes. Iv. 22, 23.[163]

The reliance on an inner revelation led to a down-playing of Scripture in relation to direct knowledge of God, of Biblical events in relation to inner experience. It encouraged a dismissal of the outward forms, laws or authorities of organised religion, a devaluing of the role of education in the religious life (William Dell was particularly outspoken on this theme) and resistance to the involvement of civil authorities in the religious life.[164] Although this emphasis did not deny the historical event of Adam's Fall it raised questions relevant to this study about how and whether this ahistorical and apolitical personal focus could intersect with the broader historical telling of the narrative of man's Fall. These will be explored in relation to Winstanley, the author among the subjects of the following chapters whose work owes most to this tradition of mysticism. In this connection it is interesting to view how one of the mystical thinkers, Mary Pocock, in her 1649 pamphlet *The Mystery of the Deity in Humanity*, reflected the Adam typology back into the political circumstances of her day. In Pocock's typology Adam stands for the king, and Adam in Paradise for that perfect harmony between 'the representative, king and Parliament, whose happy condition is bound up in the enjoyment of each other, in the union of the manhood, in the power of the Godhead'. The Fall occurs when the king, Adam, loves only himself and his own self-seeing reason rather than dwelling with Eve who is divine reason, and so the proper relationship between substance and shadow is inverted, the king made himself the substance rather than the shadow by seeking to be God himself 'and so grew into earthly mindedness'.[165]

The universal story

While the mystics took Adam's story deep into man's soul, scholars and explorers spread it abroad to cover new peoples and places. The interpretation of the story shifts from inner exploration to external manifestations. The expansion of knowledge and journeys of discovery opened Christian Europe to a wide diversity of humanity, of human experience and human behaviour. Publications about other places and other cultures, past and present, proliferated during the early modern era, geographies, histories and ethnographies.[166] Perhaps the most significant of these, Iohan Boemus's 1520 *Omnium gentium mores,* was translated in 1555 as *The Fardle of Fashions* and widely consulted for well over 100 years.[167] Locke was a compiler of travel literature (he recommended ethnographical titles as proper reading for the gentleman); so too was Milton.[168] Williams and Eliot produced their own travel accounts as, for different reasons, they described their experiences of encounter with the Indians. Kristina Bross records the classification by a contemporary Newcastle bookseller of John Eliot's *A Further Narrative of the Progress of the Gospel amongst the Indians in New England* as one of 'the most vendible Books in *England*'.[169]

There were some signs of a shift of interest away from origins and the original (in both senses as beginnings and pattern) exemplified in the writings of Jean Bodin, whose work was very influential in England.[170] He tended to adopt an approach that took societies as given and analysed them on this basis. Tyrell characterised Bodin's method as follows:

> As for *Bodin,* and divers others that have writ on this subject, they do no more than follow others, who have asserted this Absolute Power, upon no other grounds than the *Jewish* or *Roman* Municipal Laws; but have never troubled themselves to look into the true Original of Paternal Authority, or Filial Subjection, according to the Laws of Nature or Reason.[171]

So in *Sovereignty* for example, Bodin employed an inductive method, comparing states, explaining their schemes of public law, describing the locus of sovereignty in each and then identifying common principles and variants. He paid particular attention to the difference that environmental factors make to human societies, to variations of climate and topography. In several of his histories he took incessant mutability and change to be a constant (colonies starting up around family groupings or as overflows from existing colonies) and avoided their incorporation into an overarching story. However, in spite of Bodin's popularity and influence, genealogical thinking and scriptural authority still dominated and presented a challenge to new learning – how to reconcile this diversity of histories and current realities with Biblical chronology and in particular with descent from Adam.[172] Reconciling these tensions became something of a preoccupation. In her study of early anthropology Margaret Hodgen remarked that 'no one embarked on a substantial piece of work in which the problem of cultural diversity was at issue without taking into account both Genesis and commentaries on Genesis' – a point illustrated by citing among others Purchas's

Pilgrimage of 1613, Grafton's *Chronicles* of the 1560s, and Ralegh's *History of the World* of 1614.[173] The debate continued into the later years of the seventeenth century, so that Matthew Hale could write in his 1677 publication, *The Primitive Origination of Mankind Considered and Examined According to the Light of Nature*:

> The late Discovery of the vast Continent of America and Islands adjacent, which appears to be populous with Men, as well as stored with Cattell almost as any part of Europe, Asia, or Africa, hath occasioned some difficulty and dispute touching the traduction of all Mankind from two common Parents supposed of all Mankind, namely Adam and Eve.

For Hale the resolution of this question was absolutely crucial in a battle against atheism for, 'I do not see any better Cure of it, or Preservative against it, next to the Grace of God, than the dire Consideration of the Origination of Mankind'.[174]

It has already been observed that many English colonists did not view the natural condition of the Indians as their original condition; their use of terms such as 'reduce' and 'recall' implied that they had fallen from a higher state of grace to which they needed to be brought back. The idea developed that these people had wandered away (both figuratively and literally) from their starting point and lost much of what they had *en route*. Boemus described this movement when he traced the journeys of Noah's son Ham and his descendants away from their paternal home, 'swarme after swarme into other habitations'. During their travels their language changed 'and knowledge of the true God and all godlie worship vanished out of mind'.[175] Ralegh picked up this theme in his commentary on Indian religious customs:

> But as men once fallen away from undoubled truth, doe then after wander for evermore in vices unknown ... so did these grosse and blind idolaters every Age after other descend lower and lower and shrinke and slide downwards.[176]

The tropes of 'wandering' and of 'lost' were used of the Indians in settler literature (both were employed by Williams) and given more weight by the semi-nomadic nature of many of their lives. The idea of the Indians as lost tribes of Israel was a common subject for discussion and debate on both sides of the Atlantic. The English divine, Thomas Thorowgood, published a book in 1650 with the subtitle: *Probabilities that the Americans are Jewes,* in which he argued that Jewish origins could be discerned in some of the rites and fashions, ceremonies and opinions of the Indians of his time. When Roger L'Estrange countered with *Americans No Jewes,* Eliot was brought into the debate in a 1660 edition in which Thorowgood reaffirmed his original case with the new subtitle *that those Indians are Judaical, Made more Probable by Some Additional ... learned Conjectures of Reverend Mr. John Eliot.*[177]

The debate was not merely curiosity and conjecture, nor was it entirely directed at the Indians' past as children of Adam; it had a future orientation, for the belief in the conversion of the Jews as preliminary to the coming of Christ's kingdom was integral to the eschatological expectation of the New England Settlers and their compatriots across the Atlantic. This association of Indians with lost tribes of Israel did not just bring them into the story but made the story's resolution impossible without them.

The idea of 'wandering away' did not answer all of the questions raised by a plurality of peoples. The obvious differences between them, cultural and, even more so, physical, made the idea of common ancestry problematic. Added to this was an awareness of some intertextual contradictions within the Biblical text, which seemed to point towards a polygenic solution to the problem; Adam was not the only 'first ancestor' created by God, and indeed he may well not have been the first of these firsts. The long-standing theory (or heresy) of pre-Adamitism was given new credence in an age of discovery and textual criticism.[178] In 1591, for example, Giordano Bruno argued that the Jews and Ethiopians could not be of the same parentage, and so God must have either created separate Adams or the Africans must have been descended from pre-Adamite races. Isaac La Peyrère, whose work was translated into English in 1656, argued for separate origins for New World people, on the basis of rational interrogation of Biblical texts. He found that certain Old and New Testament verses and passages were inconsistent with the idea of Adam's being the first and sole man directly created.[179] There is scriptural evidence for there being other people than Adam's family on the face of the earth; it seems, for example, that the men who might find and kill Adam's son Cain in Genesis 4 had a different descent. Winstanley noted this when he wrote, 'for the Scriptures seem to declare, that there were men in the world before that time'.[180]

La Peyrère's readings of the Bible could easily have been applied to the experience of those early Virginian and New England colonists who frequently saw themselves as latter-day Adams extending his divinely ordained task of dressing the garden and tilling the earth in new lands and yet were aware of other human presences already in there.[181] Such conclusions drawn from particular readings of the Bible, or from clashes between Biblical and other forms of knowledge, were deemed to be dangerous by more orthodox thinkers, however; Francis Turretin refuted the idea that men existed before Adam in his *Institutes*.[182] In his *Cosmographie* (1652), Peter Heylyn acknowledged the difficulties caused by new knowledge and encounter with different types of people and society but resolved it with a geographical determinism (with shades of Bodin) that would marry nicely with the theories of wandering found in Boemus and Ralegh:

> It came to pass that though they were all descended from one common Root, yet, by the situations of their several dwellings, they came to be of several tempers and affections; in which they were so different

from one another; that it might seem they had been made at first out of severall Principles and not all derived from one common Parent.[183]

However, it was explained, the concept of shared origins in the family of Adam and of Noah gave further reasons to the English for interest in Indian societies and their political structures, for the traces of this earlier existence and the persistence of an original condition, and as the starting points for the restoration to their original condition of civility and knowledge of the true God. They provided experimental grounds for political society.

This survey of contemporary conversations demonstrates that there is not a single Adamic thread during the seventeenth century but an interweaving of plural significances for the first man and first father. Taken individually and in their interplay with each other, these significances tend towards a variety of political and theological conclusions. The categories of state and story and, within these, distinctions among nature, decree and condition and between genealogical and eschatological narratives have revealed some creative tensions in interpretations of Adam: the difference between Adam as the original for a political order or as an original for man the foundation of the political order; the prominence given to God's or to man's activity; whether the polity originates from a pre-lapsarian perfection or fallen condition; the different dynamic that the story brings when its cuts across the original created order; the different levels (individual, national, global, cosmological) in which that story is worked out. The following four chapters will illustrate this interplay of significances by focusing on five selected authors and showing how various interpretations of Adam were incorporated into their writing and shaped their thinking. The conversations introduced in this chapter provide the background and reference points for those individual studies, and the analysis of the authors' work will remain alert to the tensions noted, though also free to follow new directions. The first of this series of chapters brings together two New England authors, Roger Williams and John Eliot, with a particular emphasis on their Indian writings.

Notes

1. The version of Filmer used for references in this book is *Sir Robert Filmer's Patriarcha and Other Writings*, edited by Johann P. Somerville (Cambridge: Cambridge University Press, 1991).
2. *Patriarcha* was probably written in the 1620s and 1630s; it was revived in several editions in the 1680s – see Johann P. Somerville's introduction to *Patriarcha and Other Writings* for debates about the time of writing.
3. Published posthumously in 1698.
4. Algernon Sidney, *Colonel Sidney's Speech Delivered to the Sheriff on the Scaffold December 7th 1683* (London, 1683).
5. Edmund Bohun, *A Defence of Sir Robert Filmer, against the Mistakes and Misrepresentations of Algernon Sidney, Esq., in a Paper Delivered by Him to the*

Sheriffs upon the Scaffold on Tower-Hill, on Fryday December the 7th 1683 before His Execution There (London: Kettily, 1684).
6. James Daly, *Sir Robert Filmer and English Political Thought* (Toronto: University of Toronto Press, 1979); Gordon Schochet, *Patriarchalism in Political Thought* (Oxford: Blackwell, 1975). Filmer died in 1653. Here the term 'Whigs' is used for those who argued for the right of resistance to a tyrannical monarch.
7. The perceived usefulness of Filmer's writings to the establishment is evident in the support given by Archbishop William Sancroft to Edmund Bodun for his 1685 improved edition of *Patriarcha*.
8. Levin-Walman, *Reconceiving Liberalism*, 38–39. References to Locke as providing the political foundation of liberal America, 'a nation sprouting from the seed of Enlightenment principles', are commonplace. As an example, see Michael Anthony Lawrence *Radicals in their Own Time: Four Hundred Years of Struggle for Liberty and Equal Justice in America* (New York: Harper Collins, 2000), 2, 7. He has been afforded the distinction of being the original not just of America but of modernity itself where modernity is viewed as synonymous with liberalism, the man who 'helped preside over the birth of modernity'. Lee Ward, *John Locke and Modern Life* (Cambridge: Cambridge University Press, 2010), 3, 9.
9. In Peter Laslett's introduction to his 1960 Cambridge edition of *Locke's Two Treatises of Government*, 68. See also John Dunn, *The Political Thought of John Locke: An Historical Account of the Argument of the 'Two Treatises of Government* (Cambridge: Cambridge University Press, 1969), 244, and Daly, *Sir Robert Filmer*, 163: 'John Locke bounced his ideas off the hulk of Filmerism into the minds of even 'conservative' contemporaries'. Although Filmer presented Locke with particular questions to engage with, both Laslett and Dunn perhaps underestimate Locke's interest in Adam quite apart from Filmer's argument, as evidenced in his theological writing.
10. The work of Locke and Tyrell is so close as to suggest some form of collaboration, or at least of preliminary discussion.
11. Daly, *Sir Robert Filmer*, 17. See also Filmer's words; 'It is not possible for the wit of man to search out the first grounds or principles of government ... except he know that at the creation one man alone was made, to whom the dominion of all things was given, and from whom all men derive their title. This point can only be learnt from the scriptures', *OG*, 252–53.
12. Algernon Sidney, *Discourses Concerning Government, Vol. 2* (Edinburgh: G. Hamilton and J. Balfour, 1750), 27f.
13. This argument is made in James Tyrell, *De patriarcha non monarcha* (London: Richard Janeway, 1681) and in John Locke's *First Treatise of Government*.
14. *1TG*, 164.
15. *ALMM*, 144.
16. *ALMM*, 138.
17. *ALMM*, 138.
18. *PA*, 35.
19. *OG*, 197 and *ALMM*, 138.
20. *PA*, 35.
21. *OG*, 188.
22. *ALMM*, 144.

76 Conversations about Adam

23. Tensions in Filmer's theories of heirship and God's sanction are discussed in Gordon Schochet, *The Authoritarian Family and Political Attitudes in 17th Century England: Patriarchalism in Political Thought*, new edn. (New Brunswick: Transaction Inc., 1988), 155f.
24. *ALMM*, 144.
25. For interpretations of the Fifth Commandment in official Church catechisms to link patriarchy to the magistrate dating back into the Middle Ages and continuing through the seventeenth century, see Schochet, *Authoritarian Family*, 78f.
26. Schochet, *Authoritarian Family*, 107. See Daly, *Sir Robert Filmer*, 79 for these and other examples. This argument is also used by critics of patriarchalism, notably by Locke in Chapter XI of *1TG*.
27. Cited in Daly, *Sir Robert Filmer*, 102.
28. Corneliu C. Simut, *The Doctrine of Salvation in the Sermons of Richard Hooker* (Berlin: Walter de Gruyter, 2005), 28.
29. Daly, *op. cit.*, 20.
30. Schochet *op. cit.*, 4f.
31. John Overall, *The Convocation Book of 1606: Commonly Called Bishop Overall's Convocation Book, concerning the Government of God's Catholic Church and the Kingdoms of the Whole World* (Oxford: J. H. Parker, 1844), Chapter 2.
32. *OG*, 187.
33. The fact that the Fifth Commandment requires obedience to father and mother constitutes a weakness in patriarchal theory (see Locke's criticism of Filmer on this, *1TG*, 184). Such honour is also due to those with spiritual authority over the people.
34. Edward Gee, *The Divine Right and Originall of the Civill Magistrate from God. Illustrated and Vindicated* (London, 1658) contained a comprehensive repost to Filmer's *Patriarcha*.
35. According to Daly, Filmer 'wrote as if the Elizabethan picture of the world had never existed' – Daly, *Sir Robert Filmer*, 34.
36. James P. Young, *Reconsidering American Liberalism: The Troubled Odyssey of the Liberal Idea* (Boulder, CO: Westview Press, 1996).
37. *PA*, 2.
38. Thomas Aquinas, *The Summa Theologica of St. Thomas Aquinas*, trans. by Fathers of the English Dominican Province, rev. edn. (London: Burns Oates and Washbourne,1920) in *New Advent Online* <http://www.newadvent.org/summa/> [accessed 6 June 2012], I–II qq. 90–106. http://www.newadvent.org/summa/2091.htm#article2.; *Summa Theologica* I–II q94, a2.
39. 'Now among all others, the rational creature is subject to Divine providence in the most excellent way, in so far as it partakes of a share of providence, by being provident both for itself and for others. Wherefore it has a share of the Eternal Reason, whereby it has a natural inclination to its proper act and end: and this participation of the eternal law in the rational creature is called the natural law' (Summa Theologica I–II q91, a2).
40. 'But since man is naturally a civic and social animal as is proved in Polit. I, 2 a third order is necessary, whereby man is directed in relation to other men among whom he has to dwell' (Summa Theologica I–II q.72, a4).
41. *PA*, Chapter II, 1: 'The ignorance of the Creation occasioned several errors amongst the heathen philosophers'; Robert South, 'The Happiness of Adam',

from 'Sermons preached upon Several Occasions', in *English Prose, Vol. III: Seventeenth Century*, ed. Henry Craik (New York: MacMillan, 1916).
42. Lee Ward, *The Politics of Liberty in England and Revolutionary America* (Cambridge: Cambridge University Press, 2004), 37.
43. Jon Parkin, 'Foreword' to Richard Cumberland, *'A Treatise of the Laws of Nature'*, translated, with Introduction and Appendix, by John Maxwell (1727), edited by Jon Parkin (Indianapolis: Liberty Fund, 2005).
44. Hooker had even greater influence in the seventeenth century than in the sixteenth, when he was writing; there are several citations of Hooker in Locke's *Treatises of Government*; In both *Some Thoughts concerning Education* (1693) and *Some Thoughts concerning Reading and Study for a Gentleman* (1689), Locke recommended that Pufendorf be part of the curriculum for education of gentlemen.
45. In his inclusion of *the freeholder* in the dialogue, Tyrell is perhaps making reference to Filmer's *The Freeholders Grand Inquest* (1648).
46. *PA*, 232.
47. Hunton, *Treatise of Monarchy*, 2.
48. Rom. 2:13-14.
49. 'Those general and universal Causes, which procure the preservation, or mischief of Mankind, do depend on such fixt Principles in Nature, as are not to be altered by the judgment of any judge, whether he be a single man in the state of Nature, or the Supream Powers in the Commonwealth' – Tyrell, *Patriarcha*, 62.
50. *OG*, 218. Filmer is arguing from economic rather than psychological interpretations of conflict.
51. Ward, *Politics of Liberty*, 82; J. P. Somerville disputes this reading of Selden in J. P. Somerville, 'John Selden, the Law of Nature, and the Origins of Government', *Historical Journal* Vol 27 no. 2 (1984), 437–47.
52. *OG*, 218.
53. Augustine, *City of God*, edited by David Knowles (Harmondsworth: Penguin, 1972) xix, 12, 868–69.
54. Thomas Hobbes, *On The Citizen (De Cive)*, edited by Richard Tuck and Michael Silverthorne (Cambridge: Cambridge University Press, 1998), 188; Thomas Hobbes, *Leviathan*, edited by C.B. Macpherson (Harmondsworth: Penguin, 1968), 227.
55. Hobbes, *De Cive*, 188.
56. Helen Thornton, *State of Nature or Eden? Thomas Hobbes and his Contemporaries on the Natural Condition of Human Beings* (Rochester: University of Rochester Press, 2005), 37.
57. Thornton, *State of Nature*, 37; William Whateley, *Prototypes, or, The Primary Presidents out of the Booke of Genesis. Shewing, the Good and Bad Things They Did and Had. Practically Applied to our Information and Reformation* (London, 1640), 4–5.
58. Thornton, *State of Nature*, 38; John Salkeld, *A Treatise of Paradise 1617* (Georgia: Emory University, 1968), 150.
59. Hugo Grotius, *De Iure Praedae Commentarius: A Translation of the Original Manuscript of 1604* trans. Gladys L. Williams (Oxford: Clarendon Press, 1950), II: i.; In *De Jure belli ac pacis libri tres*, I. 10, Grotius writes: 'The Law of Nature is so unalterable, that God himself cannot change it. For tho' the Power of God be infinite, yet we may say, that there are some Things to

which this infinite Power does not extend, because they cannot be expressed by Propositions that contain any Sense, but manifestly imply a Contradiction'; God cannot effect 'that what is intrinsically Evil 13 should not be Evil' – Hugo Grotius, *The Rights of War and Peace,* edited by Richard Tuck, (Indianapolis, Liberty Fund) <http://files.libertyfund.org/files/1425/1032-01_LFeBk.pdf> [accessed 4 November 2012], 155. There is a shift in Grotius's position since his 1607 *De Jurae Praedae*: 'What God has shown to be his will, that is law'.

60. Grotius, *Rights of War*, 89.
61. John Locke, *Essays on the Law of Nature: the Latin Text with a Translation,* edited by Wolfgang von Leyden, new edn. (Oxford: Clarendon Press, 2002).
62. Alessandro Passerin d'Entrevès, *Natural Law: an Introduction to Legal Philosophy* (New Brunswick, NJ: Transaction Publishers), 55.
63. A. John Simmons, *The Lockean Theory of Rights* (Princeton: University of Princeton Press, 1992), 96f.
64. Robert South, 'The Fatal Imposture, and Force of Words Set Forth in a Sermon Preached on Isaiah V.20, May the 9th 1686', in *Twelve Sermons Preached on Several Occasions, first volume* (London, 1692), 448–49, cited in Thornton, 25.
65. Dudley Digges, *The Unforgiveableness of Subjects, Taking up Armes against their Sovereigne* (n.p., 1644), cited in Richard Tuck, *Natural Rights Theories: Their Origin and Development* (Cambridge: Cambridge University Press, 1979), 102–103. See also in Hobbes' *Leviathan*, 189: 'A Law of Nature, (*Lex Naturalis*,) is a precept, or generall Rule, found out by Reason, by which a man is forbidden to do that which is destructive of his life, or taketh away the means of preserving the same ... For though they that speak of this subject used to confound *Jus* and *Lex*, *Right* and *Law*, yet they ought to be distinguished, because RIGHT consisteth in liberty to do, or forbeare; Whereas LAW, determineth and bindeth to one of them: so that Law. and Right differ as much, as Obligation, and Liberty.'
66. *Eccl. Pol. Lib. I. Sect. 10*, cited by Locke, *2TG*, 277.
67. Grotius, *De Iure Belli* I.3.8.1 and I.3.2.1.; Digges, *The Unlawfulness of Subjects Taking up Armes against Their Soveraigne*, cited in Tuck, *Natural Right*, 103; Ibid., 94.
68. This identification of the two models is located in a discussion of Locke's theory of rights and the author is careful to note Locke's tendency to move in between the two as his theory develops.
69. Locke interprets the Biblical relationship between Adam and Eve to show that it cannot be used as evidence of Adam's wider patriarchal power –*1TG*, Chapters IV and V. Milton's portrayal of the relationship between the first parents in *Paradise Lost* also has some application to wider human society.
70. *OG*, 237; *1TG*, 151.
71. *OG*, 188.
72. *OG*, 187.
73. Gordon Schochet, *Patriarchialism in Political Thought* (Oxford: Blackwell, 1975), 147.
74. Bernard Sheehan, *Savagism and Civility: Indians and Englishmen in Colonial Virginia* (Cambridge: Cambridge University Press, 1980), 70–71.
75. Hobbes, *Leviathan*, 186.
76. Robert Johnson, *Nova Britannia Offering Most Excellent Fruites by Planting in Virginia* (London: Samuel Macham, 1609), 6; Robert Gray, *A Good Speed to Virginia (1609)* (EEBO editions: Proquest, 2010).

77. Overall, *Canon II*.
78. Cited in Sheehan, *Savagism*, 117; Ibid., 117.
79. Critics' misinterpretation and evaluation of Hobbes's term 'in nature' may have led to this misunderstanding (Thornton, *State of Nature*, 31).
80. As an example of the ambiguity of the term 'natural' Pat Moloney finds three different states of nature in James Tyrell's political theory: absence of government and civil law; Edenic state of innocence; after Fall but before establishment of government – Pat Moloney, 'Leaving the Garden of Eden: Linguistic and Political Authority in Thomas Hobbes', *History of Political Thought*, 18 (1997), 242–66; 249.
81. God 'did not wish the rational being, made in his own image, to have dominion over any but irrational creature, not man over man, but man over the beasts.' – Augustine, *City of God* XIV: I.
82. W. R. Lund, 'The Historical and Political Origins of Civil Society: Hobbes on Presumption and Certainty', in *Thomas Hobbes Critical Assessments Vol. III: Politics and Law*, edited by Preston T. King (London: Routledge, 1993), 730; See *Leviathan* III: Chapter 38 for Hobbes's distinction between the 'first World' from Adam to the Flood, the 'present World' and the 'World to come', in which direct divine rule will be restored in Christ – Hobbes, *Leviathan*, 495.
83. Hobbes, *Leviathan*, 480f. In *Leviathan* Hobbes treats sacred history separately (in Part III) from his main political arguments in Parts I and II.
84. Thomas Hobbes, 'A Dialogue between a Philosopher and a Student of the Common Laws of England' in *The English Works of Thomas Hobbes, of Malmesbury*, vol. 6, edited by Sir William Molesworth (London: John Bohn, 1839), 146; in *Patriarcha* Filmer comments on evidence of patriarchalism in Hobbes's writing in *PA*, 185.
85. Lund, *Historical and Political*, 734.
86. Ibid., 734.
87. Hobbes, *Leviathan*, 728.
88. Ibid., 187.
89. Ibid., 227.
90. Fiametta Palladini, 'Pufendorf Disciple of Hobbes: The Nature of Man and the State of Nature: The Doctrine of *Socialitas*', *History of European Ideas* 34 (2008), 26–60, 44–45.
91. Hobbes, *Leviathan*, 187.
92. *OG*, 187.
93. *2TG*, 297; *2TG*, 301.
94. Margaret Hodgen, *Early Anthropology in the 16th and 17th Centuries* (Philadelphia: University of Pennsylvania Press, 1971), 198.
95. Alexander was a literary figure and leader of Scottish colonial enterprises.
96. Karen Ordahl Kupperman, *Indians and English: Facing off in Early America* (Ithaca: Cornell University Press, 2000), 78. Robert Johnson, Virginia Company promoter, never went to America.
97. *A Brief Disquisition of the Law of Nature, According to the Principles and Method laid down in the Reverend Dr. Cumberland's (now Lord Bishop of Peterborough's) Latin Treatise on that Subject, as also His Confutations of Mr. Hobb's Principles, Put into another Method. The Second Edition Corrected, and Somewhat Enlarged. By* James Tyrell, *Esq; with the Right Reverend Author's Approbation. LONDON, Printed for W. Rogers in Fleet-Street,*

80 Conversations about Adam

R. *Knaplock* in St. *Paul's* Church-yard, *A. Bell* in *Cornhil*, and *T. Cockeril* in the *Poultry*. 1701. Para 2.

98. Interest in physiological make-up is found in Cumberland's writing (and Tyrell's expansion of the same), closely interwoven as it is in contemporary scientific thought. Tyrell, *A Brief Disposition*.
99. Citing Carl Becker.
100. J. Budziszewski, *Written on the Heart: The Case for Natural Law* (Downers Grove, IL: IVP Academic, 1997).
101. *Summa Theologica* II-II q15, a1. <http://www.newadvent.org/summa/3015.htm> [accessed 2012] Budziszewski, *Written on the Heart*, 109f.
102. Margot Todd's study of Oxford and Cambridge curricula demonstrates the large part that classical authors (especially Seneca, Cicero, Quintilian, Ovid, Virgil, Plutarch, Pythagoras and Isocrates) and the Christian humanists played in the education of seventeenth century Puritans – Margot Todd, *Christian Humanism and the Puritan Social Order* (Cambridge: Cambridge University Press, 1987).
103. John 1:18; Martin Luther, 'Commentary on the Gospel of John', *Luther's Works*, ed. Jaroslav Pelikan (St Louis, MO: Concordia, 1958–1986), vol. 22, 150.
104. W. J. Torrance Kirby, 'Richard Hooker's Discourse on Natural Law in the Context of The Magisterial Reformation', *Animus 3* (1998): 33 <http://www.mun.ca/animus/1998vol3/kirby3.htm#N_1_> [accessed 20 August 2011].
105. *A Christian Letter of certaine English Protestantes, unfayned favourers of the present state of religion, authorized and professed in England: unto that Reverend and Learned man Mr. R. Hoo[ker] requiring resolution in certayne matters of doctrine (which seeme to overthrowe the foundation of Christian Religion, and of the Church among us) expreslie contayned in his five bookes of Ecclesiasticall Policie [ACL]* (Middelburg: R. Schilders,1599), cited in Kirby.
106. *Ecc. Pol. 1.3 Sect 9*, cited 2TG, 136.
107. Stephen John Grabill, *Rediscovering the Natural Law in Reformed Theological Ethics* (Grand Rapid, Michigan: Wm. B. Eerdmans, 2006), 88.
108. Westminster Assembly, *Westminster Confession of Faith* (Westminster, 1647), 1.1, <http://www.churchofscotland.org.uk/__data/assets/pdf_file/0011/650/westminster_confession.pdf> [accessed 4 December 2012].
109. 'Pre-lapsarian theology' here denotes a theology that relates to the time and human condition before the Fall, not a reference to Reformed theologies of election.
110. Lee W. Gibbs, 'The Puritan Natural Law Theory of William Ames,' *Harvard Theological Review* Volume 64 Issue 01 (January 1971): 37–57, p. 37.
111. William Ames, *Conscience with the Power and Cases thereof* trans. (London: s.n. 1639), in *Internet Archive* <http://archive.org/details/conscpo00ames> [accessed 4 November 2011], 108.
112. Reason and conscience were closely aligned in seventeenth-century thought but conscience is often given an added moral weight associated as it is with personal integrity and soul-searching. Hunton is able to make a distinction between 'honest men [who] go according to their Conscience, and Reasonable men' [who go] according to evidence – 'A Vindication of the Treatise of Monarchy Containing an Answer to Objection Made against It,' included in Hunton, *Treatise of Monarchy*, 85.
113. From the preamble, 'To the Reader', Ames, 2.

114. *Westminster Confession* 10.3.
115. Perry Miller, *The New England Mind: The Seventeenth Century* (New York: MacMillan, 1939).
116. Hunton, *Treatise of Monarchy*, 14.
117. *REW*, 40. In a different political context, Roger Williams interpreted his quarrel with the Massachusetts Bay ministers (leading to his exile in 1635 for his 'diverse new and dangerous opinions') as an assault on his freedom of conscience. Williams's protagonist John Cotton declared that the individual's conscience was only at liberty as far as it was 'rightly informed' – Edwin S. Gaustad, *Liberty of Conscience: Roger Williams in America* (Valley Forge: Judson Press, 1999), 73f.
118. Ames, *Conscience*, 28f; Edmund S. Morgan, new edn. *Roger Williams The Church and State* New York: W.W. North and Company, 2006), 130f.
119. See Perkins's *Discourse 5*: 'God knows perfectly all the doings of man, though they be never so hid and concealed: and man by a gift given him of God; knows together with God the same things of himself: and this gift is named Conscience'; William Perkins, *The Work of William Perkins*, edited by Ian Breward (Abingdon: Sutton Courtenay Press, 1970), 519.
120. Glenn Moots, *Politics Reformed: The Anglo-American Legacy of Covenant Theology* (Colombia: University of Missouri Press, 2010), 64.
121. Evidence of these discussions among the Marian exiles includes, for example, Christopher Goodwin's religious arguments for resistance to tyranny. Moots, *Politics Reformed*.
122. Margaret Steele, 'The 'Politick Christian': The Theological Background to the National Covenant' in *The Scottish National Covenant in its British Context 1638–1651*, edited by John Morrill (Edinburgh: Edinburgh University Press, 1990), 31–67.
123. *WW, CW* vol. 2, 83; Ibid., 83; 88.
124. *REW*, 220–21.
125. There was also a Covenant of Redemption being the covenant between Father and Son that underlay Christ's redeeming work.
126. Moots, *Politics Reformed*, 77f.; this was evident in the debate about the 'Half-Way Covenant', which allowed the baptism (though not communion) of infant children of church members drafted by Richard Mather and formerly approved in 1662 though rejected by many others in the Massachusetts Bay community.
127. Moots, *Politics Reformed*; Michael McGiffert, 'From Moses to Adam: The Making of the Covenant of Works', *Sixteenth Century Journal* Vol 19 No.2 (1988), 131–55; A covenant is not mentioned in Genesis and had to be extrapolated from God's command not to eat. There is a brief reference to a covenant broken by Adam in Hosea 6.7.
128. *Westminster Confession*, 19.
129. John Eliot, 'A Late and Further Manifestation of the Progress of the Gospel amongst the Indians in New England', in John Eliot, *The Eliot Tracts: With Letters from John Eliot to Thomas Thorowgood and Richard Baxter*, edited by Michael P. Clark (Westport, CT: Praeger Publishers, 2003), 314.
130. Wheat and tares, Mt. 13:24–30.
131. David Weir, *Early New England: A Covenanted Society* (Grand Rapids, MI: Wm. B. Eerdmans Publishing Co., 2005).
132. Moots, *Politics Reformed*, 81.

82 Conversations about Adam

133. Carl R. Trueman, *John Owen: Reformed Catholic, Renaissance Man* (Aldershot: Ashgate Publishing Company, 2007), 67.
134. James Mark Beach, *Christ and the Covenant: Francis Turretin's Federal Theology as a Defense of the Doctrine of Grace* (Göttingen: Vandenhoeck and Ruprecht, 2007).
135. John Owen, *Works 3 100*, cited in Trueman, *John Owen*, 69.
136. Ibid., 69.
137. James T. Dennison Jr, *Francis Turretin's Institutes of Elenctic Theology (1679–85)* (Phillipsburg, NJ: P&R Publishing, 1992–97) 8 III xi. Cited in Beach, 67.
138. MG – CW II, 55.
139. Cited in Trueman, *John Owen*, 75.
140. Beach, *Christ and Covenant*, 75.
141. Cited in Avihu Zakai, 'Thomas Brightman and English Apocalyptic Tradition,' in *Menasseh Ben Israel and His World*, edited by Yosef Kaplan, Henry Méchoulan and Richard H. Popkin (Leiden: E. J. Brill, 1989), 31–44, p. 37.
142. Matthew Poole, *Commentary on the Holy Bible: Vol III Matthew to Revelation* (McLean, VA: MacDonald, 1985), 976; The dates AD 390–96 were associated with the rise of the Pope as the antichrist. Some interpreters also saw the rise of the Pope as 400–6, making 1666 a significant date. This seventeenth-century dispensationalism is to be distinguished from the nineteenth century dispensationalism of the Brethren Movement.
143. Alexandra Walsham, *Providence in Early Modern England* (Oxford: Oxford University Press, 1999).
144. Joseph Mede, *A Translation of Mede's Clavis Apocalyptica*, trans. by R. Bransby Cooper (London: J. G. and F. Rivington, 1833), 423.
145. RE, 6.
146. Zakai, *Thomas Brightman*, 37.
147. Rev. 3:16.
148. Walsham, *Providence in Early Modern England*.
149. Ibid., 281.
150. John Winthrop, *Winthrop Papers*, edited by Allyn Baily Forbes (Boston: Massachusetts Historical Society, 1944), Vol. 2, 293; Winthrop, Vol. 3, 54; the sermon was named after the ship on which they travelled – Gilpin, *Millenarian Piety*, 14. Winthrop Papers edited by Allyn Baily, Forbes and Stewart.
151. Kristina Bross, *Dry Bones and Indian Sermons: Praying Indians in Colonial America* (Ithaca and London: Cornell University Press, 2004), 5.
152. Delbamco is cited in Bross, *Dry Bones*, 6; for example, to take the potential leaders of the colony, out of 24 Harvard students who graduated 1642–1646, only 10 remained in New England the rest returning to England and Ireland, and out of the 20 or so who graduated in 1647, 1649 and 1650, only 8 remained.
153. John Wilson, *Prophet in Parliament: Puritanism during the Civil Wars 1640–1648* (Princeton: Princeton University Press, 1969).
154. Ibid., 207.
155. Ibid., 208.
156. Hobbes, *Leviathan*, 409.
157. George Sabine, ed., *The Works of Gerrard Winstanley* (New York: Russell and Russell, 1965), 'Introduction', 31.
158. See for example Mary Pocock's pamphlet *The Mystery of the Deity in Humanity*, in Nigel Smith, *Perfection Proclaimed: Language and Literature in English Radical Religion 1640–1660* (Oxford: Clarendon Press, 1989).

159. J. Andrew Mendelsohn, 'Alchemy and Politics in England 1649–1665,' *Past and Present* 135, 1 (1992): 30–78, 34f. Translators and champions included Charles and Durant Hotham, John Sparrow, John Ellistone, John Pordage, Francis Ellington Henry and Thomas Vaughan – see Rufus M. Jones, 'John Boehme's Influence in England,' in *Spiritual Reformers in the 16th and 17th Centuries* (London: Macmillan and Co., 1914); B. J. Gibbons, *Gender in Mystical and Occult Thought: Behmenism and its Development in England* (Cambridge: Cambridge University Press, 1996).
160. John Sparrow, 'Introduction' to Jakob Boehme, *A Description of The Three Principles of the Divine Essence*, trans. John Sparrow (London, 1648).
161. Richard Coppin, *A hint of the glorious mysterie of the divine teachings between God, Christ and the Saints* (London: Giles Calvert, 1649).
162. 1 Cor. 15:45 'And it is also written, The first man Adam was made a living soule; and the last Adam was made a quickening Spirit'.
163. John Saltmarsh, *Sparkles of Glory or some Beams of the Morning Star: Wherein Are Many Discoveries as to Truth and Peace to the Establishment and Pure Enlargement of a Christian in Spirit and Truth* (London: E. Huntington, High St Bloomsbury, 1811), 33.
164. William Dell, *The Trial of Spirits, Both in Teachers and Hearers* (London, 1666).
165. Smith, *Perfection Proclaimed*, 211.
166. Anthony Grafton, *New Worlds, Ancient Texts: The Power of Tradition and the Shock of Discovery* (Cambridge, MA: Belknap Press of Harvard University Press, 1992).
167. Hodgen, *Early Anthropology*. The full titles of Boemus's two works are as follows: *Omnium gentium mores, leges & ritus ex multis clarissimis rerum scriptoribus* (1520) and *The fardle of façions, containing the aunciente maners, customes, and laws, of the peoples enhabiting the two partes of the earth called Affrike and Asie* (1555).
168. On Locke, see Hodgen, *Early Anthropology*, 188. One example of this interest is Milton, *A Brief History of Moscovia and of Other Less-Known Countries Lying Eastward of Russia as far as Cathay, Gathered from the Writings of Several Eye-Witnesses* (EEBO Editions: Proquest, 2010).
169. Bross, *Dry Bones*, 1. John Eliot's *Further Narrative* was also known as *Tears of Repentance*, likely to be a reference to Bartolomé de Las Casas's *The Tears of the Indians* (1542).
170. Mentioned by Wm Harrison, Holinshed, Sidney, Nash, Spenser, Bolton, Hobbes, Wheare, Heylyn, Robert Burton, Carpenter (Hodgen, *Early Anthropology*, 283); in England by 1579 it could be said that 'you cannot steppe into a scholars studye but (ten to one) you shall likely finde open either Bodin *De Reppublica* or Le Royes *exposition on Aristotles politiques*' – Gabriel Harvey, cited in Tuck, *Natural Rights*, 44.
171. Tyrell, *Patriarcha*, 20. The reference is to *Bodin*, de Rep. l.1. c. 4.
172. Anthony Grafton notes that the ancient texts of the classical world (Cicero, Plato, Aristotle) further complicated the picture by offering alternative models for the interpretation of human diversity – Grafton, *New Worlds*, passim.
173. Hodgen, *Early Anthropology*, 223.
174. Matthew Hale, *The Primitive Origination of Mankind Considered and Examined According to the Light of Nature* (London: printed by William Godbid,

84 *Conversations about Adam*

for William Shrowsbery at the Sign of the Bible in Duke Lane, 1677). 'To the Reader', vii.
175. Cited in Hodgen, *op. cit.*, 234.
176. Walter Ralegh's *History of the World* (1614), cited in Hodgen, *op. cit.*, 267.
177. Roger L'Estrange, *Americans No Jewes* (London, 1652); Thomas Thorowgood, *Jewes in America* (London: 1660).
178. Even Bodin came close to the theories of those who viewed Adam and Eve as parents of the Jewish people alone when he remarked that the Bible gave 'only the origins of that people whom God alone chose ... not of the others' – Grafton, *New Worlds*, 152.
179. This rational enquiry into the text and canon of the Scriptures in the sixteenth and seventeenth centuries was initiated by philosophers, e.g. Paracelsus, Bruno, Hobbes, Spinoza (Hodgen, *Early Anthropology*, 272).
180. *LFP* – CW, II, 75.
181. See William Symonds, *A Sermon Preached at Whitechapel in the Presence of the Adventurers and Planters for Virginia, 1609* (New York: Theatrum Orbis Terrarum, 1968): 'Let us be cheerfull to go to the place that God will shew us to possess in peace and plenty, a Land more like the Garden of Eden, which the Lord planted, then any part else of all the earth,' and 'To the same effect is that spoken of *Adam*, after his fall, that *God sent him forth of the Garden of Eden to till the earth* (Gen. 3:23)'.
182. The idea is refuted in Francis Turretin, *Institutes of Elenctic Theology 1679–85*, edited by James T. Dennison Jr. (Phillipsburg, NJ: P & R Publishing, 1992–97) – Vol. I, 452.
183. Peter Heylyn, *Cosmographie* – cited in Hodgen, *op. cit.*, 234. Joyce Chaplin, traces colonists' fears that (following the logic of environmentalism) their new American environment would wreak changes on their bodies, and their eventual coming to the conclusion 'more heartening to their prospects if chilling in historical perspective' that English bodies were remarkably tough and that they were better suited to America than the Indians and could supplant them as natives of the New World – Joyce Chaplin, *Subject Matter: Technology, the Body, and Science on the Anglo-American Frontier 1500–1676* (Cambridge, MA: Harvard University Press, 2001), 156.

3 Roger Williams and John Eliot's Indian writings and the story of Adam

Introduction: shared origins, diverging models

John Eliot, minister of Roxbury, Massachusetts, and evangelist to the Indians, recalled a conversation with a Narragansett sachim.[1] As they discussed together the Law of God and salvation by Christ, he had asked the sachim, 'Why they did not learn of Mr *Williams* who hath lived among them divers yeers?' The sachim answered that they 'did not care to learn of him, because he is no good man but goes out and workes upon the Sabbath day'.[2] It is difficult to reconstruct this encounter as it happened. Eliot, whose writings suggest a man ever aware of message and audience, may not have been reporting the sachim's meaning exactly, or the sachim himself may have been giving the missionary the words he knew he wanted to hear. Nevertheless, these words suggest much about the differences between the two men who are the subject of this chapter: Eliot, with his focus on teaching the Indians the kind of moral, religious civility of which observance of the Sabbath is an important element, and Roger Williams who spent years living and dealing with the Indians as exile, trader and diplomat, yet became increasingly sure that drawing them into the observances and practices of the Church was not his, nor anyone else's role. Williams himself did not conform to the expectations of a Christian society that Eliot so firmly held. These more surface differences reflect a deeper divergence of theology that in turn generated quite different political models, one very structured and Scripture-based, the other much more pragmatic and cognisant of local customs and preferences.

The fact of this difference was acknowledged in the rather anachronistic categorisation of the two New England authors in the first *Cambridge History of American Literature* where Eliot was given a place in the conservative 'theocratic group' and Williams in the progressive 'democratic group', the latter's political theory described as a 'profoundly modern conception'.[3] Like Winstanley, with his socialist admirers, Williams too became the darling of later politically defined movements; Edmund S. Morgan remarked that the nineteenth- and twentieth-century liberals had 'claimed him for their own'.[4]

In 1940 a major biography of Williams was given the title *The Irrepressible Democrat*.[5] Since that time scholarly attempts have been made to restore him to the Biblically framed world of John Eliot, though his credentials as a modern liberal have been given a new airing recently with the publication of John H. Barry's popular biography-cum-treatise on American values, *Roger Williams and the Creation of the American Soul*, which portrays him as the father of the modern idea of liberty, the man who first articulated American individualism.[6] Perry Miller, who did much to restore the status of the Puritans in historical and literature studies, tried to reclaim Williams from the liberals in his short biography of 1953, by pouring scorn on the popular idea of him as the precursor of Jefferson, liberalism and rationalism and emphasising the theological basis of his thought.[7] Morgan, in his 1967 essay on Williams, described him as 'a man of his time and very much part of it', whose thinking developed from ideas he shared and debated with those around him, though he sometimes pushed these ideas to their limits.[8] Other scholars (such as W. Clark Gilpin, James Byrd) have emphasised the seventeenth-century grounding of Williams's preoccupations and methods – millenarian expectation, Biblical example.[9]

Focus on the Indian element in the authors' experience and writing has led to an interest (fed by feminist and post-colonial critique) in the themes of coloniser-colonised hegemony and of self-and-other intersubjectivity. Ivy Schweitzer, Thomas Scanlan and Kristina Bross have all applied such perspectives to the authors' Indian material, the last of these giving the greatest attention in her work to the contemporary Christian underpinning of the Indian project.[10] Such studies have produced valuable detailed analyses of the texts in question. A trend of these more modern critical approaches is to start from the experience of alterity and assess the authors by the degree to which they are complicit in or able to overcome the binary opposition of English and Indian.[11] To approach the relationship through Adamic eyes, however, is to assume their underlying unity as children of the same father and their joint participation in his story. This chapter will demonstrate how Eliot's and Williams's political models, different though they may be, are both rooted in a seventeenth-century frame of interpretation as differing responses to the story of man's fall with Adam and his restoration with Christ.

Both men belonged to the same world, and the similarities in their backgrounds and experiences make the differences of their conclusions all the more interesting as examples of seventeenth-century theorising of the origins, foundation and direction of the polity. Both attended Cambridge at the same time, and both were ministers. Both arrived in Massachusetts in 1631 as part of the Puritan exodus from Laudian England. Due to his increasingly separatist views about Christianity, Roger Williams became an exile from the Massachusetts Bay Colony, while Eliot remained within, generally respected, the only point of embarrassment being when his politically radical writing was so out of keeping with the restored monarchist regime that it was banned from the colony in 1661. Both men had practical, direct engagement in the construction of a political society and government, on a small and in many ways experimental scale. Eliot established Indian towns and explored Biblical models for their governance, while Williams was involved

Roger Williams and John Eliot's Indian writings and the story of Adam 87

in setting up political structures for the rather difficult and mismatched collection of individuals who formed the colony of Rhode Island. Both, too, kept their eyes on the unfolding of events and political changes in old England and contributed through their own political treatises to the accompanying debates. Both men had close dealings with the Indians and an interest in interpreting them for an English audience.

The content of this chapter will largely be drawn from the authors' Indian writings. For Eliot these include his *Indian Dialogues*, fictionalised missionary dialogues between praying Indians and other Indians; his *Brief Narratives*, reports on the progress of his praying towns; and letters to funders of his Indian missions.[12] For Williams the primary source will be *A Key to the Language of America*, his Indian vocabulary augmented with detailed observations on their lives and customs. Other writings by the authors make sense of the Indian experience within their wider conceptualisation of the social and political order, and so reference will also be made to these, notably to Eliot's *Christian Commonwealth* (1659), Williams's *Christenings Make Not Christians* (1645), his *Bloudy Tenent of Persecution for Cause of Conscience* (1644), plus other literature from his controversy with John Cotton.[13] This focus on the Indian writings reflects contemporary interest in the lives of the Indians, their physical appearance, their customs and their polities. Karen Ordahl Kupperman explains this interest by likening it to a mirror, the image of the Indian reflecting back to the English a better understanding of their own society.[14] She characterises English culture of this era as 'marked by fears and misgivings as much as confidence', a time of self-reflection and examination.[15] English men and women (whether New England settlers or old England readers of travel literature) could bring to their encounter with this previously isolated branch of the human family the questions uppermost in their minds at home about the validity of different norms of social living and political organisation.[16] This study recognises that seventeenth-century English men already had a powerful frame of reference for the understanding of their lives and society in Adam, his creation, his fall, its consequences and resolution. The questions asked of the Indians then also involved questions of how they fit within this Adamic frame and what further illumination they might contribute to that universal story. The Indians' lives and customs are incorporated into conversations about origins, man's natural state, persistence and loss, and the themes of wildness and civility, of wilderness and garden are given new prominence.

Origins in Adam

References to the first chapters of Genesis do not figure more prominently than other Biblical texts in John Eliot's and Roger Williams's writings, and there are few chapter and verse citations, so few that James Byrd's study of Williams's use of the Bible does not include his readings of Adam.[17]

Bross's study, by analogy and correspondence, links Eliot, in his missionary activity, to the prophets Ezekiel and Moses but makes little reference to Adam.[18] However, when Eliot and Williams are reproducing or imagining religious conversations with and between the non-Christian or newly converted Indians, it is notable that the story of Adam's creation and fall is absolutely central. The Indians were starting from a state of ignorance of Biblical history, and so what might have been assumed, or taken for granted (though foundational to that history) among English readers, needed to be spelt out for Indian audiences. Adam was very prominent both in the explanation of God's activity and in the positioning of the Indians themselves (who they are, where they have come from and the parameters and purposes of their existence) in relation to this tale of Fall and Regeneration. So Eliot in his first sermon to the Indians used themes of Creation and Fall; the examination in Christian knowledge that the Indians underwent as a preliminary to church membership included questions about Adam ('What Covenant did God make with Adam?'; 'What was the sin of Adam?'; 'When Adam sinned what befell him?'; 'Seeing but one man Adam sinned, how came all to die?'); the Indians' own testimonies to church elders made frequent reference to the story of Adam and their inclusion in its consequences.[19] In Eliot's *Indian Dialogues* (1671), the characters Peneovot and Waban grapple with these themes as the key components of their religious learning and conversion:

PEN: Now he informed me, that Adam, the first man, sinned by the temptation of angels, which rebelled against God, and turned devils. And his judgement and condemnation on all his posterity.[20]

WABAN: He made man, and gave him dominion over all his works in this world, and a law of life, under the penalty of damnation ... But man by the temptation of evil angels, who by their sin became to be devils, I say man broke the law which God gave him and sinned against God, turned rebel against God and served the Devil. And in this rebellion all the children of men go to this day ... And this is the condition of all mankind, and it is our estate.[21]

Williams recorded how staying among some wild island Indians, he had occasion, through the help of God, to speak 'of the true and *Living only Wise God,* of the Creation: of Man, and *his fall* from God &c'.[22] To facilitate other such conversations between English and Indians, he included in his book useful phrases in the language of the Narragansetts, phrases for God's creation of Adam and Eve: '*Wuttàke wuchè wuckkeésittin penashimwock wamè*' ('Last of all He made one man'); '*Ka wesuonckgonna – kaûnes Adam*' ('And He called him Adam'); '*Ká wuchè peteaúgon. Wukkeesitinnes paũsuck squàw*' ('And of that rib he made one woman').[23] In his preface to the *Key,* Williams offered an account that was the closest he approached to Eliot's Indian dialogues and conversion accounts. This is the story of his

Roger Williams and John Eliot's Indian writings and the story of Adam 89

visit to the Pequot captain, Wequash. As he lay on his death bed, Wequash reminded Williams of a conversation they had had three years previously:

> I acquainted him with the *Condition of all mankind* & his Own in particular, how *God* created *Man* and *All things:* how Man fell from God, and of his present *Enmity* against *God,* and the *wrath* of God against *Him* until *Repentance.*[24]

According to the dying captain, in Williams's telling, those words had never been out of his heart until that day. The Indians were being incorporated into a story with a beginning (in the Creation and Fall of Adam) and an end (salvation in Christ). A personal identification with the story's starting point and its conclusion was expected in the question used to examine Eliot's Indians: 'When you heare that Adam by his sin deserved eternal death, and when you hear of the grace of God sending Jesus to save you, which of these break your heart most?'[25] Dane Morrison has suggested that the centrality of origin myths in the religious culture of the Algonquians made them receptive to the Genesis narrative, and the recent trauma they had experienced through devastating plague coupled with an understanding of disease as supernaturally inspired and directed, gave the account of Fall and hope of Redemption a particular relevance to their own condition.[26]

The story was a spiritual but also a physical one of generation from a common ancestor. In spite of the existence of polygenic and pre-Adamite theories among some English observers at this time or the alternative Indian aetiologies that he recorded, Williams had no doubt that the Indians were indeed the children of Adam and presented this fact as received wisdom:

> From *Adam* and *Noah* that they spring, it is granted on all hands.[27]

It was the Indians' later descent and subsequent history that posed more of a puzzle. Thus, he reported English speculations about their origins in Tartaria, Indian traditions about the location of their forefathers' souls and migration of their own, the affinity of some of their customs with the Jews and of their language with the Greeks, and concluded that 'it is as hard to finde the *wellhead* of some fresh *Streame,* which running many miles out of the *Countrey* to the salt *Ocean,* hath met with many mixing *Streames* by the way'. Though their identity was certain, their movements since and their relationships with the other peoples of the world were so unsure that Williams left the question open ('I dare not conjecture in these Vncertainties'), focusing instead on their present condition.[28]

Eliot, equally sure about the origins of the Indians in Adam, was more prepared to theorise their subsequent history. He was drawn into the debates of the 1650s about whether or not the Indians could be regarded as the lost tribes of Israel and so were in reality the Jews that need to be gathered in before Christ's kingdom could come.[29] This identification of the Indians with the lost Jews, and with prophecies of the coming of the Kingdom, was beneficial to Eliot's missionary work; as he wrote in a letter to potential funders: '*I know every believing heart ... longeth to hear of the Conversion of our poor Indians, whereby such Prophesies are in part begun to be accomplished*'.[30] Thomas Thorowgood included Eliot's writings as support for his argument in a tract, *Jews in America or Probabilities that Those Indians are Judaical, Made More Probable by Some Additionals to Former Conjectures* (1660).[31] Though incorporated with enthusiastic reference into Thorowgood's tract, Eliot's contribution may not have given the Norfolk clergyman's theory the full endorsement (nor the empirical evidence from direct observations of the Indians) that he wished. Eliot granted that a few of the lost Israelites may have made their way to America. The bulk of them, though Hebrews, he suggested were of an early branch (descendants of Shem and of Eber) not included within Abraham's covenant and Moses' law. Eliot gave a careful, Scripture-based exposition of how these peoples might have moved in different stages with different generations before arriving in America. The different sources of Williams's and Eliot's discussion on origins, one including observation and Indian knowledge, the other purely scriptural, are instances of the different approaches of the two men to the interpretation of the Indian experience.

By relating the story of Adam, Creation and Fall to the American Indians, Williams, Eliot and their compatriots were answering the question of how the Indians fitted within what they already knew about God, the world and mankind, the first chapters of Genesis being fundamental to that knowledge. By hearing and telling Adam's story as part of their own, the Indians were being incorporated into a universal history. They shared universal origins and the universal consequences of the Fall. As Williams wrote in his *Key*:

> Nature knows no difference between *Europe* and *Americans* in blood, birth, bodies, &c. God having of one blood made all mankind, *Acts 17*. And all by nature being children of wrath, *Ephes. 2*.[32]

The Indians and English were so much elements of the same story that they were as parts of the same body, thus Eliot with his missionary impetus and millenarian worldview, compared the Lord's ability to 'find these lost and scattered Israelites' to His ability to 'gather the scattered and lost dust of our bodies at the Resurrection.'[33]

Wandering away

Given these convictions of the common origin and ancestry of English and Indian, and indeed of all peoples of the world, the differences between them required explanation. In his *Key*, Williams wrote of differences in clothing, both literal clothes and the figurative clothing of religion.

> What should be the reason of this mighty difference of One man's children that all the Sonnes of men on this side the way (in Europe, Asia and Africa) should have such plenteous clothing for Body for Soule! And the rest of Adams sonnes and Daughters on the other side, or America (some thinke as big as the other three) should neither have nor desire clothing for their naked Soules, or Bodies.[34]

In the writings of Williams and Eliot, to different degrees, we find ways of linking current experiences and knowledge of the Indians with their common ancestry in Adam. The theme of wandering away, found in other commentators on the American Indian, is present in both authors, and a summons to the Indians to return home was part of Eliot's mission.[35] The *Indian Dialogues* were written 'for their instruction in that great service of Christ in calling home their countrymen to the Knowledge of God And of themselves and Iesus Christ'.[36] There were aspects of Indian life and thought that could be seen as the persistence or the remnant of something that they received as human beings through Adam's Creation, what was natural to them as humans. Williams's *Key* in particular stresses these; for example, he wrote of Indians' natural wisdom and natural sociability.[37] Similarities between their practices (for example, the segregation of women during menstruation) and language and those of the Hebrews were also mentioned as possible remnants of Hebrew origins.[38]

A second aspect is the losing, as they wander away from the source, of what they once had. Both men used the stark yet conventional formula of depravity and degeneration for the Indians to convey this sense of movement away from original knowledge and morality.[39] At the beginning of Eliot's *Indian Grammar* they are described as 'the very ruins of mankind'.[40] Williams combined depravity and the persistence of the natural (and good) in his description of the Narragansetts:

> In the *ruines* of depraved *mankinde* are yet to be founde *Natures distinctions*, and *Nature's affections*.[41]

Another theme is the acquisition of particular custom and tradition that either overlays the original or replaces what has been lost. In a letter, Eliot explained how Indian custom has 'drowned' their original natural virtues:

> There is in them a great measure of natural ingenuity, and ingeniosity, only it is drowned in theire wild, and rude manner of liveing.[42]

Eliot was almost entirely negative in his assessment of Indian customs, described as 'filth and folly', and his *Indian Dialogues* present the tension between these and the path towards redemption that he and his native missionaries urged the Indians to take.[43] The customs they had acquired had to be set aside before salvation could be gained.[44] In one of the dialogues the missionary Waban explains how his status as a 'praying Indian' is dependent on leaving behind Indian customs that are an obstacle to right knowledge of God:

> WABAN: ... I am a praying Indian. I have left our old Indian customs, laws, fashions, lusts, pauwauings and whatever else as contrary to the right knowledge of the true God and Jesus Christ our redeemer.[45]

Eliot's ventriloquising of the Indian responses to this missionary imperative shows a degree of sympathy from the author for those who find it difficult to set aside their accustomed ways:[46]

> To change our Gods, and laws and customs are great things and not easily to be obtained and accomplished. Let us alone that we may be quiet in the ways which we like and love, as we let you alone in your changes and ways.[47]

In his *Key*, Williams too relates the elements of loss and acquisition when he describes how false religion fills the gap left by the loss of the true religion:

> The wandring Generations of *Adams* lost posteritie, having lost the true and living God their Maker, have created out of the nothing of their owne inventions many false and fained Gods and Creators.[48]

The context of this comment is an account of the Indians' religion, but, characteristically, Williams broadens the application of his observation to include under 'the wandring Generations' of Adam's lost posterity people from all nations of mankind, whether they are without knowledge of God or have knowledge but are not 'meeke' in their obedience, whether they are 'Indian', 'Turk', 'Iew' or 'Christian false'.[49] His criticism of the accumulation of false religious tradition in civilised and Christian, European nations is as sharp as if not sharper than that of Indian religious custom; it is a prominent theme in *The Bloudy Tenent* (1644).

If Williams's opinions on the falseness of their religious customs are put aside, his *Key* offers a dispassionate, sometimes neutral, often appreciative, account of the customs of the Indians that he records. It is a very different picture from the 'filth and folly' reported by Eliot and indicates a contrasting perspective on what he sees and hears in his contacts with his Indian neighbours that is more in tune with scientific, Baconian observation and inductive methods than with the theology-led and teleological interpretations of Eliot. Perry Miller goes so far as to describe Williams's *Key* as 'the nearest approach to an objective, anthropological study that anyone was to achieve in America for a century or more'.[50] He offers more than anthropology, however, as he uses his observations to make (often critical) comments about his English compatriots as well as to extract more generalised moral or theological messages. Williams's anthropology supplies a moral and spiritual exercise for his readers. As David Read argues, in his study of knowledge formation in the New World, Williams's 'field of inquiry' in the lives of the Narragansetts moves his exploration of the workings of Providence away from the familiar turf of his readers 'so that one can see rightly the multiple, recondite, unanticipated, sometimes shocking ways that God acts in the quotidian and preeminently *social* space that Williams so often designates as a "wilderness." The use of the unfamiliar language of the Indians is part of this educative destabilisation.[51] Adopting this approach, Williams is attuned to the particular as well as the general. In Chapter II of the *Key*, for example, he begins his lesson with the question, '*A Scúmetesímmis?*' ('Have you not yet eaten?'), describes Indian customs of eating and entertaining, follows with the general observation that there is 'more free entertainment and refreshment amongst these *Barbarians* then amongst thousands that call themselves *Christians*', and in conclusion relates what he has observed to the *a priori* surety that God is great, God will provide and God will judge.[52]

On several occasions Williams shows how Indian customs are responses to their particular circumstances. Their skill in harvesting, processing and using the fruits of the land in which they live, reported by Williams, are among these adaptations to their environment; the chapter 'Of Travell' describes how well adapted they are through custom (including the stretching and binding of their legs as babies to strengthen them for running) to the vast wilderness in which they live.[53] In this Williams comes close to the geographical determinism of Heylyn and the concept that, though all men were descended from a common root, they came to be different from each other due to 'the situations of their several dwellings'.[54]

Williams's portrait of the Narragansetts as well as adapted to and comfortable in their setting, and the approval he gives to many of their customs, implies that there is not the imperative for them to change, to set aside old ways and take on the new style of living that Eliot's missionaries urge on their Indian brothers. It appears that Williams is willing to let them alone and quiet in the ways they 'like and love'. The different approaches of Eliot and Williams to the Indians whom they both acknowledge as bound to them through common descent from Adam become more evident through analysis of their handling of the themes of civility and of wilderness commonly included in contemporary conversations about America and in the understandings of the history of mankind since Adam that frame their work.

Wildness and civility

The association of civility with Christianity has already been mentioned in Chapter 2 with reference to Carleill and Hakluyt's contribution to contemporary conversations of this theme. They held to the established convention that civility is a precursor to godliness. Another example of this association is found in a 1643 tract by Thomas Weld and Hugh Peter, of particular relevance to this chapter because these men had been sent by the

Massachusetts General Court to obtain a patent for the same territory, the Narragansett country, as was Williams when he visited England at about that time.[55] In their *New England's First Fruits*, they anticipated criticism of Massachusetts Bay's poor record on mission by offering a pre-emptive justification for the small number of Indian conversions:

> [W]onder not that we mention no more instances at present: but consider, First their infinite distance from Christianity, having never been prepared thereunto by any Civility at all.[56]

Thus lack of civility is an obstacle, and increase in civility a preparation for conversion to Christianity.[57]

This discouraging assessment was echoed by Eliot in his writings and more so in his life's work of the conversion of his 'poor, blind Natives' to the civilised state of preparedness for God's grace.[58] It was a process he explained to the Indians themselves:

> I declared unto them how necessary it was that they should first be Civilized by being brought from their scattered and wild course of life, unto civill Cohabitation and Government ... And therefore I propounded unto them that they should look out some fit place to begin a Towne, unto which they might resort, and there dwell together, enjoy Government, and be made ready and prepared to be a people among whom the Lord might delight to dwell and rule.[59]

As has been seen, the Indian missionaries in Eliot's *Dialogues* preached the necessity of giving up Indian customs as part of turning to God. In their place they were encouraged to adopt 'the virtues and good ways of the English' (as opposed to the bad ways of the English) and so civility was associated with the Protestant and Puritan lives of the Massachusetts Bay colonists, 'would they but doe as wee doe in these things, they would be all one with English men'.[60] Eliot's praying towns project was predicated on this: 'they must have visible civility before they can rightly injoy visible sanctities in ecclesiastical communion'.[61] The necessary items for visible civility included English-style clothes, particular forms of homes with internal walls set in individual plots of land demarcated with fences, organisation of government that accorded with Biblical precedent and participation in forms of labour ('good imployments') that conformed to the working patterns of the settlers.[62] Letters to potential funders in England are a record of this 'civilising' process and reveal the practicalities involved. A letter to Mr Hamner, for example, explains that 'because our Indians are now come in cohabitation and labour, they much delight in linnen to work in', and gives instructions on how and where to send library supplies, linen and cotton.[63] Substantial amounts of money were involved in clothing the Indians according to English standards and fashion. Another letter to

Mr Nicholls records £50 given by Mr Speacot 'to be sent in linen and canvas goods for Indians to wear'.[64] The transformation from 'wildness' to 'civility' not only entailed conformity to English forms of living and labour but also the acceptance of a disciplinary regime regulating private morals. One convert, Nishohku, confessing his weaknesses for drink and women, recounted the difficulties of this transition for himself as a young man:

> For if I now sin, or commit lust, I shall be punished, or put in prison; but if I run wilde, I have liberty to sin without danger: but I was ashamed of such thoughts, and repented; but yet I doubted.[65]

Underlying this whole process was Eliot's conception of the relationship between the spiritual and civil and of the history of mankind as it rolled out from Adam's Creation and Fall. In his study of Eliot's millennialism, James Holstun identifies four historical stages of man in Eliot's writing: the unfallen saints Adam and Eve who would have founded the perfect polity had they not fallen; the Fall and reign of degenerate man whose 'natural state' in fact is decayed civility; civil man whose personal and political lives are characterised by Protestant discipline and popular government; and the regenerate saint who is the product of the regenerate *civis*.[66]

Relating these stages to the condition of the Indians Eliot encountered, they were in the stage of degenerate man and could not achieve the status of regenerate until they had passed through the third stage of civil man. This is clearly expressed in *The Day Breaking*:

> As in nature there is no progress *ab extreme ad extremum nisi per media*, so in religion such as are so extremely degenerate must be brought to some civility before religion can prosper.[67]

Eliot's tracts anticipate and mark progress towards an end. The *Indian Dialogues* are an important part of this story-telling and provide examples of individual life histories where this movement between stages has taken place. The passionate language used shows the dynamism and drama of the process. In *Dialogue II* the Indian convert, Peneovot exclaims:

> Oh I am surprised, I am amazed. You have ravished my soul. I wonder at myself. Where have I been? What have I done? I am like one raised out of a dark pit. You have brought me forth into the sunshine.[68]

And the change is confirmed later with: 'I will never live again as I have formerly done'.[69]

In his *Brief Narratives*, Eliot gave short reports on the progress in each of his Indian towns and his references to individuals within those towns gave indications of their spiritual status whether they are 'sound' or 'godly', they 'pray unto God' or, in the case of unfortunate backsliders, have 'fallen into sin'. Eliot's conceptualisation of the relationship between civility and Christianity was fairly conventional, though his telling of the story was given extra force by his involvement in a practical experiment of civilisation as preparation for regeneration and by his presentation of the Indian experience through what are purportedly their own experiences and forms of speech.[70]

Williams's position, and the interpretation of his writing, is less straightforward. J. Patrick Cesarini, in a 2003 article, drew attention to the influence of the circumstances of the publication of the *Key* on his presentation of his themes.[71] The book was written as Williams travelled to England to obtain a charter for his new Rhode Island colony. In this quest he was in competition with Weld and Peter who were applying for a patent for the same territory and who framed their request in the logic of a conversion project. It is thus likely that Williams's *Key* was a response to his rivals and their interest in the mission to the Indians. In the preface, Williams notes that 'the great Inquiry of all is what Indians have been converted'.[72] He makes the conventional link between civility and Christianity, when he expresses the hope that the *Key* itself might become a tool for civilising the Indian, though with the qualification that the spreading of both is dependent on the Father's pleasure, and uses the conventional device of negative description to signal the Indians' current lack of civility: 'they have no Clothes, Bookes, nor Letters'.[73] Like Eliot, he puts forward the English way of civility as something to aspire to:

> But when [the Indians] heare that about sixteen hundred years agoe, *England* and the *Inhabitants* thereof were like unto *themselves,* and since have received from *God, Clothes, Bookes, &c* they are greatly affected with a secret hope concerning *themselves.*[74]

Elsewhere in his work, however, Williams diverges from Eliot to present a quite different understanding of the civility or lack of civility of the Indians, and a different relationship between those two presences, the English and the American Indians, in his text. A recurrent theme (one he shares with some other contemporary observers such as Thomas Morton and James Rossier) is that the Indians too manifest many of the marks of civility on which the English pride themselves.[75] It is a message that is conveyed with particular emphasis in the verses he uses as emblems to encapsulate the concluding lesson of each chapter. Thus the verse at the end of Chapter I, Of *Eating* and *Entertainment,* includes the lines:

> *Let none sing* blessings *to their soules,*
> *For that they Courteous are:*
> *The wild* Barbarians *with no more*
> *Then Nature, goe so farre:*

In the lists of Narragansett vocabulary Williams records Indian salutations. From these salutations his observation in generall is that 'there is a civility and courtesie even amongst these wild Americans'.[76]

Roger Williams and John Eliot's Indian writings and the story of Adam

Williams takes several of the Indians' customs (family structures, political organisation, legal custom, the 'high and honourable esteem of the Mariage bed') and shows how they too are signs of civility when assessed against European criteria of civilisation. Labour is used by Eliot as a sign of civility, but Williams shows not just that the Indians work hard and productively but that they do so in sociability and co-operation – 'with friendly joining they breake up their fields, build their Forts, hunt the Woods, stop and kill fish in the Rivers'.[77] He shows them trading, for though they are 'ignorant of *Europes* Coyne' yet they have their own in the form of shells.[78] He writes of 'families, cohabitation and association of houses and townes together'. Even where the customs appear quite wild, Williams is able to show that they are in fact based on civility. When the Indians sleep outside by the fire, for example, they do it for comfort, substituting the warmth of the fire for that of the bedclothes or for hospitality so that visitors might have the benefit of their shelter, or, tellingly, they might do it because the English, out of suspicion, will not open their homes to them.[79]

This last reason is one of many instances recorded by Williams that not only portray the Indians as civil, but show them to be more civilised than their English counterparts. The kindness and hospitality with which the Indians greet strangers is such that it puts to shame the English Christians:

> It is a strange truth, that a man shall generally finde more free entertainment and refreshment amongst these *Barbarians,* then amongst thousands that call themselves *Christians*.[80]

The manner in which Williams's descriptions of the Indians serve to throw bad light onto the English has similarities with the approach taken by Thomas Morton, another exile from the Massachusetts Bay community, and so could be a backhanded criticism of the English, Christian society that had thrown him out. It could also be a form of provocation to warn a privileged race not to take for granted and thus lose its advantages, similar in effect to the warnings of divines Richard Mather and Henry Whitfield that, just as God had once transferred his favour from the Jews to the gentiles, so he might remove it from the English and bestow it upon the Indians.[81] The following couplet implies that to warn was part of Williams's purpose:

> Make sure thy second birth, else thou shalt see,
> Heaven ope to Indians wild, but shut to thee.[82]

Elsewhere in the *Key* he writes 'The Courteous Pagan shall condemne / Uncourteous Englishmen', and puts into their mouths several criticisms of English practice, lies, broken promises, 'whoredoms', and violence.[83] The word Eliot uses for Indian custom, Williams's Indians use for the English and Irish when they express their shock at their 'horrid filth'.[84] There are numerous other examples where the language and associations of civility are turned upon their heads. Just as Williams has used the language of civility for the Indians, so he and his Indians use the language of degeneracy for the English. Williams attributes to the Indians surprise that those who wear clothes ('doe goe in Cloaths' 'they're richly clad') or who know God should behave in such a disgraceful way.[85] The English are described as 'Beasts nor men', as 'Barbarians', as 'pagans'.[86] The long hair styles of the English that contrast with the shorter style of the Indians are a sign of what English men have 'degenerated to'.[87] Such writing is more than the consequence of personal grievance and does more than challenge the English to improve their morals and be watchful; rather, it is an expression of Williams's theological conviction about the nature of man and the relation of human history. As such, it confuses and confounds Eliot's fourfold categorisation of the kinds and stages of man.

Scholars of Williams's work, John Teunissen and Evelyn Hinx, found an alternative history in the *Key* that would upend Eliot's understanding.[88] In the introduction to their 1973 edition of the text, they argued that different sections of the *Key* represent respectively Edenic man before the Fall and degenerate man after the Fall. They claimed that by the end of the first two sections of *Key* Williams has created a picture not of the 'noble savage' but 'of the closest possible seventeenth century approximation of the Garden and its pre-lapsarian attributes'.[89] Indications in the text of the Indians' closeness to nature and of their superior physical fitness and adaptability to their environment would all seem to support this reading, as well as the harmony and kindness seen to characterise their relationships in various chapters. References to God's creation of the sun and moon to direct the day and night and the Indian children's naming of the stars are evocative of the Genesis story and pre-lapsarian Eden.[90] This paradisiacal state cannot last, however, for, in contrast to Thomas Morton's arcadian vision, the world Williams portrayed is beset by a 'tragic primitivism', and the tragedy is, according to Teunissen and Hinx's perspective, brought on by the very people who claim to come with a civilising mission.[91] In an article on the same topic, they wrote:

> The first half of *Key* likewise moves through a series of observations concerning the perfections of natural man, but in the latter half (following from the chapter on Indian religion) it is the degeneration of the native's natural virtue as a result of their contact with civilising Christians that becomes Williams' subject.[92]

Teunissen and Hinx's model does not capture the essence of Williams's *Key*, however, for several reasons. First there is greater differentiation in Williams's representation of his Indians than a pre-lapsarian understanding would allow. Not all possess the natural dignity and generous hospitality he attributes to many of them. In fact the first chapter of the *Key* begins with a distinction that shows that, like the English, the Indians are of different types, and so at the same time we get both internal diversity and similarity with the other culture in this context of encounter:

> The Natives are of two sorts, (as the English are.) Some more Rude and Clownish ... Others, and the generall, are *sober* and *grave*.[93]

Williams does not reserve his negative comments for the English but includes the violence of the Indians towards one another in one of his verses, '*The Indians count of Men as Dogs / It is no Wonder then: / They teare out one anothers throats!*'[94] Williams's own experiences ensure that he is not naïve in his interpretation of the Indians. In a letter to Winthrop, while on a diplomatic mission to the Pequots, he writes of 'the bloody Pequod ambassadors, whose hands and arms, methought, wreaked with the blood of my countrymen, murdered and massacred by them on Connecticut river'.[95] He also conveys reports of the most repulsive and apparently degenerate customs of some nearby tribes, those three or four hundred miles west who live off the bark of trees which they dry and eat with the fat of beasts and even of men, who terrorise their neighbours or the Mauquaûogs or Men-eaters who make a 'delicious monstrous dish' out of the heads and brains of their enemies.[96] These Indians are not just vague threats in background of the picture like wild beasts in the forest as Williams incorporates them as men into the scheme of salvation.[97]

A further problem with Teunissen and Hinx's theory is that it is dependent on a typological reading of the text foreign to the kind of spiritual typology Williams adopts; for him all types have collapsed into Christ and His Kingdom, and his followers have superseded the Jew as God's holy nation.[98] Although he is prepared to use figurative language and metaphor, he avoids typology in his interpretation of the peoples of the world. To use the Indians in the American wilderness as a type for Adam in the garden would not be in keeping with his method or theology. The Indians' significance cannot be other than what they are, fallen men awaiting regeneration like everyone else.

There may also be a confusion of the terms 'nature', 'natural' as in 'natural man' with modern understandings of what nature and being close to nature might signify. What Williams is remarking on is not the Indians' loss of natural virtue through the contamination of civilisation but the persistence of natural virtue even in their wild and degenerate state:

> In the ruines of depraved mankind are *yet* to be founde Natures distinctions, and Natures affections.[99]

When Williams states that 'the sociablenesse of the nature of man appeares in the wildest of them, who love societie', he does not mean that natural sociability appears exclusively or particularly in the wildest of men but that (perhaps unexpectedly for his readers) it appears in them, too.[100] Natural wisdom is a fire that has not been quenched by this wildness.[101] Elsewhere he defines it as 'that Candle or Light remaining in a man', his choice of the word 'remaining' emphasising the persistence of the guidance God gave to mankind at Adam's creation, into man's present post-lapsarian state.[102]

In the *Examiner Defended* (1652), Williams distinguishes between two forms of natural wisdom that correspond to different degrees of civility:

> I ask If natural wisdom (that Candle or Light remaining in man) be not two fold? – first that which is Common to all mankind in general; people, lowest, vulgar ... second that which is noble and high (in degrees) refined and elevated by finer animal spirits, by Education, by Study, by Observation, by experience.[103]

The distinction that Williams is making between 'lowest' and 'high' is not a spiritual one. The civil man whose natural wisdom is refined and elevated by learning does not thereby gain access to a spiritual and saving knowledge of God. In the same text, Williams warns that the second candle can be misapplied and end up misleading in matters of religion. Man, however 'refined and elevated', cannot come to a full knowledge or true love of God through his own natural resources, even if those resources are God-given; to think so would be 'a downright Doctrine of *Freewill,* in depraved nature' and 'to run pointblank against all the Histories of the Nations, and all present *Experience* of mankind, in all known parts of the world'.[104] But lack of true knowledge of God does not disqualify '*Nature's Sons both* wild *and* tame' from a moral and upright life.[105] Williams's work contains recognition both of the virtues (even civility) that nature in its first, uneducated, character can produce in the pagan Indian and of the moral virtues that nature in its second, refined, character can produce in civic man. In *The Bloudy Tenent*, for example, Williams argues that even non-Christian magistrates may be imbued by God with civil or moral goodness that is commendable and beautiful, as well as with 'the many excellent gifts wherewith it has pleased God to furnish many enabling them for public service in their countries', though the 'infinitely more beautiful godliness' that goes with true knowledge of God be wanting.[106]

An aim of Williams's writing was to break the link between civility and spirituality. In contrast to Eliot's three stages to the restoration of fallen man (degenerate man, civil man, regenerate saint), Williams recognised only two spiritual states, that of 'natural man' (or 'nature's sons') and that of the 'sons of God', these latter being the small number of elect who will share fully in God's salvation. Civility does not belong on one side or other of this distinction; it may be found among natural men or even be found lacking among the chosen. The verse at the end of Chapter I of *Key* encapsulates these ideas:

> *If Natures Sons both* wild *and* tame,
> *Humane and Courteous be:*
> *How ill becomes it Sonnes of God*
> *To want Humanity?*[107]

Contrary to the ideas behind Eliot's missionary work, civility in Williams's understanding was neither a guarantor of Grace nor a preparation for conversion. It is a point he made in several of his writings:

> For it is not a forme, nor the change of one forme into another, a finer and a finer, and yet more fine, that makes a man a convert I meane such a convert as is acceptable to God in Jesus.[108]

Someone may appear in all outward performance to be a true Christian and preach and pray and yet be no more than a natural man.[109] Nor is lack of civility a bar from grace. Among his Indian friends, Williams hoped that '(in the Lords holy season) some of the wildest of them shall be found to share in the blood of the Son of God'.[110] Even the most obnoxious and savage of peoples, the man-eating Indians of the west, are not outside God's mercy; their unsavoury practice of eating their enemies' heads and brains 'is yet no barre (when the time shall approach) against God's call'.[111] The choice of who is or is not saved is entirely God's.

In his Indian writings, Eliot told a story of transformation that was closely bound to his concept of a transition through civility to Christianity and regeneration. Williams's *Key* has several references to the beginning of man's story with discussion of his origins in Adam, and of the end, with anticipation of the day when man, whether Indian or English, will stand naked before 'Christs most dreadfull barre' awaiting judgement.[112] Williams's theology meant he might hope, but could not predict the salvation or otherwise of his Indian associates. In the end his descriptions, observations and dealings with the Indians could not inform his readers about their spiritual state, their progress towards salvation or future promises. The closest Williams came to the kind of pilgrim's progress report found in Eliot's work was the story of Wequash in the introduction to the *Key*, the telling of which was prompted by other writers and by political interests. Even then he expressed his uncertainty in his account about the outcomes of Wequash's interest – 'I dare not be so confident as others' – and so reduced considerably its power as a story.

The detail of Williams's descriptions of Indian practices indicates that the focus of his writing was more their present than their future state. His text does not have the movement of Eliot's story because the state of his characters is one of waiting on the Lord, rather than acting to advance his kingdom. Instead, it has close interest in the current lives of the Indians and attention to the practicalities of the here and now. For Eliot the present activities of the Indians were bound up in their spiritual journey; for Williams there were two levels and spheres of activity that did not overlap. In the earthly sphere the Indians and English are active but in the spiritual, their activity is on hold until they hear God's summons:

> English and Indians busie are
> In parts of their abode

Yet both stand idle, till God's call
Set them to worke for God.[113]

The differences between Williams's and Eliot's interpretations of mankind's history are further evident in their handling of the related concepts of the wilderness and the garden.

Wilderness and garden

The story of Adam's Creation and Fall, foundational to both men's perspectives on the world, is present more often in the association of words, images and meanings than in explicit chapter and verse reference to Biblical text. Thus, the image of the garden, particularly the walled garden (reflecting the etymology and tradition of Eden and Paradise), and of the wilderness outside, both frame and illustrate their interpretations of the world and the societies in which they lived.[114] Important too is the concept of labour as activity proper to the garden and of fruitfulness as its outcome. The two men's movement to and within the great expanses of the New World and their experience of establishing new communities in these territories gave the garden and wilderness distinction, and the image of labouring in the garden, experiential as well as theoretical significance.

Eliot's view of the America to which he and his fellow Massachusetts Bay colonists travelled in 1631 could hardly be more different from Thomas Morton's Arcadian image of the same territory with its 'goodly groves', 'round rising hillucks', 'sweete cristall fountains' and clear running streams that lull the senses to sleep.[115] In a letter to Thomas Thorowgood, Eliot recalled how the colonists had chosen what seemed to be land of little promise without the richness of the furs to the north or gold and tobacco to the south and 'nothing in probability to be expected but religion, poverty and hard labour'.[116] The language Eliot employed presented the settlers' new life as analogous to Adam's condition after the Fall; like him they had changed a 'comfortable being for the outward man into a condition full of labour, toile, sorrow, wants and temptations of a wilderness'.[117] Eliot's assessment appears more negative than that of Winthrop, whose call to migration presented the American project as a continuation of Adam's pre-lapsarian activity of improvement, 'the whole world is the Lord's garden and he hath given it to the sons of Adam to be tilled and improved by them', but Eliot was interested not only in the improvement of the promising, but also in the transformation of the challenging.[118] His was essentially a post-lapsarian outlook, exiled from the garden and seeking return. Understood in this way, his Indians, in their pit of darkness, made ideal material for Eliot to work with, and the imagery of the garden and his own task as labourer in the garden were transferred to them. In an early tract he linked land and people as fields of transformation, writing that, though the settlers had thought that the Indians would be 'dry and rocky ground', they would soon find them 'better soil for the Gospel than we can think' just as they had been surprised to find the soil of New England to be 'scarce inferior to English tillage'.[119]

Indeed, the imagery of the garden threaded through much of the activity that Eliot was interested in, whether it was tending the garden, gathering in its fruits or protecting the garden from the encroachment of the wilderness. In one of his *Indian Dialogues* it was used to describe the need for self-examination and vigilance among the converted, that they might not fall back into their former state of degeneration. With an inward-looking orientation reminiscent of Winstanley's work, he wrote:

> So will our hearts be sending forth new weeds of sin but we must be daily diligent to watch and weed them out.[120]

This gardening activity takes place at the micro-level of the individual's spiritual journey, but the same image was also applied at the macro-level of political society. In *The Christian Commonwealth* Eliot warned that within the commonwealth 'sin will grow apace like ill weeds if it be not always watched'.[121] In this tract he proposed a way to combat the creeping wilderness through weekly meetings in groups of 10 to address grievances so the gardening task was carried out through political institution. Ultimately, though, all missionaries and institutional bodies were acting as agents for Christ, whom Eliot described in his *Brief Narrative* on the progress of his praying towns, as 'Lord of the Harvest'.[122] Though Eliot used the garden analogy for the conversion of his Indians, the soul's self-searching and the ordering of the polity shows the unity in Eliot's scheme, a unity of activity that Williams does not share.

Using Biblical imagery, Eliot likened his missionary project to the gathering in of grain. Writing of New England he observed, 'there God hath some graine to gather into his garner some elect to call into his kingdom'.[123] Eliot anticipated this final gathering with his praying towns, though the Indian inhabitants of these were the hopeful rather than the elect. The Indian praying towns were models of separation, for this experiment in godly, civil living was conducted in isolation from both the English community and the Indian communities from which the Indian converts had come. Holstun identifies them with Christopher Hill's 'Robinson Crusoe situation', a place for Puritan spiritual growth in a context of isolation, which in turn has parallels with Adam and Eve's existence in the walled garden in Milton's *Paradise Lost*.[124] Where Eliot's model differs from that of Crusoe is in its collective nature, dealing with a group of like-minded godly people, rather than a virtuous individual. An aim of his praying towns mission was to train the Indians to be 'the Lord's people only, ruled by his Word in all things'.[125] There was also a broader aim, expressed explicitly in *The Christian Commonwealth*, that the towns might be the beginning and model of a regeneration of England.[126] Eliot's project is another example of the Puritan combining of the individual and collective dimensions noted by Theodore Bozeman and other scholars of their theology.[127]

A physical echo of the marking out of a spiritual space may be found in the walls of the Indians' new homes and fenced enclosures that characterised the town, safeguarding the personal spaces and tamed plots of land of individual households. Within these towns the Indians replicated the activity of the inhabitants of the first gardens for Eliot's intention was that they should 'labour and pray'. As with the paradise that is lost in Milton's poem, Eliot's praying town garden was not entirely secure from contamination from outside. Thus in his *Brief Narratives* (1670) he reported the invasion of drunkenness into one of his towns; a ruler in another, otherwise of 'sound and godly' character, who was 'overtaken by a passion'; and several encounters with the fierce and murderous Mauquaogs who do not belong in the garden but who 'haunt', 'molest' and 'annoy' the inhabitants and have killed members of those praying Indians who venture out against them.[128] As the destruction of Indian praying towns during King Philip's War, just a few years after these reports, was to prove, the walls of spiritual and moral separation between garden and wilderness, though carefully constructed, were still permeable.

While Eliot was working figuratively and literally to build up the walls, Williams was breaking them down, or rather promulgating the message that the wall between garden and wilderness has been irretrievably broken down, until, that is, God restores his garden on the last day. This question of the division between wilderness and garden was at the root of Williams's initial exile from the Massachusetts Bay colony in January 1636, an exile that afforded him the experience of 14 weeks' sojourn in the real physical wilderness where he was 'exposed to the mercy of an howling Wilderness in Frost and Snow &c'.[129] Williams rehearsed his language of walls, wildernesses and gardens during his long-standing controversy with John Cotton, one of the principal ministers of the colony. Cotton identified four charges against Williams: that he denied the colonists right by king's patent to land he claimed belonged to the Indians; that he claimed 'a wicked person' should not be called upon to take an oath or join in prayer; that he insisted the New England Puritans should not participate in worship of the Church of England and that he argued 'that the Civil Magistrate's power extended only to the Bodies and Goods, and outward state of men'. Behind these was Williams's objection to Cotton's regulatory principle that 'Church and Commonweal' are one. In a response entitled *Mr. Cotton's Letter Lately Printed, Examined and Answered*, he employed the following metaphor:

> The faithful labors of many witnesses of Jesus Christ, extant to the world, abundantly proving that the church of the Jews under the Old Testament is the type, and the church of the Christians under the New Testament in the antitype, were both separate from the world;

> and when they have opened a gap in the hedge or wall of separation between the garden of the church and the wilderness of the world, God hath ever broken down the wall itself, removed the candlestick, and made His garden a wilderness, as at this day. And that therefore if He will ever please to restore His garden and paradise again, it must of necessity be walled in peculiarly unto Himself from the world; and that all that shall be saved out of the world are to be transplanted out of the wilderness of the world, and added unto His church or garden.[130]

Here and elsewhere Williams developed the argument that Christ's true church of God's elect as the antitype has put an end to all types, the historical Christian church has become inextricably enmeshed in the ways of the world, and the Christians of the true church are scattered throughout the nations.[131] Figuratively speaking, the wall between garden and wilderness is destroyed; all of mankind is now in the wilderness, and only God will restore the garden in the last days 'if He will ever please to'. Thus no nation, society or congregation can make claim to the status of God's chosen people or Christ's Church, nor can any know with certainty who those chosen people might be.[132] The imagery of the garden and wilderness is used again in *The Bloudy Tenent* to make this second point in an argument against the rejection of heretics from the polity:

> As if because briars, thorns and thistles may not be in the garden of the church, therefore they must all be plucked out of the wilderness. Whereas he that is a briar, that is a Jew, a Turk, a pagan, an anti-christian to-day, may be, when the word of the Lord runs freely, a member of Jesus Christ tomorrow, cut out of the wild olive and planted into the true.[133]

The idea that political authorities, such as the leaders of the Massachusetts Bay colony, can have sway over spiritual as well as civil affairs is abhorrent. Like his friend Milton, he was outspoken in opposition to John Owens's *15 Proposals for the Furtherance and Propagation of the Gospel* (1652) and petition to Parliament to suppress notorious heresies. *The Bloudy Tenent*, published on his 1651–54 visit to London, was a response to this.[134]

Williams's work contains frequent reference to the state of 'wilderness'. It is sometimes used negatively to denote a place of hardship (his own experiences in the physical wilderness give him reason for this) or of sin. In the *Key*, the Indians tell the English that, on account of their sins 'your Land's the Wildernesse' and they are no more than barbarians and 'Pagans wild'.[135] But insistence that the garden has gone and that men are all in the wilderness is not a counsel of despair; the wilderness is not that bad, and God is not absent. From his own experience in physical wilderness and the hospitality of the non-Christian natives he met, Williams was able to say, 'God makes a Path, provides a Guide/ And feeds in Wildernesses':[136]

> As the same Sun shines on the Wildernesse that doth on a Garden! So the same faithful and all sufficient God, can comfort feede and safely guide even through a desolate howling Wildernesses.

Some limited knowledge of God might be had in the wilderness by all men, whether or not they have access to Biblical text: 'God hath not left himselfe without wit'. We learn that the birds in all coasts of the world 'preach unto Men the prayse of their Makers Wisedome, Power, and Goodnesse', and the fruitful rains and seasons, the earth and trees and plants that fill man's heart with food and gladness, are witnesses to God and his kindness.[137]

The breaking down of barriers that Williams chronicles is exactly that. Just as the 'Sons and daughters of God' are scattered across the nations, so there are reminiscences of the garden in the wilderness, as we find in one of Williams's verses:

> Yeares thousands since, God gave command (as we in Scripture find)
> That Earth and Trees & Plants should bring
> Forth fruits each in his kind
> The Wildernesses remembers this,
> The wild and howling land
> Answers the toyling labour of
> The wildest Indian hand.[138]

These lines evoke, in the wilderness, images of Adam and Eve's cultivation of the Garden of Eden. There are parallels between the ideas expressed here and Williams's observations on the natural wisdom and natural sociability of the wild Indians. He is presenting evidence of the persistence, through the crisis of the Fall, of much of the order of the first Creation. If the Indians sometimes appear to be like the pre-lapsarian Adam and Eve, and the wilderness occasionally evokes the garden, it is not because they exist in an Edenic state of innocence, but because they enjoy some of the positive as well as the negative inheritances from their first ancestors. Although there may not be the joy of the 'infinitely more beautiful godliness' that the elect future inhabitants will find (in God's time) in the restored garden, existence in the wilderness has its own goodness.[139] This verse indicates that labour is the key to establishing the proper relationship between humanity and God's creation, and so Williams emphasises the busyness of the Indians as they cultivate, harvest and process the fruits of the land or map out and use their territory for hunting. They are required to be not just thankful (to God) but also fruitful and will be condemned for failing on either count.[140] Man's proper activity in the wilderness is to live in it and make it as good as it can be in the present, rather than to try to transform it back into the garden; only God can bring in the new order. Williams's theories of the polity depend on this position.

The polity

Although for Eliot the focus of this chapter has been on his Indian writings, these cannot be understood without reference to his political writings, which put them in the context of his overall vision of the transformation of England and indeed of political society in general. In the preface to his treatise, *The Christian Commonwealth* (1651), Eliot himself made explicit links between his work to bring civil government and order to 'our poor, dark and blind Indians' and his vision for the ordering of the English polity; indeed, he suggested that it was his work with the Indians that caused him to reflect more deeply on the most desireable form of government for any Christian people.[141] The times and circumstances in which Eliot was writing seem to present unparalleled opportunities for fulfilment. His perceptions on arrival in the New World, of the very wildness of the American wilderness and the nakedness of the American Indians that he characterised as *abrasa tabula* appeared to provide possibilities for the creation of a new society, based not on human invention but on God's ordinance.[142] Very soon after his move to America, events in England appeared to sweep away the obstacles and clear the ground for the advent of a Christian utopia there and one that would be the beginning of Christ's kingdom in all the world. He wrote that England was 'in a capacity to chuse unto themselves a new Government and in such deep perplexity about that great Question' and urged them:

> To set open the door, to let in the Lord Jesus to give them rest; who hath been all this while knocking at the door, by these perplexing troubles.[143]

The Christian Commonwealth emerged from this climate of political expectation and debate. Its immediate context was the Engagement Controversy of 1649 during which Parliament responded to the Levellers' questions about its political authority with a call upon all men to swear true and faithful allegiance to the commonwealth 'as it is now established without a king or house of Lords'. This controversy earned written responses from other writers – including Gerrard Winstanley, whose tract *Englands Spirit Unfoulded or an Encouragement to Take the Engagement* supported Parliament's stance.[144] Eliot himself rejected the idea of *de facto* political power and proposed a new social contract based on Scriptural precedent, an appeal to God as the source of all authority. It would be idolatry to recognise authority in anyone but Christ, and all oaths and covenants taken by God's people were for the advancement of His kingdom.

Timing is important in Eliot's work, the sense that the Indians, the English, the peoples of the world were coming to a significant point in their history, the point of completion of the story that began with Adam's Fall. Reporting the lives of the Indians he used the language of 'readiness and preparation' and the crucial question in the assessment of the Indians' path to salvation was at what point could they be deemed to have repented sufficiently of their sins to be ready to enter into church membership? At what point, through God's grace, is an Indian community sufficiently freed from its former blindness and depravity to merit their own church?[145]

Eliot's view that England had, through the purging of the civil war, reached the crucial point in time for salvation appears in the language of *The Christian Commonwealth*: 'after all these clouds and storms, the peaceable Kingdom of Christ may rise up and the Lord may rise up and the Lord may reign in England'; 'the Lord Christ is *now* accomplishing these things in Great Britain'; he is '*now* come to take possession of his kingdom and England is first in that blessed work'; 'English worthies' are called '*now* to advance Christ'.[146] And it is not just England but the world 'the time being come that the Lord is about to shake all the Earth'. For an individual or a people to enter into covenant with the Lord and subjection to Him, the prerequisite is 'that they do humbly confess their corruption by nature and lost condition'; thus it is through acknowledgement of that early episode of mankind's history that they can arrive at the last.[147]

In Eliot's scheme the political and the spiritual are inextricably bound up together. There is in fact no validity for a political model outside this combination; Eliot declared it to be the Lord's commandment that a people should enter into covenant with Him and become His people, 'in their Civil Society as well as in their Church Society'.[148] The words of the covenant he used with his Indians make this clear:

> Wee doe give ourselves and our Children unto God to be his people, Hee shall rule us in all our affaires, not onely in our Religion, and affaires of the Church (these wee desire as soone as wee can, if God will) but also, in all our works and affaires in this world, God shall rule over us.[149]

John Cotton, when consulted by Eliot, suggested an addition to the covenant that placed this stage in the Indians' journey firmly within the narrative of Fall and Redemption:

> Wee are the sonnes of Adam, we and our forefathers have a long time been lost in our sinnes, but now the mercy of the Lord beginneth to finde us out againe; therefore the grace of Christ helping us, wee doe give ourselves and our Children &c.[150]

Eliot both trained his Indians and urged his English compatriots to accept a form of government that was ordained by God and set out in the Scriptures. In his tract *Strength out of Weaknesse*, Eliot offered a model for the organisation of his Indian communities as established for the Israelites through Moses in Exodus 18. It is a hierarchy of political assemblies to the order of tens, hundreds and thousands and was presented again (with reference to Revelation, Matthew and Hebrews) in *The Christian Commonwealth*

Roger Williams and John Eliot's Indian writings and the story of Adam 109

as the model Eliot urged English worthies to adopt for their country. Eliot employed the ideas of assembly and the people's covenant with their leader, but this covenant included God, and the emphasis was firmly placed on God's institution of the polity rather than men's; they were to be guided not by their own natural wisdom, or any principle of natural rights and freedom, but by the Scriptures alone. Thus he swept aside the symbol of the Englishmen's natural rights given iconic status in the debates of the civil war; 'it is the holy scriptures of God onely that I do urge to be your onely Magna Charta'.[151] His tract is in many ways an argument against trusting in the light of nature, whether construed as wisdom, rights or freedoms, for the ordering of men's affairs. It is reliance on these that Christ will destroy. He will 'throw down that great idol of Humane Wisdom in Government and set up Scripture-Government in room thereof not natural laws or liberties'; down will come 'all Dominions and Governments of man, by Humane policy, forms of Government and Laws in all places'. England's job now was 'not to search humane Polities and Platformes of Government, contrived by the wisdom of man'. This emphasis in no way denies the role of human agency in the establishment of government, for Eliot saw it as the role of men to seek the only valid ordering of their nations in the Scriptures (this is the basis of his praying towns project) and establish these as a preliminary to, rather than consequence of, Christ's reign; 'And then Christ reigneth, when all things among men, are done by the direction of the word of his mouth'.[152] Thus Eliot found an institutional and political solution to the depravity of man.

Williams's political theory could hardly be more different from that of Eliot, though both are dependent on the present fallen condition of man and his need for salvation. While Eliot saw the establishment of a Christian commonwealth as a means to that salvation and a way of advancing Christ's kingdom, Williams's view was that it is only at the millennial advent that the members of the mystical nation of the church, now scattered through all the world, will be brought together and the conclusion of mankind's story be achieved. Eliot's vision is what Wilson has classified as a 'prophetic' eschatology that sees men as instruments of God in the preparation of His kingdom. Williams, on the other hand, manifested an 'apocalyptic eschatology' whereby God's kingdom comes in an instant as an 'intrusion upon the present' and without the aid of his servants.[153] For the present there is not (and in the future until Christ's coming, there cannot be) any nation or congregation with a valid claim to being God's people.

> What land, what country now is Israel's parallel and antitype, but that holy, mystical nation, the church of God, peculiar and called to him out of every nation and country. (I Pet ii 9)[154]

The denial of providential status to any nation (now that types are ended) and the scattered nature of God's true church, so that it consists of small numbers in all nations, has a levelling effect; 'what difference between Asia and Africa, between Europe and America, between England and Turkey, London and Constantinople'.[155] And so observations of the governments, existing and historical, within these states and all their diversity, can provide examples of how nations are and might be governed in the present state, which is one of waiting. Williams considered the different states of the world and found that 'so many glorious and flourishing cities of the world maintain their civil peace; yea, the very Americans and wildest pagans keep the peace of their towns and cities, though neither in one nor the other can any man prove a true church of God'.[156] Behind his observations is a belief in the validity of human (as opposed to religious) activity, associations and institutions, outside the story of redemption and the criteria of degeneracy and regeneration this story applies, a perspective very evident in his treatment of the Narragansett people and society in the *Key*. In *The Bloudy Tenent*, he declared the 'wildest Indians'' civil and earthly governments to be 'as lawful and true as any in the world'.[157] The worthiness of the earthly and the civil, as opposed to the spiritual and (truly) Christian, was endorsed by God at Creation. Williams tells us that when God created all things out of nothing 'he saw and acknowledged divers sorts of goodness which must still be acknowledged in their distinct kinds'.[158] These move from the natural 'a good tree', 'a good sheep', to the artificial, 'a good house', to the social 'a good city', 'a good company', 'a good husband, father, master', and to those who are 'morally, civilly good in their several civil respects and employments' such as physician, lawyer, merchant and magistrate.

By inductive reasoning, Williams finds commonalities in the formation and rationale of different civil societies:

> We have formerly viewed the very matter and essence of a civil magistrate and find it the same in all parts of the world, wherever people live upon the face of the earth, agreeing together in towns, cities, provinces, kingdoms: – I say the same essentially civil, both from,
>
> 1. The rise and fountain whence it springs, to wit, the people's choice and free consent
> 2. The object of it viz., the common weal, or safety of such a people in their bodies and goods, as the authors of this model have themselves confessed.[159]

Here he sets out two key principles of his political theory. The first is that government is created by the people on the basis of free agreement and that the people remain the source of the power of the magistrates they thus create. Earlier in *The Bloudy Tenent* Williams acknowledges as 'most true' that civil government is an ordinance of God but infers from this that the people are 'the sovereign, original and foundation of civil power' and may choose whatever form of civil government they 'in their wisdom' find to be most suitable.[160] He later re-emphasises the point that 'all true civil magistrates have not the least inch of power but what is measured out to them from the free consent of the whole'.[161] Behind his theory is the concept of 'natural freedom'.[162] His emphasis on the human foundation of government originating in natural wisdom that is in itself a gift from God contrasts sharply with Eliot's concern to show how human wisdom is swept aside by the divine institution of a prescribed form of government but is in many respects a precursor of Locke's model as set out in his *Two Treatises of Government*.

The second principle of Williams's political theory gives the reason for consent to government. It is a reflection of a general observation made in the *Key* that, prompted by his experience with the wild Narragansetts, underlines the naturalness of a human impulse towards political society:

> The wildest of the sonnes of Men have ever found a necessity, (for the preservation of themselves, their Families and Properties) to cast themselves into some Mould or forme of Government.[163]

This understanding, as well as the flexibility of Williams's politics that allows for a variety of forms of government, demonstrates a pragmatism that sees government as being more about preservation than transformation.[164] Indeed, in his own position as leader of the troublesome colony of Rhode Island and Providence Plantation, Williams found that pragmatic requirements for the peaceful ordering of a state might require taking a firm line against ideologically framed opposition to his authority. Likening himself to the commander of a ship, he argued that if any threaten mutiny, or 'shall preach or write that there ought to be no Commanders, nor Officers, because all are equal in Christ' then, as captain he 'may judge, resist, compel and punish such Transgressors, according to their Deserts and Merits'.[165]

Again Williams's ideas are far removed from Eliot's interpretation of the commonwealth. For Williams, government is necessitated by the sinfulness of fallen man that puts other people's lives and property at risk; political association and the appointment of a civil magistrate is a solution to this, but he did not see as an aim of civil government the curing or punishing of sins unless they have a direct impact on the peace of the state:

> I dare not assent to that assertion, 'That even original [sin] remotely hurts the civil state.' It is true some do, as inclination to murder, theft, whoredom, slander, disobedience to parents, and magistrates; but blindness of mind, hardness of heart, inclination to choose or worship this or that God, this or that Christ, beside the true, these hurt not remotely the civil state, as not concerning it, but the spiritual.[166]

Both authors, then, were agreed about the beginning of all mankind in Adam, his Creation and Fall and both that these events as described in Genesis determine all human experience thereafter; they are the assumed basis of human history. Both placed their New England experiences, of wilderness and of encounter with the Indians, within that context of this universal story. They saw it as the Indians' story too; they were included in the telling of it; they were told it, and they told it to each other. But in spite of this shared foundation, there were different understandings of how the story plays out. For Eliot, the history of man rolls out in a continuous story of Creation, Fall degeneracy, return to civility and, finally, hope of restoration. He both drew the Indians into that story as fellow sons of Adam and hoped that by their involvement and progress through civility to Christianity they would move that story forward. They are the fruits that need to be garnered in the last days, or they are the model of transformed society that can be applied more widely and advance the advent of the kingdom. The script is predetermined and the Indians, and the English, are being asked to conform to it. For Eliot human history is the playing out of a drama. Adam is an actor in that drama, but more than that, his act constitutes the event that sets the play in motion. Eliot's work was tempered with millennial expectation understood in political terms, and he was keen to see the glorious ending of the story begun with Adam.

Williams's historical sense was very different. He was clear about the beginning of human history and about what will happen at the end, but there is no movement at present. For Williams it is history interrupted. He compared the church of his own time to a 'vessel becalmed at sea'.[167] If God's Church (God's people) is becalmed at sea then there is no big ongoing story; Williams had no secular teleology to tell a different tale. If men can only wait upon the Lord for final part of story, then what they are experiencing is one long intermission. Williams's world is very different from Eliot's; it is static rather than dynamic, an interest in mankind's state rather than his story. The key to his interpretation of his fellow humans is not what it is about them that shows where they are bound and how far along the route they have advanced, rather it is what it is that shows what they are, the elements that explain or determine how they behave now in this period of waiting, and so Williams offers his readers a detailed description of Narragansett society as it is currently lived.

Adam takes on a different significance in Williams's scheme, as state-of-being rather than as event in a story. Williams uses the Indians' identity as Adam's children to explain who they are now more than where they are going; his writing has a present rather than future orientation. The Indians share signs of Adam's fallen state,[168] for example in those tendencies towards sin that require the establishment of a polity to keep them under control. They also inherit those natural guides (wisdom, freedom, sociability and so on) that were given by God to pre-lapsarian Adam and that have not been wiped out by the Fall but have persisted through it to direct his children now. Similarities between the Indians and English are signs of a common humanity, possessed through a common ancestry; differences between their cultures are explained through the acquisition of skills and customs and the response to differences of environment, rather than different levels of depravity. Rather than being one big story, in this intermission there are many small stories, belonging to particular groups of people in particular places, and so we have the seeds of anthropology noted by Perry Miller in Williams's method. The particularity of Williams's understanding of human society is closely aligned to the pragmatism of his political theory, by which 'a people may erect and establish what form of government seems to them most meet for their civil condition'.[169] As these small stories are not integrated into the big story in Williams's strict separation of the civil and the spiritual, the status of the government or magistrate within the larger story (i.e. whether or not they are a Christian) has no bearing on their political role, and the religion of their subjects is of equal irrelevance to them. With politics thus understood it would be easy for the frame of the story of man's fall and restoration to disappear as a reference for the understanding of people's political lives, however crucial it might be to understanding their spiritual state.

Notes

1. The Indians with whom Williams had dealings were largely the Narragansetts and for Eliot they were Algonquian.
2. These words were reported to Thomas Shephard, a publicist of Eliot's work, *CSS – ET*, 134.
3. William Peterfield Trent, John Erskine, Stuart P. Sherman, Carl van Doren, ed., *The Cambridge History of American Literature* (New York: G. P. Putnam's Sons, 1917 to 1921). Book I, Chapter III para 5. Note also the distinction between 'apostolic John Eliot' and 'tolerant Roger Williams' in William P. Trent and Benjamin W. Wells, ed., *Colonial Prose and Poetry. 1901. Vol. I. The Transplanting of Culture: 1607–1650* (New York: Thomas Y. Crowell & Co., 1901).
4. Morgan, *Roger Williams*, 142.
5. Brockunier, Samuel Hugh, *The Irrepressible Democrat, Roger Williams* (New York: The Ronald Press Company, 1940).
6. John H. Barry, *Roger Williams and the Creation of the American Soul: Church, State and the Birth of Liberty* (New York: Viking, 2012).
7. Perry Miller, *Roger Williams: His Contribution to the American Tradition* (New York: Atheneum, 1939).
8. Morgan, *Roger Williams*, 5.
9. Gilpin, *Millenarian Piety*; Byrd, *Challenges*.
10. Ivy Schweitzer, *The Work of Self-Representation: Lyric Poetry in Colonial New England*, (Chapel Hill: University of North Carolina Press, 1991); Thomas Scanlan, *Colonial Writings and the New World 1583–1671* (Cambridge: Cambridge University Press, 1999); Kristina Bross, *Dry Bones and Indian Sermons: Praying Indians in Colonial America* (Ithaca: Cornell University Press, 2004).
11. Scanlan, 136; Schweitzer, 181f.
12. Some of these works have been collected together with other authors' accounts of Eliot's missionary activities to form what have become known as '*The Eliot Tracts*'. The first published edition of these, the 2003 volume edited by

Michael P. Clark, is the edition being used for this book. Kathryn Gray's 2015 book examines how Eliot's Indian letters, reports and dialogues helped to create a transatlantic community around interests in the missions to the Indians. Kathryn N. Gray, *John Eliot and the Praying Indians of Massachusetts Bay: Communities and Connections in Puritan New England* (Lanham, MD: Bucknell University Press, 2013).

13. Roger Williams, *Letters of Roger Williams 1632–1682*, edited by John Russell Bartlett (Providence: Narragansett Club, 1874).
14. Kupperman, *Facing off*, 19.
15. Ibid., 18.
16. Kupperman, *Facing off*, 19.
17. Byrd, *Challenges*.
18. Bross, Chapter 2 'Seeing with Ezekiel's Eyes,' 28–51.
19. Eliot's first sermon was preached on the River Charles near Watertown. William Kellaway, *The New England Company 1649–1776 Missionary Society to the American Indians* (Glasgow: The University Press, 1961), 83. The examination questions are reported in *LFM – ET*, 314–15. Examples are the testimonies of Nishóhkou, (377), Wutasakompaiun, (389), of Monotunquanit, (391), of Anthony (383), *FAP, ET*.
20. *ID*, 114.
21. *ID*, 97–98.
22. *Key*, 20.
23. *Key*, 133.
24. *Key*, Preface.
25. *Key*, 315.
26. Dane Morrison 'A Praying People: Massachusetts Acculturation and the Failure of the Puritan Mission 1600–1690' *American Indian Studies, vol. 2* (New York: Peter Lang, 1995).
27. *Key*, A4. One of the Indian aetiologies is a monogenetic understanding akin to the Genesis version, by which the god, Kautántowwit made one man and woman of a tree 'which were Fontaines of all mankind' (*Key*, 135); in another, the Indians said that 'they have *sprung* and *growne* up in that very place, like the very *trees* of the *wildernesse*' (*Key*, A4), a polygenetic understanding of human origins.
28. Not conjecturing on either the past or future histories of the Indians is characteristic of Williams's method.
29. In Deuteronomy (Dt. 32:21) the Lord scattered the ten tribes into the corners of the world so they were lost, but has promised to gather them again.
30. *TR – ET*, 261.
31. *LC – ET*, 410–27.
32. *Key*, 53.
33. *LAM – ET*, 185.
34. *Key*, 121.
35. Prominent among the other commentators is Boemus, cited in Hodgen, *Early Anthropology*, 234.
36. *ID*, 42.
37. *ID*, 67; *ID*, 47.
38. *Key*, A4. See also James Holstun, *A Rational Millenium: Puritan Utopias of Seventeenth Century England and America* (Oxford: Oxford University Press, 1987), 138.

Roger Williams and John Eliot's Indian writings and the story of Adam 115

39. A formula which was used by Thomas Hooker (1586–1647) and Cotton Mather (1663–1728) and thus spans the century.
40. *IG*, A3.
41. *Key*, 30.
42. A letter dated Roxbury August 29th in *John Eliot and the Indians 1652–1657 Being Letters Addressed to Rev. John Hamner of Barnstable, England* (New York: The Adams and Grace Press, 1915).
43. *ID*, 64. Eliot was also critical of some European customs' vaine, and frothy fashions, follies wanton dresses, and madnesses of the times' in a letter to Thomas Thorowgood, *ET*, 426.
44. Eliot writes in a letter (to Thorowgood) that his scope is 'to write and imprint no other but Scripture principles in the *abrasa tabula* scraped board of these naked people, that so they may be in all their principles a choice people unto the lord' – *ET*, 426.
45. *ET*, 95–96.
46. In his introduction to the Eliot Tracts, Michael Clark notes the pragmatic approach to customs in Algonquian culture and preparedness to shift allegiance to more powerful political and spiritual agents if they are successfully challenged – *ET*, 17.
47. *ID*, 87.
48. *Key* 139.
49. *Key*, 140.
50. Perry Miller, *Roger Williams*, 52–53.
51. David Read, *New World, Known World: Shaping Knowledge in Early Anglo-American Writing*, (Columbia: University of Missouri Press, 2005).
52. *Key*, 16.
53. *Key*, 95–102, 68–78.
54. Peter Heylyn, *Cosmographie* – cited in Hodgen, *Early Anthropology*, 234.
55. Weld and Peter were sent to England in1641; Williams went in 1643.
56. Thomas Weld and Hugh Peter, *New England's First Fruits* (London: Henry Overton, 1643), 4 (included in the *Eliot Tracts*).
57. James Axtell, *The Invasion Within: The Contest of Cultures in Colonial North America* (New York: Oxford University. Press, 1985).
58. Gilpin, *Millenarian Piety*, 130. The phrase 'poor blind natives' was used in the long title of John Eliot's *A Brief Narrative of the Progress of the Gospel amongst the Indians in New England, in the Year 1670* (London: John Allen, 1670).
59. *LFM – ET*, 303.
60. *Letter of Mr Eliot to T.S. concerning the late work among the Indians Cleare Sunshine ET*, 124.
61. Letter dated Roxbury July 19 1652, *JEI*.
62. Letter dated Roxbury August 29 1654, *JEI*.
63. Letter Roxbury Oct 7 1652, *JEI*.
64. See letters referring to this transaction in JEI. At Eliot's first Indian sermon one of the positive features of the event commented upon was the fact that the adaptation of the Indians to English fashion meant that it was not always easy to tell the Indians and English apart – Kellaway, *New England Company*, 83.
65. *FAP – ET*, 362.
66. Holstun, *Rational Millennium*, Chapter 3, 'John Eliot's Empirical Millennialism'. For the civil man see Eliot's description; 'He that is willing to serve Christ by

116   *Roger Williams and John Eliot's Indian writings and the story of Adam*

the Polity of the second Table civilly, is in some degree of preparation to serve him, by the Polity of the first Table Ecclesiastically' – CC, 3.
67. *DB – ET*, 88. This tract is anonymous. It may have been written by John Eliot or by Thomas Shepard or John Wilson who publicised his work. Whoever wrote it, it expressed the principles of the Praying Indian project.
68. *ID*, 96.
69. *ID*, 103.
70. Similar views of the relationship between civility and Christianity are found in the Virginia literature referenced in Chapter 2, for example.
71. J. Patrick Cesarini 'The Ambivalent Uses of Roger Williams's 'A Key into the Language of America', *Early American Literature* September 22 (2003), 469–94.
72. *Key*, A4. Williams's telling of his version of Wequash's story reflects Weld and Peter's use of the same example of conversion without reference to Williams's role: 'Since it hath pleased some of my Worthy *Country-men* to mention (of late in print) *Wequash*, the *Péqut Captaine*, I shall be bold so farre to second their *Relations*, as to relate mine owne Hopes of Him (though I dare not be so confident as others)'.
73. *Key*, A3, A4.
74. *Key*, A4. It seems likely that the *Key* did contribute to his success in convincing the authorities to grant the charter as a 1644 letter from the Parliamentary commissioners mentioned Williams's 'printed Indian labours' – Cesarini, *Ambivalent Uses*.
75. There is ambivalence in English accounts of the Indians, e.g. James Rossier praised the Indians of New England for their 'exceeding good invention, quicke understanding and ready capacitie' and for their 'kinde civility', though he was also prepared to write of their ignorance and inability to exploit the riches of the land in the midst of which they 'they live sensually content with the barke and outward rinde'. 'A True Relation of the Most Prosperous Voyage ... in the Discovery of the Land of Virginia, 1605', in *The English New England Voyages 1602–1608*, edited by David B. Quinn and Alison M. Quinn (London 1983) 269–71, p. 297.
76. *Key*, 9–10.
77. *Key*, 99.
78. *Key*, 152.
79. *Key*, 18–19.
80. *Key*, 16.
81. Richard Mather raises this as a possibility in Tracts 224–25, and Henry Whitfield warns that these Indians may 'rise up in judgement against us and our children at the last day ... and leave us in Indian darkness' (146–47), Holstun, *Rational Millennium*, 115.
82. *Key*, 53.
83. *Key*, 9.
84. *Key*, 145.
85. *Key*, 151.
86. *Key*, 151, 145.
87. *Key*, 49.
88. John J. Teunissen and Evelyn J. Hinx, ed. *Roger Williams: A Key into the Language of America* (Detroit: Wayne State Uni. Press, 1973).

89. Teunissen and Hinx, *op. cit.*, 41.
90. *Key*, 64, 80.
91. Teunissen and Hinx, *op. cit.*, 37.
92. John J. Teunissen and Evelyn J. Hinx, 'Roger Williams, Thomas More, and the Narragansett Utopia', *Early American Literature* 11, 3 (Winter 1976–1977): 281–95, p. 292.
93. *Key*, 1.
94. *Key*, 190.
95. *LRW*, 231–32.
96. *Key*, 13, 49.
97. Even of his friends the Narragansett Williams wrote: Though I would not fear a jar with them yet I would send off from being foul and deal with them wisely as with wolves endowed with men's brains' (*LRW*, 38–39).
98. *CNC – CWRW*, vol. 7, 32.
99. *Key*, 30. My emphasis.
100. *Key*, 47.
101. *Key*, 16.
102. *ED – CWRW*, vol. 7, 241.
103. *ED – CWRW*, vol. 7, 241.
104. *ED – CWRW*, vol. 7, 242. Williams sets out in strong terms the inadequacy of the light of nature alone to guide men towards true worship: 'I ask ... If it be not to run pointblank against all the Histories of the Nations, and all present *Experience* of mankind, in all known parts of the world to attribute so much *Light* to any of the *Eldest* and *Gallantest* sons of Nature, as to attain a *Spiritual* and saving knowledge of God, to attain a love unto God in all their knowledge ... without the Revelation of the Word and Spirit of God out of his absolute, free and peculiar Grace and Mercy in Christ Jesus' (*CWRW – ED*, 242). This passage is used wrongly by Teunissen and Hinx to demonstrate inconsistency in Williams's attitude to the Indians - Teunissen and Hinx, *Roger Williams*, 37).
105. *Key*, 10.
106. *BT*, 211, 285.
107. *Key*, 10.
108. *CNC – CWRW*, vol. 7, 37.
109. *BT*, 260.
110. *Key*, A4.
111. *Key*, 49.
112. *Key*, 204.
113. *Key*, 48.
114. The word paradise has its roots in the old Iranian noun *pairidaēza*, 'a wall enclosing a garden or orchard'; Milton's Paradise is a walled garden.
115. Morton's *New English Canaan* 1637 and his colony at Merrymount provided a counter narrative to Puritan New England and an alternative pattern on living. Thomas Morton, *The New English Canaan of Thomas Morton: with Introductory Matter and Notes* edited by Charles Francis Adams Jr. 1883 reprint (Boston: IndyPublish, 2008).
116. *ET – LC*, 23; *ET*, 424.
117. *ET*, 423.

118. John Winthrop, 'General Considerations for the Plantations in New England (1629)' *Chronicles of the First Planters of the Colony of Massachusetts Bay 1623–1636*, edited by Alexander Young (Boston: Charles C. Little and James Brown, 1846), 274.
119. *Eliot Tracts* 15 in Holstun, 108; continuing the gardening theme, a 1652 letter to English supporters of his mission suggests they send over a Godly messenger to see 'what fruit appeareth of that love of theires' Letter dated Roxbury Oct 7 1652, *JEI*.
120. *ID*, 108.
121. *CC*, 149 Holstun, *Rational Millennium*, 157.
122. *BN*, 6 in John Eliot. In a letter dated Roxbury July 19th 1652, he writes; 'the lord seemed to ripen and prepare them for holy church covenant', *JEI*.
123. Letter dated May 1657, *JEI*.
124. Holstun, *op. cit.*, 108–109.
125. Letter dated Roxbury July 19 1652, *JEI*. In the preface of *Christian Commonwealth* he uses a parallel phrase: 'that so they may be the Lord's people'.
126. In his study of Puritan millennialism, Holstun writes of an 'expansive withdrawal' – withdrawing to one's own Godly community in order to be a model for the wider world. Holstun, 156.
127. Walsham writes that to draw a 'clean contrast between the individual and collective dimension is to misrepresent 'the overall dialectical weave of Puritan theology' – Walsham, *Providence*, 306.
128. *BN – ET*, 403–404.
129. *CLE*, 367.
130. Roger Williams, 'Mr. Cottons Letter Lately Printed, Examined and Answered', in *CWRW* vol. 1, 108.
131. In *BT*, Williams expands on the history of this destruction of the wall between church and world with reference to Constantine's confusion of church and polity. By maintaining religion through the material sword (Williams claimed), Constantine and the good emperors did more harm to the name and crown of Lord Jesus than the persecuting Neros, and by their influence the garden of the church and field of the world made all one: 'Babel, or confusion was ushered in, and by degrees the gardens of the churches of saints were turned into the wilderness of whole nations until the whole world became Christian or Christendom' – *BT*, 155.
132. Williams expressed a sense of the incompleteness of reformation of the church – e.g. when he wrote to Winthrop 'though you have come farr yet you never came out of the Wildernes to this Day' *Winthrop Papers* vol. 3, 316–17. See also Gilpin, *Millenarian Piety*, 54.
133. *BT*, 166.
134. For Milton's involvement in the same controversy see Lewalski, *Life*, 284f.
135. *Key*, 145.
136. *Key*, 78.
137. *Key*, 93, 101.
138. *Key*, 102.
139. The different forms of goodness in the world and society is a theme in *Bloudy Tenent, BT*, 211.
140. *Key*, 102.
141. The 'poor, dark and blind Indians' are found in *CC*, Preface.

142. Indians as *abrasa tabula* found in *LC – ET*.
143. *CC*, Preface.
144. *CW*, II, 161f.
145. The procedure for the Indian examinations is described in Kellaway, *New England Company*, 89.
146. My emphasis.
147. *CC*, 2.
148. *CC*, Preface.
149. Translated into English, *SW – ET*, 227.
150. *SW – ET*, 228.
151. *CC*, Preface.
152. *CC*, Preface.
153. Wilson, *Prophet in Parliament*, 207f. See the discussion in this book 2.2.1.
154. *BT*, 277.
155. *BT*, 275; In his study of Williams, Scanlan claims that throughout the *Key* Williams is offering England the best hope of securing a colonial project that would set it apart from other nations and through a stringent adherence to Protestant belief would allow it to integrate its religious and national identities through colonial enterprise. There is little evidence of this political goal and this English particularism in the text. Scanlan, 132.
156. *BT*, 46.
157. *BT*, 215.
158. *BT*, 211.
159. *BT*, 304.
160. *BT*, 214.
161. *BT*, 315.
162. *BT*, 215.
163. *Key*, 145.
164. Gaustad, *Liberty of Conscience*, 145.
165. Ibid., 145.
166. *BT*, 331–32.
167. 'The Church and people of God since the Apostles is an Army routed, and can hardly preserve and secure itselfe, much lesse subdue and conquer others like a vessel becalmed at sea', *HM – CWRW*, vol. 7.
168. 'how lamentably doe we see before our eyes the daily and continued effects of that first *wrath* upon mankind, in so many sorrows of all sorts for the first transgressions', *CNC – CWRW*, vol. 7, 109.
169. *BT*, 214.

4 Gerrard Winstanley and Adam for Millennium and Commonwealth

Introduction: language of politics and of theology

The corpus of Gerrard Winstanley's works appeared during an intense period of writing and publishing between 1648 and 1652. Reading off the titles gives the character of his writings a combination of religious mysticism and call for radical political reform.[1] They include, among others, *Mysterie of God concerning the Whole of Creation* (1648), *The Saints Paradice* (1648), *The Truth Lifting up Its Head above Scandals* (1649, dedication 1648), *The New Law of Righteousness* (1649), *The True Levellers Standard Advanced* (1649), *A New-yeers Gift for the Parliament and Armie* (1650), *Fire in the Bush* (1650), *The Law of Freedom in a Platform* (1652; dedication 1651), and various direct appeals to those in positions of power, whether Fairfax, Cromwell, Parliament, the City of London, ministers of the universities or lawyers of the Inns of Court.[2] A consistent theme in his politics, the equal rights of all Englishmen to the land of England (and of all humans to the whole of physical creation), means he has been beloved of historians from the political left, notably Christopher Hill, who viewed Winstanley as a kind of proto-Marxist and played a large role in popularising his work through his Penguin edited edition of a selection of his writings.[3] Weighted against such perceptions of Winstanley as a precursor of a 'modern' age is the apocalyptic tenor of his work, the central role of the battle between good and evil, light and darkness, St Michael and the Dragon, the references to the book of Daniel and Revelation and also his experimental mysticism, which resonates with some of the writings of the Quakers, Ranters and Familialists and their emphasis on inner experience, on God within and on love. Mark Jendrysik describes him as problematic among the political thinkers of his time being 'at once the most modern and the least modern'.[4] In addition to Winstanley's writings, his actions, too, speak of his politics and his theology.

There has been a wide divergence in interpretations of Winstanley's writing, partly as a result of the combination of equal rights communitarianism that had such appeal for twentieth-century commentators, with the mystical language and Biblical reference of his time. For the socialist and communist historians to whom we owe the revived academic interest in Winstanley, this language was viewed as a 'theological camouflage', a 'cloak to conceal the revolutionary design of the author'.[5] Hill acknowledged the prominence

Gerrard Winstanley and Adam for Millennium and Commonwealth 121

of Adam's story in Winstanley's texts but claimed that he approached the story of the Fall of Man in the manner of a modern anthropologist, 'as a myth which conceals a profound social truth'; the politics came first and religion was just a dressing.[6] Other scholars have reversed this relationship between politics and religious mysticism in their interpretation of the author. Rather than religious language disguising the political, John Burgess suggests, Winstanley's 'political language helped to describe the significance of the inner transformation, which the 'saints' already experience'; rather than religion cloaking revolutionary intent, Paul Emen argues that it was only because of his theological conviction that Winstanley commenced on a project of land communisation that any other criterion of judgement would have told him was impossible.[7] What Hill presents as a myth to describe a social reality, the Fall of Man, is identified by Timothy Kenyon, as 'the fulcrum' of Winstanley's political thought.[8] Those who argue against socio-economic-political interpretations of Winstanley place emphasis in their studies either on the mystical Adam within each man or on the restoration of fallen mankind and eschatological transformation of the cosmos.

The intensity of Winstanley's period of writing means that the work that is sometimes distinguished as his earlier work was written only very few years earlier than that distinguished as his later work, the experience of the failure of his Digger experiment is often viewed as the watershed.[9] In 1649 Winstanley and a group of like-minded men set out to cultivate the common land of St George's Hill, Surrey, as a sign of their creation rights to common ownership of that land. These 'Diggers' found themselves up against the combined forces of the law and the local landowners and the project ended in failure as they were, after about a year's activity, finally evicted from their last stronghold at Cobham. Scholars have given different significance to the events and eventual collapse of the Digger experiment in Winstanley's political thinking and in his religious understanding and expectations of God's activity in the world.

In his study of the faith and politics of Münster and Winstanley, Andrew Bradstock ventures a twofold categorisation of Winstanley scholars: those who focus more on his politics and those who focus on his theology.[10] The former stress a transformation in his thinking after the Digger experience, and the latter emphasise its continuity. Thus George Juretic wrote of a rapid secularisation of Winstanley's thought once the digging experiment, as well as his abandonment of mysticism as it was found not to provide a solution to political problems he encountered, was underway. J. C. Davis uses the subtitle of Winstanley's *Platform*, '*True Magistracy Restored*', to argue for a decisive shift in his thought from millenarianism and anarchy to the remodelling of the state by men: 'Cromwell, not Christ, is to be the agent of change'.[11] Against this those who stress the millenarian hope through his works note how, even in this last tract, Winstanley wrote that 'the spirit of the whole Creation (who is God) is about the Reformation of the World and He will go forward in His work'.[12] Jendrysik sees the proper interpretation of Winstanley's later writing as a programme that integrates secular reform and spiritual renewal.[13] This chapter will demonstrate that there are shifts, and indeed inconsistencies, in Winstanley's writing but that they do not constitute a religious versus secular opposition; rather they illustrate differing religious and scriptural interpretations of the foundations of political society. In particular it will note the multiple understandings of the figure of Adam and the significance they had on Winstanley's political thinking.

The different emphases and directions in Winstanley's writing may be explained by the vicissitudes of seventeenth-century politics, the ups and downs of his own career and the variety of contemporary influences on his thought. In times of political and theological turmoil it is understandable that a thinking man such as Winstanley might engage with a variety of concepts and theories that make sense of and give meaning to what he is experiencing and provide foundations for his own his political theories and actions. This chapter will demonstrate the difficulty of drawing out a single unifying political thread from Winstanley's work and examine instead the Adamic knot that binds so many disparate threads together. Although Winstanley in several places wrote of his distrust of teachers and scholars, it is evident that he was aware, if only at second hand, of several of the conversations of his time about human society and man's place in God's scheme. He seemed to be familiar with Robert Filmer's argument for Adamic patriarchy when he wrote 'some may say here that Adam was under no law, but his will was a law to him'.[14] Similarly he showed a familiarity with Natural Law theories when he set out his own position in opposition to a Hobbesian understanding, 'now this same power in men that causes divisions and war is called by some men the state of nature which every man brings into the world with him ... but this law of darknesse is not the State of Nature' and when he proposed common preservation rather than self-preservation as the root of government.[15] Winstanley expressed a moral objection to political theories based on the desire or right for self-preservation seeing it as the selfish covetousness that results in one man enslaving his brother.[16]

The fascination with eschatology of much of Winstanley's writing reflected a contemporary preoccupation. Joseph Mede's 1627 *Clavis Apocalyptica* was reissued in 1643 by order of Long Parliament, an indication of public interest in the coming of the final days and the special place of England within that, and John Wilson's analysis of sermons before Parliament concludes that triumphant millenarianism that promoted a transformist eschatology (expecting dramatic changes within this world) was a characteristic of this preaching from 1642.[17] There are echoes in Winstanley's mystical writings of continental mystics probably as mediated through English preachers of the time such as John Everard, John Saltmarsh and William Dell. All of these were interested in the inward working and revelation of God; like Winstanley, Everard saw the Bible as a cosmic spiritual drama with Christ and Satan, Heaven and Hell present within the individual's soul, and Saltmarsh's language of the two Adams, the flesh and the spirit, and his typology of Cain, Esau and Ishmael as the First Adam of iniquity, their younger brothers, Abel,

Jacob and Isaac being types of Christ the Second Adam, matches the language of Winstanley.[18] To follow the thread of Adam through Winstanley's writings is thus to work with the variety and interplay of theological and political discourses. This work forms the main body of this chapter but first it sets out the context of those interpretations, the story and man's part in it.

The story and the waiting

The dates of Winstanley's publications make him, as an author, a close contemporary of Williams and Eliot. The 1648 publishing or dedication dates of earlier work *Mysterie of God, Breaking of Day of God, Saints Paradice, Truth Lifting up its Heade against Scandals*, means they were produced just a few years later than the texts of Williams examined earlier, and his later work is contemporary with Eliot's earlier work, especially with *The Christian Commonwealth*. He was writing into the same context of expectation. As with both of these men, the content of Winstanley's thinking was framed by the events of Adam's Fall and the restoration of mankind at the end of time.[19] According to long-established tradition he used St Paul's distinction to write of the restoration of man, fallen in the first Adam, at the coming of Christ, the second Adam; Adam is both the beginning and the end.[20] Like Eliot, it seems Winstanley was (temporarily) caught up in the millenarian fervour of years approaching 1650, the sense that the fulfilment of that story begun with (the first) Adam was about to be achieved. The insistent 'now ... now ... now' of *The Christian Commonwealth* echoes Winstanley's 'now is the time come', 'he is now rising' (*Saints Paradice*), 'the time is now come' (*True Leveller's Standard*), 'now the time is come', 'it is the fulnesse or fittest time now' (*New Law of Righteousness*) and his memorable phrase 'the old world that is running up like parchment in the fire' (*True Levellers Standard*).[21] Although Winstanley himself stopped short of mathematical calculations in his texts, his writing contains frequent Biblical allusions to the 'time, times and dividing of time' during which the Lord gives 'the beast' toleration to rule, and reference to the fact that these times are now drawing to an end.[22] Winstanley would have been familiar with the calculation of this time as being three and a half years each of 360 prophetical days.[23] When the beginning of the time is dated to AD390, seen as the date of the rise of the Pope as Anti-Christ, then 1650 becomes the time when the new order begins.[24] The Digger experiment of 1649 to 1650 coincided with this significant date.

Events in England at this time fuelled this sense of expectation of Christ's imminent return and rule and supported Winstanley's understanding of the leading role that England would play, of the significance of the recent political and military struggle in that land and of the Diggers' part in it, as explicated on the title page of *A New-Yeer's Gift* (1650; dedication 1649):

> The CAUSE of those They call DIGGERS is the life and marrow of that Cause the Parliament hath Declared for, and the Army Fought for; The perfecting of which work will prove England to be the first of

> Nations, or the tenth part of the city of Babylon, that falls off from the Beast first, and that sets the Crown upon Christ's head to govern the World in Righteousness.[25]

Winstanley, who explicitly put more trust in experience than in the teachings of scholars, readily found signs around him of the expected millennium, not only in the wars and execution of the king, but in the persecution of sectaries in the 1640s and later that of his own Digger movement.[26] In *The Mysterie* he wrote of this persecution as part of the rage of the serpent in the last days:

> The great bitternesse, envy, reproachfull languages, and expressions of malicious wrath in, and among men and women in these days, against others whom they brand Sectaries, by severall names, will prove part of the smoak of her torment, and part of the restlessnesse of her Spirit, day and night, which is the beginnings of her sorrowes.[27]

While in Eliot's scheme the end of the story, in the coming of Christ and fulfilment of all prophecy, was joined to the establishment of a model of government based on the Scriptures rather than on human wisdom or natural law, Winstanley saw the story finishing where it started, with restoration of pre-lapsarian freedoms, 'the pure Law of righteousnesse before the Fall, which made all things, unto which all things are to be restored'.[28] When final fulfilment is reached men will have done away with government, and the only rule will be that of the Law of Righteousness that directs them from within. What he proposed in the *New Law of Righteousness* is a kind of anarchy where there need be no ruler appointed and no written law, for all will be led by an inner law of righteousness to do nothing but what is good for themselves and one another; it is a return to Eden.[29]

John Eliot's strong view of human agency in the bringing in of the kingdom is in evidence both in his writing of *The Christian Commonwealth* and in the practical project of his Indian towns. In spite of the prominent action he took in digging up St George's Hill, Winstanley was more ambivalent about the role of human activity in the advancement of the Kingdom. His recommendations to people and politicians, and his own conduct, appear to swing between active and passive modes. In *The New-yeer's Gift*, there is an emphasis on action. He urged the powers that be, Parliament and the army, to complete the reformation of the order that they have begun:

> The Parliament after this have made an act to cast out kingly power, and to make England a free commonwealth. These acts the people are much rejoiced with, as being words forerunning their freedom, and they wait for their accomplishment that their joy may be full.[30]

He warned that 'bare talking of righteousness and not acting, hath ruled and yet does rule king of darkness in creation'.[31] Indeed digging up of St George's Hill by Winstanley's Diggers might be seen as a prime example of action rather than idle talk, a kind of storming of the Bastille of the old order to hurry in the new. But Winstanley also stresses the limits to human actions. Christopher Hill portrays him as a revolutionary aiming at 'rousing the poorer classes to political action', but Winstanley was not a revolutionary.[32] His repeated declaration that he had no intent to use force to bring about the new order, or to 'meddle with any man's Inclosures or propriety til it be freely given to us by themselves', was not just playing safe by the authorities; to act otherwise would have been against his understanding of the relationship between man and God's activity, for God cannot be hurried by the actions of man.[33] When Jendrysik claimed that Winstanley's Calvinist-influenced religion required action for the furtherance of the kingdom ('The faithful could not merely wait on God'), he did not do justice to the earnestness of the debate among Reformed thinkers about the degree to which man can prepare for his personal redemption or contribute by his own actions to the coming of Christ's kingdom.[34] Winstanley too struggled with this question, but a conviction that man should not try to force the hand of God was part of his answer; the honour for the day of restoration will be God's alone, 'it must be his own handy work'.[35] The urgency of his millenarian insistence that the time has come was tempered with an emphasis on the importance of waiting on God and the argument that it is sinful covetousness to take from God the liberty to do what He will with His own creation. As he wrote in *The Breaking of the Day of God*:

> God is more honoured by our waiting, than by the multitude of our self-acting ... for the flesh grudges to give God his liberty to do with his own what he will, and the flesh would have something in itself'.[36]

In *Saints Paradice* he advised his readers to 'stand still, wait with a quiet peaceable heart on God, and see what deliverance he will work for you'.[37] In *The New Law of Righteousnesse* they were 'to wait with patience and quietnesse of spirit under all temptations, till the Fathers turn come ...'.[38] Indeed Winstanley signed himself at the end of the *New Law of Righteousness* as 'a waiter for the consolation of Israel'.[39]

Another factor that confuses the acting and the waiting in Winstanley's work is the nature of the event he is awaiting and the nature of the God who is to effect the transformation. His use of Biblical analogy for a man's inner struggles between forces of good and evil, and his correlation of the Godhead with the 'spirit of reason within a man' encourages an immanentist interpretation.[40] Christ is to come as a rising up within each individual rather than a coming down in glory. In *Truth Lifting up its Head* he told his readers that they were not to be saved by a 'Jesus Christ at a distance from thee' but by a 'Christ within'.[41] This internal, personal experiencing of Christ does not take away the universal significance of the rising or the sense that it is the key event in mankind's story, for the end of days for which all are waiting is the time when all men and women experience this rising within, and this will be the age when all live and act according to the law of righteousness. As Winstanley explained in the *New Law of Righteousness*:

> Everyone is to wait till the Lord Christ do spread himself in multiplicities of bodies, making them all of one heart and one mind acting in the righteousnesse one to another. It must be one power in all, making all to give consent to confirm this law of righteousnesse and reason.[42]

Acting in righteousness may be a sign of a rising that has happened within rather than a cause of that rising, and the millennium will have come when all act towards each other in moderation, peace and love.[43] It may come quickly as Christ sweeps through all Creation. Readers of the *New Law of Righteousness* are told that 'The Lord will do this work speedily, Babylon shall fall in one hour, Israel shall rise in one hour'.[44]

In his book *The Sword of the Spirit*, James Knott describes the digging as a 'symbolic witness to the impending age of the Spirit', but it was more than a symbol.[45] The millenarian fervour of the times and the righteous acts that had freed England from 'the Head of oppression which is Kingly power' had given Winstanley and his fellow Diggers cause to hope that the time of deliverance had truly come.[46] If this was so, then reclaiming this parcel of what God had ordained to be the common treasury of the earth was their act of righteousness and a sign of Christ ruling in them. If others too would display the victory of Christ within them through their good deeds, then this would be proved to be the dawn of the new age. What the Diggers met with instead was a rude reminder that the time had not come in the unrighteous acts of those who vigorously opposed their experiment, through violence, through the taking away of their liberty (by imprisonment) of their money (in fines) of their homes and clothing. The itemised bill of account in *A New-yeer's Gift* and the naming of names of the perpetrators of these injustices are set out as evidence of the continuation of the age of darkness. Using imagery from Revelation, the opposition to the Diggers' project is described as 'the red dragon's power', and 'the dragonly enemy'.[47] The verses that accompany the bill of account place emphasis on the deeds of unrighteousness:

> But what deeds were they you can see?
> No herb, but stinking weed.
> For Persecution ever was
> the Work that came from them,
> And deadly foes they ever were,
> To Christ and righteous men.[48]

Winstanley's concern was that, in spite of all the outward signs of hope in the acts and words of the Parliament and Army, the king of darkness, the dragon, the beast, might yet rule behind these professions of reformation:

> For if this Kingly power of Covetousness, which is the unrighteous Divider, did not yet Rule: both Parliament, Army and rich People, would cheerfully give consent that those we call Poor should Dig and freely Plant the Waste and Common Land for a livelihood.[49]

Paradoxically, the persecution of sectaries viewed by Winstanley elsewhere as a sign of the coming of the final age, as applied to himself and his fellow Diggers, constituted a sign that that age had not dawned; unrighteousness still had the upper hand. This must have been a grave disappointment to Winstanley personally and, as has been mentioned above, the experience of failure has been understood by several scholars of his work to have prompted a revision of his thought. In particular *The Law of Freedom in a Platform* (published 1652; dedicated 1651) addressed to Cromwell as a proposal for the ordering of the new commonwealth, is taken to be an indicator of new thinking. Those with a particular interest in his politics note the pragmatic turn of his writing. Loewenstein observes that the harsher features of his *Platform* 'restraining idle behaviour, punishing disruption, patriarchal authority and government (paternal parliament rather than king) suggest a writer who has endured the disappointments of Digger defeat'.[50] George Sabine noted a 'change of mood' arguing that millenarian expectations appropriate to the first stage of his revolutionary activity had given place to a more sober consideration of ways and means and a greater willingness to rely on changes in law and institutions.[51]

An increasing secularisation of Winstanley's thought has been a common theme over decades of study.[52] However, attention has also been drawn to references to continuing millennial expectation in *The Law of Freedom in a Platform;* 'But surely light is so broke out that it will cover the earth', Winstanley wrote, and the foreword itself contains the confidence that God will go forward in that work, which is the reformation of the world.[53] There is still evidence of orientation towards a divinely ordained order in Chapter II, where Winstanley noted that the commonwealth's government by governing the earth without buying and selling will become thereby 'a man of peace, and the Restorer of ancient Peace and Freedom'.[54] He assured his reader, 'all Nations of the earth shall come flocking thither to see his beauty, and to learn the ways thereof; and the Law shall go forth from that *Sion,* and that Word of the Lord from that *Jerusalem,* which shall govern the whole Earth'.[55] Nor, with all the talk of government and law, so different from the harmonious anarchy Winstanley previously set forth as the end and ideal, had he entirely left behind the idea of a rising of righteousness within each man to govern his actions. The government of his commonwealth did not depend on the will of any particular man or group of men;

'for it is seated in the spirit of Mankinde, and it is called the *light*, or *son of righteousness and peace*'.[56] He wrote:

> The great Lawgiver in Commonwealths Government is the spirit of universal Righteousness dwelling in Mankinde, now rising up to teach every one to do to another as he would have another do to him ... And if these be the days of his resurrection to power, as we may hope, because the name of the commonwealth is risen and established in England by a law, then we and our posterity shall see comfortable effects.[57]

This elevated language and expectation for his commonwealth is reminiscent of Eliot's visionary *Christian Commonwealth*. However, the tenor of most of the treatise is more mundane. His proposals for the ordering of the new commonwealth address man's present condition. Although the *Platform* seeks for righteousness in the rulers it does not assume it in the ruled but is rather working with the existing frailties and inclinations to error that require government and written law in first place. The chapters set out the structures and laws to guard against a variety of human faults and misdemeanours; there are sections that set up officers to monitor, safeguard and punish, 'the work of an overseer'; 'what is the office of a soldier?;' 'the work of an executioner', and laws that guard against weakness and wickedness 'laws against idleness'; 'laws against treachery'; 'laws for such as have lost their freedom'.[58]

A different type of politics is required and a different relationship between the political and religious order depending on whether the completion of Christ's return is now upon us or there is still an indefinite time to wait. The *Platform* is less a strategy to advance the new age than an attempt to answer the question raised earlier in *Truth Lifting up Its Head above Scandals* (1649; dedicated 1648): what 'meanes' men and women are to use during the period of waiting for Christ's coming.[59] The answers given largely concern the way the individual conducts himself or herself according to the Law of Righteousness as ordained at Creation. There is also reference to the way the powers of the land should conduct themselves, particularly in matters of religion. Advice for them is chiefly to support and protect those who are acting righteously and to punish unrighteousness against others.

In the *Platform,* the association in the preface of Cromwell with Moses is significant, for this places the English state in the age of Moses and written law.[60] In the *Platform* Winstanley celebrated a return to Moses and the laws of Israel's Commonwealth after the years of ignorance that buried those laws in oppression and deceit; nevertheless this constitutes a shift backwards from the coming age of the Son of Man that was to replace Moses and from the fullness of time that the Diggers' action announced, to an age that Winstanley recognised in *The True Levellers' Standard Advanced* as 'a weak time', a time of mankind's infancy and dependence, requiring the kind of patriarchal system that he advocated in his later *Platform*.[61] It is a system built on a particular interpretation of the significance of our first ancestor and the condition of man as created. For this period of waiting and the ordering of human society during this time, new thinking was required about the condition of man, for whom and by whom the polity is established and a reworking of the significance of Adam in Winstanley's theme.

Millenarian Adam

Adam is an active, dynamic figure or a dynamic power in the writings that set out Winstanley's millenarian hopes and expectations. Whether the focus is on the individual, on society or the cosmos, Adam acts within that context to effect change. The verb used frequently to describe Adam's activity is 'rising', and it is one that is used, by way of balance, to refer both to the Fall associated with the first Adam and to the coming of the second Adam in Christ. In these two risings of Adam, the beginning and the ending, we have the story of each individual severally and of everything taken as a whole.

Winstanley often appears to discourage an interest in the historical Adam by directing his readers' attention very firmly to the Adam within, but there are occasional references to our first ancestor's historical and physical existence and the universal implications of his fall.[62] Adam as an historical event is after all important to the calculations of millenarian expectation; it is this consciousness of time passing that gives mankind a story with a future as well as a past:

> Since the time that our Bibles speak of *Adam* to this day is about 6000 yeers; and this time hath been the night time of mankind ... the seventh thousand yeer which is now dawning, will be the rising of the Son of universal Love again.[63]

Contrary to Hill's description of the Fall as myth concealing social truth, Winstanley was able to link an historical Adam and his fall by cause and consequence to the present condition of all mankind and indeed of all that is in the earth. In *Truth Lifting His Head*, he offered a materialistic explanation of the spread of this first sin throughout Creation through the corruption of the ground of earth on which all creatures depend by the body of Adam buried after his death.[64] The same text proposes a threefold way of looking at Adam.[65] The first of these is Adam the historical figure, 'Adam, or first man, that went astray from his Maker which lived upon the earth many thousand years ago, which the eyes of every man is upon'. For the second, Winstanley declares every man and woman that lives on objects of creation is a son or daughter of Adam, and taken together they make up that one first man, 'so that you may see *Adam* every day before our eyes walking up and downe the street'. Third, he wrote that he sees two Adams in every man: the first who 'must act his part in me, till the fulnesse of time', and the second *Adam, Christ,* who shall come and deliver him from bondage 'and so rule King of Righteousnesse for ever after in me'.[66]

In the first way of looking at Adam the phrase 'which the eyes of every man is upon' is significant as Winstanley was here registering his disapproval, not because he had doubts about the existence of this historical Adam, but because he thought that people should be directing their attention elsewhere. The comment accords with his repeated urgings to his readers to avert their gaze from what happened 6000 years ago to focus on their own internal state, the Adam, or the Adams, in every man. So he admonishes his readers in *The New Law of Righteousnesse*: 'when a man fals let him not blame a man that died 6000 years ago but blame himself'.[67] History, he declares, has been made into an idol when in fact 'all is to be seen and felt within you', 'Heaven and hell, light and darknesse, sorrow and comforts'.[68] The clergy in particular are deemed blameworthy; they have led men astray to focus on the story of one single man and, by historicising and exteriorising the story of Fall and Restoration have claimed a spiritual authority that is not theirs and act rather to hinder than support the rising of Christ in the poor.[69] Winstanley uses the negative language of 'imagination' associated with self-deception and refers to Judas's treachery to reinforce his point that the inner man is the site of the unfolding of the story of redemption:

> And that which hath by imagination, or *Judas* Ministry, been held forth to us to be without us, as *Adam*; the Serpent, the Garden, the Tree of Knowledge, of Good and evill; and the Tree of Life; and the fall of Man, and promise of redemption, all to be without; yet all these are within the heart of man clearly.[70]

The duality of the internal Adams is important. Readers are encouraged to be aware of a struggle between the first and second Adam, the powers of darkness and light, 'for both these powers are to be felt within a man fighting against each other' and unless an individual recognises both powers within, he is deceived and still subject to the powers of darkness.[71] That the story in which Adam is a key player is the story within each individual as well as of mankind in general and the world as a whole is demonstrated by Winstanley's chronicling of his own personal history. *The New Law of Righteousness* bears testimony to his own inner experience of the battle of the two Adams ('both of which powers I have seen and felt manifested in this body of my flesh') and of the redeeming power that rises within ('the beholding and feeling of the Law of Righteousness within, fils my whole soul with precious peace').[72]

Although it may seem at first sight to be so, this focus on Adam within is neither a retreat from the world into interiority nor a disintegration of the universal narrative into a myriad personal histories. According to Winstanley it is through the rising of the second Adam within each individual and a multitude of internal victories that mankind as a whole will be restored and men will live in liberty, equality and peace with each other;

and it is only through these risings in each man's heart that God's will is felt throughout the world. The *New Law of Righteousness* is a millenarian document addressed to 'the twelve Tribes of Israel that are uncircumcised in Heart' and declares in the introductory address that 'you are the firmament, in whom the Son of righteousnesse will rise up and from you will declare himself to the whole Creation' – hence the urgency behind his directions to them to look to the inner Adam rather than the Adam of history.[73]

It is significant that Winstanley effects some dissociation of mankind as first created from Adam himself. This dissociation begins with the plurality of Adams within each individual, for if there are two Adams fighting it out within a person, that person is not Adam so much as the theatre within which the war of the Adams takes place.[74] Winstanley's allegories are not consistent on this point even within a single text, but when he uses the analogy of the Garden of Eden for mankind, Adam becomes something that works within or upon mankind rather than being mankind itself.[75] Some of the language Winstanley uses tends towards the separation of Adam and mankind, portraying the former as the selfish power that acts upon and imprisons mankind. He writes in the *New Law of Righteousness*:

> Adam, that man that appeared first to rule the earth, man-kinde, and by his unrighteousnesse make it a land of barrennesse: For this first Adam is such a selfish power, that he seeks to compasse all the creatures of the earth into his own hands, to make himself a Lord, and all other his slaves.[76]

And in *The New-yeers Gift*:

> When self love began to arise in the earth, then man began to fall ... This *Adam* or dark power was small at the first, but he is risen to great strength, and the whole Earth is now filled with him, as *Isaiah* saith *Darknes hath covered the Earth*, mankind.[77]

Winstanley's treatment of Adam here is similar to his interpretation of other Biblical figures so that the names by which they are commonly known do not so much denote the physical person as the power within them. By this understanding, Abraham is not primarily the man of flesh but the law of righteousness and peace that ruled in that body commonly recognised as Abraham, and it was the spirit rather than the body that was the Christ.[78] So the name Adam comes to stand for something other than the person of Biblical history, the powers of unrighteousness that inhabited that body. This identity is signalled by Winstanley's play upon the name:

> Adam is the comer in of bondage and is the curse that hath taken hold of the Creation: And he may be called A-dam for indeed he does dam and stop up the streams of the waters of life and libertie.[79]

Covetousness, or self-love; is the dam, the letter A: before declares that he is a preparer to miserie, and is delivered by way of Lamentation, Ah: or A-dam.[80]

As well as the Adam of history – to whom, Winstanley claims, far too much attention has been given – and the Adams within each man, there is the Adam that we see every day walking up and down the street. The sinfulness of the first Adam is a public as well as private affair. In the external world, Adam is the covetousness that has suppressed universal liberty and, lifting himself up, has gathered to himself riches and the power of government. Winstanley sees the first Adam in all forms of tyranny – whether that of husbands over wives, parents over children, masters over servants or magistrates over the people; all of them are acting through covetousness and self-love, keeping power to themselves and ignoring the fact that those they are subjecting are their fellow creatures who have equal rights with them to 'the blessing of liberty'.[81] The first Adam is the raising up of one part of mankind in dominion over another and the acquisition of property at the same time as the denial of the use of that property to others; he is the cause of the present distressed state of the world, 'the first Adam yet sits in the Chair and corrupts the Creation by his unrighteous wisdom and power'.[82]

The story of Creation and Fall offers two elements that shaped Winstanley's millenarian political vision: A-dam, the curse on mankind that will be lifted by the second Adam at the end of time; mankind as he was created and lived before the Fall who is not just the story's beginning but its conclusion. Winstanley's story of Redemption has a circularity about it; it is a story of return. His millenarianism expects the Restoration of the Creation order, and his understanding of that original state of man determines his views of the nature of the transformation for which he longs.

Winstanley's Biblical references show a heavy reliance on Genesis 1:28, where God gave the newly created humankind dominion over all the earth and an expansion of this verse to emphasise the principles of freedom and equality: 'everyone was made to be a Lord over Creation', therefore all mankind was made 'to live in the freedome of the spirit' and 'In the first entrance into the Creation, every man had an equal freedom given him of his Maker to till the earth, and to have dominion over the beast'.[83] There also dwelt in mankind a spirit of universal love and righteousness that led each to live in peace with each other and respect each other's rights to the equal use of the common treasury, the earth. In *A New-yeers Gift*, Winstanley describes the state of this 'day time of mankind', which will be renewed again once the night and darkness has been dispersed:

> While the Spirit of Lordship in the last day time of mankind, was universal Love and Righteousness leading every single branch of mankind to do to another as he would be done unto; then everything was in peace, and there was sweet communion of Love in the creation: and as

the Spirit was a common Treasurie of unitie and Peace within, so the Earth was a common Treasurie of delight for the preservation of their bodies without so that there was nothing but peace upon the face of the whole Earth.[84]

This beginning is the end that Winstanley sets before his readers, a return to the freedom and peace of the first days but with the added surety that Christ has set his seal upon this condition so that it cannot change but will last for eternity: the office of Christ, 'the blessing', is to restore and deliver from death and bondage and to set man down in life and unchangeable rest.[85] The political implications of this view of the ideal and the future are that Winstanley sees the final age as a form of harmonious anarchy, an end to all human government, to all property ('*Mine* and *Thine* will be swallowed up') and to all the structures (lawyers, prisons or engines of punishment) that maintain them:[86] 'There shall be no need of these, for all shall walk and act righteously in the Creation'.[87] Winstanley's 'three doors of hope' for England to escape the wrath of the King of Righteousness when his time comes and welcome this new age, are very radical: getting rid of the shadow of learning and all teachers, for the true teacher is the inward experience of the spirit; an end to property, to buying and selling and enclosing; leaving off dominion and lordship one over another, including acts of imprisoning and corporal and capital punishment.[88] It is an end of politics and also an end of history, as Winstanley writes: 'Now mankind enters into the garden of God's rest, and lives forever'. After the drama and the conflict set in motion by the first Adam, mankind will arrive at the close of the story, the stasis of eternal rest.[89]

Commonwealth Adam

The condition of humankind at the end of time is notably different from the model of commonwealth that Winstanley advances in his *Platform*. Although they have in common a denial of private property and a sharing of the earth's riches, the structures, legislation, systems of discipline and punishment in the *Platform* have little in common with the happy anarchy described above. Despite the emphasis on Winstanley's disappointment among some scholars, *The Law of Freedom in a Platform* is far from being a counsel of despair but was in fact written in a climate of hope that the declaration of a commonwealth in England might herald something different from what he saw as the oppressive tyranny of the monarchy that went before.[90] This optimism is expressed in his preface addressed to Oliver Cromwell, 'God hath made you a successful instrument to cast out that conqueror, and to recover our land and liberties again', and in his insistence that the tide should be taken at the flood and a political order created that would remove the weight of oppression under which the English people have suffered for so long and restore land and liberty to the same.[91] The loss of confidence in the imminence of the millennium required a new question, which the *Platform* seeks to answer.[92] If the change from kingly government does not lead immediately to Christ's kingdom, then what does it lead to? In the *Platform* Winstanley asks:

> If we must be subject to men, then what men must we be subject to, seeing as no man hath as much right on earth as another, for no man now stands as a conqueror over his brethren by the law of righteousness?[93]

The character of Winstanley's commentary on the political order hitherto, his emphasis on a history of oppression, on the snatching away of the people's birthright, on the enslavement of the English by the Norman yoke and his rejoicing at the fall of the Stuart monarchy, required clarity about the legitimacy of the government he endorsed and the structures and methods of government he proposed. This legitimacy depends on the nature of the ruled, the nature of the ruler and the rightness of the relationship between them. For the foundation of his commonwealth Winstanley referred back to the first man and found in Adam both the necessity for government and the authority to govern.

Winstanley chose not to build his commonwealth on the fallen condition of man; his commonwealth was to be a wonder and source of hope to the rest of the world and could not be founded upon the iniquity, oppression and deceit he associated with the Fall and with kingly government. His image of fallen man as 'a complete devil' ruled by 'envy, covetousness, evil surmising, hypocrisy, unclean lust of the flesh, gluttony, drunkenness' made him ungovernable except through punishment, and deprivation of liberty and the forms of harsh rule associated with monarchy.[94] Winstanley rejected the 'nasty, brutish and short' that necessitated the magistrate's rule in Hobbes's scheme. He treated the self-love and overriding desire for self-preservation on which Hobbes was to build his Leviathan as a pathology, 'the root of the Tree Tyranny, and the Law of Unrighteousness'.[95] But the ideal of pre-lapsarian man presented in *New-yeers Gift* that spoke of righteousness, peace and unity did not provide the justification for government and laws that the commonwealth needed either; rather it removed the necessity for human government altogether. A different emphasis was needed.

Winstanley's commonwealth was to be established for men who were essentially good, and so it was positive, but who were not immune to sin, and so it was necessary. His interpretation of their needs was developed from a concept of pre-lapsarian man that retained the goodness of the earlier model but also emphasised its fragility. The development of this idea, so relevant to his *Platform*, can be found in the more mystical work *Fire in the Bush*.[96] Here he presents another threefold description

Gerrard Winstanley and Adam for Millennium and Commonwealth 135

of mankind. No man, he tells his readers, can know himself without these particulars:

(a) the creature or living soul, which before the curse defiles it is very good; and this is the image of God (or of the righteous spirit) in flesh, or first Adam.
(b) the mystery of iniquity or the power of deceit, and this is the god of the world, or prince of darkness, that deceives the living soul first, and takes possession.
(c) the life of God, or of the righteous spirit rising up in the living soul and casting out the power of darkness out, and bringing mankind into peace; and this is the second Adam or Lord from heaven.

This understanding of the First Adam (a), a 'plain, honest-hearted, even innocent Adam' is a far remove from the curse of A-dam, so prominent in Winstanley's millenarian writing.[97] It is an affectionate picture of humanity in his original condition, which 'is plain-heartedness without guile, quiet, patient, chaste, loving without envy: yet through weakness is flexible and open to temptation and change'.[98] This Adam is both the original state of mankind at the time of the first ancestor's creation 6000 years ago and the state of childlike simplicity that every human being passes through.[99] He links this condition to observations of a new born baby:

> Look upon a child that is new born, or till he grows up to some few years: he is innocent, harmless, humble, patient, gentle, easy to be entreated, not envious: and this is Adam, or mankind in his innocence.[100]

It is also the state to which men and women should return, though they might succumb for a while to the iniquity and deceit of (b), before Christ can be born in them and bring them unchanging peace, for, as Winstanley reminds his readers, '*Except a man be born again and become as a little child, he cannot enter heaven*, that is, into peace'.[101] This interpretation of Adam with its focus on his created rather than his fallen state, the endorsement of his condition as 'very good' yet vulnerable to change, and the positive significance given to the estate of the child, provides the foundation for Winstanley's commonwealth, his *Platform*, which was probably written at about the same time as the publication of *Fire in the Bush*, though published two years later.[102] It allows him to recognise human weaknesses without exaggeration or despair; it justifies the rule of written law and exercise of magisterial authority needed to guide and protect a child-like populace and it enables him to view his commonwealth thus ordered as just a step away from the age of righteousness, when, in God's time, the Son of Man rises. Although, like Williams, Winstanley expected Christ's Kingdom to come suddenly, independent of man's activity, there is a sense in which his scheme, like Eliot's ordering of his praying towns, was preparing the ground for that final age. While Eliot sought to bring his Indians to a state of civility, Winstanley advocated a state of childlikeness for the people of his commonwealth.

The individual human beings who constitute Winstanley's commonwealth and for whom its laws are made have the changeability and fallibility acknowledged in *Fire in the Bush*; 'some are wise, some foolish, some idle, some laborious, some rash, some mild, some loving and free to others, some envious and covetous', and it is because of this, he writes, that the law was added to rule and judge men's actions and preserve common peace and freedom.[103] In the following chapter he proceeds to interweave the theme of the people as child with that of the magistrate as father. In recognition of this state of weakness and dependency, the father/child relationship is central to Winstanley's commonwealth, and its elaboration requires another interpretation of Adam, that of Adam as patriarch.

The patriarchalism of the *Platform* is one of the most surprising elements of this text for those impressed by the radical Winstanley of his earlier works. It is a noticeable departure from *A Declaration to the Powers of England*, for example, that positions the coming in of bondage, teachers and rulers on one side and servants and slaves on the other.[104] It is the elder brother Esau in glory and ease over Jacob, the meek spirit, the act of the First Adam raising up one part of humanity in dominion over the other.[105] The First Adam is teacher and ruler in both *Standard* and *Platform*, but in one he holds these roles as oppressive tyrant and in the other as gentle patriarch. In Winstanley's commonwealth he is not associated with the domination of one brother over another but is a parent who cares for all his children equally and so keeps rivalry of Esaus and Jacobs under check.

In the *Platform* Winstanley explains how the original magistracy rose up in the first family. As first father, we are told, Adam was 'most wise in contriving and strong in labour and so fittest to be the chief governor'.[106] The role given to Adam is reminiscent of that assigned to him in Robert Filmer's writing, but Winstanley was careful to distance himself from the thesis that Adam was under no law but his own will, a will to which the people are subject.[107] Adam, he claimed, was bound not by his own will but by 'The law of necessity, that the earth should be planted for the common preservation and peace of his household, was the righteous rule and law to Adam'.[108] By nature more than by decree this law bound both Adam and his household so that because his children wanted preservation they consented to his counsel. Adam derived his authority from his children's consent; a principle that avoids the monarchical conclusions of Filmer and that is applied throughout the levels of government that administer the commonwealth, at parish level and at that of the state:

> In the first family, which is the foundation from whence all families sprang, there was the father; he is the first link of the chain magistracy. The necessity of the children that sprang from him doth say, 'Father,

do thou teach us how to plant the earth, that we may live, and we will obey'. By this choice they make him not only a father, but a master and ruler. And out of this root springs up all magistrates and officers, to see the law executed and to preserve peace in the earth, by seeing that right government is observed.[109]

The parliament of Winstanley's commonwealth thus derives its authority from the position of Adam in that first family. Just as a father shows tender care to all of his children not elevating one above the rest, so parliament is to remove all grievances from the oppressed children, irrespective of their persons great or weak.[110] Its role is to restore to them their birthright, which is freedom in the commonwealth's land, to remove old corrupted laws and enact new.[111] In the final chapter of his final work, Winstanley sets out his suggestions for what those laws might be. In so doing he hopes to encourage a return to the state of Israel's commonwealth, long since buried under ignorance and corruption, to a time when, he believes, the laws were 'few, short and pithy' and 'the people did talk of them when they lay down and when they rose up, and as they walked by the way', and they had a keen understanding of the laws on which depended their peace.[112]

The return

In *Fire in the Bush*, Winstanley describes the condition of fallen man in terms of the Prodigal Son who, let him have what he would have, is still unsatisfied, who lives without God (his Father) in the world and feeds upon the husks of riches and pleasures like swine.[113] It is an appropriate analogy as, though not developed in this text, it evokes the theme of return so important in Winstanley's later work and places it in the context of the relationship of father and child. Adam can be found in all stages of this story: Adam as the child, Adam as the self-love that leads the child astray, Adam as the prodigal and Adam as the father to whom the prodigal returns. The experience of the prodigal can be found in another text relating to Adam, *Truth Lifting up His Head*, where the dialogue format produces this answer to the vexed question of why God should allow the first man to fill the world with his unrighteousness,

> That man-kind may see, that though it spring up to an innumerable multitude of sons and daughters, all living upon creature-objects, not upon the spirit, are but still the one first man, that wearied out himself in vain, and finds no true peace thereby.[114]

Man has gained nothing by all this activity and, Winstanley's writings make clear, he only finds peace by returning to where he began. In *Fire in the Bush* he sets up two stages of return to the condition of the first creation, a return to the created state of child-like simplicity and natural innocence but of vulnerability to change and a fixing of that return when Christ rises up within man and puts a seal upon him so he shall never more be swayed away from the paths of righteousness – Christ 'sets him downe in rest, never to fall again'.[115] For the general as for the individual two stages of return can also be discerned. In *The Law of Freedom* there is the restoration of commonwealth along the model of Moses's Israel, and a government that 'may well be called the *ancient of days*; for it was before any other oppressing government crept in'.[116] There is the age brought in by the spread of the spirit of the whole creation and the rising up of the universal spirit of righteousness dwelling in mankind, which according to the logic of *New-yeers Gift*, will finally obviate the need for an external written law as all will be ruled by the light, or son of righteousness within.[117]

Winstanley occasionally employs the conventional figure of Christ the redeemer 'riding on clouds' as he comes to deliver his people, but generally the image used is not of Christ coming down in glory but of him rising up within man.[118] He warns his readers against the deceiving words of those that tell them that their God and saviour is without.[119] When Christ comes he will not be bringing something new as the corollary of all our efforts to advance Christ's kingdom (as Eliot held) or something new that will overturn completely the worldly order by which we currently lead our lives (as Williams held), but he will return us to the condition of creation where we began. After all the excitement of dragons and archangels, of beast and serpents and battles in heaven, the end is undramatic and even mundane, the enjoyment of this world as it was created to be, sharing the fruits of the earth together and acting well towards one another, living on this land in 'comfortable ease'.[120] As the end is for mankind to return to where he began, the story of the Fall and its consequences becomes an aberration framed by the reality of the created order, which is the rights and condition of man as God made him and intended him to be. Winstanley does not take man's fallen condition as the basis for his commonwealth, but rather his created state. Its structures and laws are designed to keep the populace within that righteous state, to prevent the breaking out of the story by protecting individual or society from temptation and fall. Adam has taken over from A-dam in his scheme. The story becomes an irrelevance to the commonwealth except as a warning of what might be if its actions are not conducted according to the laws of righteousness established at creation. Finally the Christ's universal rising brings man at last to dwell in his 'rest and strength of Love unchangeable', which puts even the possibility of story to rest.[121] Mankind is back where he started never to be deceived again.[122]

Notes

1. The edition of Winstanley's works being used in this book is Thomas N. Corns, Ann Hughes and David Loewenstein (eds.), *The Complete Works of Gerrard Winstanley* (Oxford: Oxford University Press, 2009).
2. *An Humble Request to the Ministers of Both Universities, and to All Lawyers in Every Inns-a-court* (April 9 1650).

3. Hill, *Winstanley*, 9; see also Christopher Hill, *The Religion of Gerrard Winstanley* (Oxford: Past and Present Society, 1978).
4. Mark Stephen Jendrysik, *Explaining the English Revolution: Hobbes and His Contemporaries* (Maryland: Lexington Books, 2007), 26.
5. Eduard Bernstein, *Cromwell and Communism: Socialism and Democracy in the Great English Revolution* (London: Allen and Unwin, 1930). Bernstein's book was originally written in German (*Kommunistische und demokratisch-sozialistische Strömungen während der englischen Revolution*) in 1895 and translated into English in 1930.
6. Hill, *Winstanley*, 30.
7. John P. Burgess, *The Problem of Scripture and Political Affairs as Reflected in the Puritan Revolution: Samuel Rutherford, Thomas Goodwin, Jon Goodwin and Gerrard Winstanley* (Unpublished DPhil thesis University of Chicago, 1986), 204; Paul Emen 'The Theological Basis of Digger Communism' *Church History* 23 (1954), 216.
8. Timothy Kenyon, *Communism and the Fall of Man: The Social Theories of Thomas More and Gerrard Winstanley* (Ph.D thesis, University of Warwick, 1981), and Timothy Kenyon, *Utopian Communism and Political Thought in Early Modern England* (London: Pinter Publishers, 1989).
9. George Juretic, 'Digger No Millenarian: The Revolutionizing of Gerrard Winstanley,' *Journal of the History of Ideas* 36 (1975): 263–80; J. C. Davis, 'Utopia and History,' *Australian Historical Studies* 13, 50, (1968): 165–76.
10. Andrew Bradstock, *Faith in the Revolution: The Political Theories of Münster and Winstanley* (London: SPCK, 1997), 82.
11. Davis, 'Utopia and History.'
12. *LFP – CW*, II, 280.
13. Jendrysik, *Explaining*, 28.
14. *LFP – CW*, II, 313 seems to be a reference to Robert Filmer's *The Anarchy of a Limited or Mixed Monarchy* 1648.
15. *FB – CW*, II, 220. Hobbes was publishing at same time so Winstanley may not have read his work directly but was aware of the conversations out of which Hobbes's theories emerged.
16. *LFP – CW*, II, 314.
17. Wilson, *Prophet in Parliament*, Ch. 7; Wilson makes a distinction between the eschatology of radical preachers and the prophecy of the Presbyterians.
18. John Saltmarsh, *Sparkles of Glory or Some Beams of the Morning Star: Wherein Are Many Discoveries as to Truth and Peace to the Establishment and Pure Enlargement of a Christian in Spirit and Truth* 1647 (London: E. Huntington, High St Bloomsbury, 1811). Echoes of Saltmarsh can be found in *NLR – CW*, I, 55; *BD – CW*, I, 139; *TLS – CW*, II, p. 9; *LFX – CW*, II, 52.
19. Kenyon argues that the Fall is 'the fulcrum' of Winstanley's political thought. Kenyon, *Communism and the Fall of Man*, 133; cf., 137. See also Bradstock *Faith in the Revolution*, 83.
20. 'As it is also written, The first man Adam was made a living soule; and the last Adam was made a quickening Spirit.' 1 Cor. 15:45.
21. *SP – CW*, 316; *SP – CW*, 356; *TLS – CW*, II, 7; *NLR – CW*, I, 479; *NLR – CW*, I, 511; *TLS – CW*, II, 5.
22. *DPO – CW*, II, 34; *TLS – CW*, II, 14; *MG – CW*, I, 289. Illusions are made to Dan. 7:25; Dan. 12:7; Rev. 12:14.

23. Examples of this calculation are found in Joseph Mede's *Clavis Apocalyptica* and are reported in Matthew Poole's Biblical commentary.
24. Pope Siricius (AD 384–399), reputed to be the first Roman Bishop to call himself "Pontifex Maximus" and "Pope" (papa).
25. NYG – CW, II, 107.
26. The preface to NLR is dated 26th January, which puts it into the midst of momentous events one day after Charles I's sentence and four days before his execution. David Loewenstein *Representing Revolution in Milton and his Contemporaries: Religion, Politics and Polemics in Radical Puritanism* (Cambridge: Cambridge University Press, 2001), 61. In other parts of his writing he also found a completely different significance in the persecution he and his Diggers suffered interpreting it as a sign that the millennium was not imminent - NYG – CW, II, 111.
27. MG – CW, I, 281.
28. LFX – CW, II, 55.
29. For example: 'no lawyers, prisons, engines of punishment' - NLR – CW, I, 506; 'no dominion and Lordship' – NLR – CW, I, 523. The same view is found in *The Breaking of the Day of God*, 'no laws and government' BD – CW, I, 184.
30. NYG – CW, II, 108.
31. NYG – CW, II, 120.
32. Hill, *Winstanley*, 10.
33. AHC – CW, II, 66.
34. Jendrysik, *Explaining*, 27.
35. NLR – CW, II, 509.
36. BD – CW, I, 154.
37. SP – CW, I, 328.
38. NLR – CW, I, 501.
39. NLR – CW, I, 477.
40. NLR – CW, I, 375. The use of the title 'Reason' for God does not however preclude the concept of a transcendent God as when Winstanley writes 'In the beginning of time, the Great Creator, Reason ...' – CW, II, 4.
41. TLH – CW, I, 420.
42. NLR – CW, I, 505. See also 'this is not done by the hands of the few, or by the unrighteous men, that would pull down the tyrannical government out of other men's hands and keep it in their own heart, as we feel this to be a burden of our age. But it is done by the universal spreading of the divine power which is Christ in mankind making them all to act in one Spirit and in and after one law of reason and equity.' NLR – CW, I, 503–504.
43. NLR – CW, I, 506f.
44. NLR – CW, I, 509.
45. Knott, *The Sword*, 102.
46. 'the Head of oppression which is Kingly power' NYG – CW, II, 108.
47. Rev. 12:3.
48. NYG – CW, II, 148–9.
49. NYG – CW, II, 111.
50. Loewenstein, *Representing Revolution*, 88. See also Hill who points to Winstanley's acknowledgement that laws are needed to counter the 'spirit of unreasonable ignorance' and punishments for wrong doing and laziness, including whipping and forced labour are recommended – Hill, *Winstanley*, 41–42.

Gerrard Winstanley and Adam for Millennium and Commonwealth 141

51. George Sabine, ed., *The Works of Gerrard Winstanley* (New York: Russell and Russell, 1965), 60.
52. Bradstock, *Faith in the Revolution*, 84; Juretic, argued that once the digging experiment was underway W's ideas rapidly secularised – Juretic, 'Digger no Millenarian', 269f; Davis argued the subtitle of *LFP* 'True Magistracy Restored' indicates the true nature of his shift in thinking 'W drops both his millenarianism and his anarchism and concerns himself with the remodelling of the state by men; and in the *LFP* addressed to the General sees 'Cromwell, not Christ to be the agent of change' – Davis, 'Utopia and History', 172.
53. *LFP – CW*, II, 348; *LFP – CW*, II, 280.
54. *LFP – CW*, II, 309.
55. *LFP – CW*, II, 311. The reference is to Mic. 4:1, 2.
56. *LFP – CW*, II, 310.
57. *LFP – CW*, II, 311.
58. *LFP – CW*, II, 323; *LFP – CW*, II, 329; *LFP – CW*, II, 331; *LFP – CW*, II, 371; *LFP – CW*, II, 375; *LFP – CW*, II, 376.
59. *TLH – CW*, II, 432.
60. The association of Cromwell with Moses was common at the time; see Derek Hirst, '"That Sober Liberty": Marvell's Cromwell in 1654' in *The Golden and the Brazen World: Papers in Literature and History 1650–1800*, edited by John Malcolm Wallace (Berkeley: University of California Press, 1985).
61. 'A time of the world that the man-child could not speak like a man' *TLS – CW*, II, 8.
62. His early text *The Mysterie of God concerning the Whole Creation, Mankind* includes a complex interplay of the allegorical and the historical: 'And when Adam put forth his hand to take, and eat of the fruit of the Tree in the Hystorie, his hand was guided thereunto by this serpent, whose secret whisperings he delighted in; and truly this delight itself was the eating, and it was the chief forbidden fruit that grew up in the middle of the living Garden, Adam, which God forbad him to eat of or delight in'. *MG – CW*, I, 261.
63. *The Curse and Blessing that is Mankinde* contained within *A New-yeers gift for the Parliament and Armie, NYG – CW*, II, 130. In the *New Law of Righteousness* he declares that the 6000 years are 'near hand expired' *NLR – CW*, I, 483.
64. *TLH – CW*, I, 421.
65. *TLH – CW*, I, 427.
66. *TLH – CW*, I, 427.
67. *NLR – CW*, I, 500.
68. *NLR – CW*, I, 538.
69. *NLR – CW*, I, 499, 526f.
70. *FB – CW*, II, 188.
71. *FB – CW*, II, 210.
72. *NLR – CW*, I, 496; *NLR – CW*, I, 526.
73. *NLR – CW*, II, 473.
74. *FB – CW*, II, 188.
75. In *The Mysterie of God* Adam is presented as a garden *MG – CW*, I, 259; and again in *Fire in the Bush*; 'Mankind, the living Earth, is the very garden of Eden, wherein that spirit of Love did walke, and delight himselfe principally' *FB – CW*, II, 176–77.
76. *NLR – CW*, I, 480.

77. *NYG – CW*, II, 135. See also: 'I shall declare what Adam the first man is, who to me appears to be the wisdome and power of the flesh carrying along the Creation, man, to live upon creature objects', *NLR – CW*, I, 480.
78. *NLR – CW*, I, 475.
79. *NLR – CW*, I, 524.
80. *NLR – CW*, I, 524. See also 'whereas the Creation, man should live in equalitie one towards another; the A-Dam hath lifted up mountains and hils of oppressing powers, and there by that, damned and stopped up that universal *communitie*' *NLR – CW*, I, 525.
81. *NLR – CW*, I, 481.
82. *NLR – CW*, I, 522.
83. *NLR – CW*, I, 502; *NLR – CW*, I, 505.
84. *NYG – CW*, II, 130.
85. *FB – CW*, II, 213f, 210.
86. *NLR – CW*, I, 506; *NLR – CW*, I, 506.
87. *NLR – CW*, I, 506.
88. *NLR – CW*, I, 523. The 'three doors of hope' is an echo of Hos. 2:15.
89. *FB – CW*, II, 178.
90. Loewenstein is one of the scholars who emphasises disappointment: Loewenstein, *Representing Revolution*.
91. *LFP – CW*, II, 279.
92. Winstanley does not present his law as *the* only answer to this question or viable government in the circumstances – he waited to see if 'Mr Peters' scriptural model' was acceptable first (*LFP – CW*, II, 287), and he suggests Cromwell 'suck out the honey and cast away the weeds' or to take it and 'frame a handsome building out of it' (*LFP – CW*, II, 291) taking the Apostle's advice 'to try all things and to hold fast to which is best'.
93. *LFP – CW*, II, 286.
94. *FB – CW*, II, 209–10.
95. *LFP – CW*, II, 314.
96. *FB – CW*, II, 202–203.
97. *FB – CW*, II, 205.
98. *FB – CW*, II, 207.
99. *FB – CW*, II, 207.
100. *FB – CW*, II, 220.
101. *FB – CW*, II, 206.
102. *FB – CW*, II, 202; See preface 'It was intended for your view above two years ago, but the disorder of the times caused me to lay it aside' *LFP – CW*, II, 287.
103. *LFP – CW*, II, 314.
104. *TLS – CW*, II, 5.
105. *TLS – CW*, II, 6.
106. *LFP – CW*, II, 313.
107. See Filmer, *ALMM*.
108. *LFP – CW*, II, 313.
109. *LFP – CW*, II, 315.
110. *LFP – CW*, II, 338.
111. *LFP – CW*, II, 337; *LFP – CW*, II, 338.
112. *LFP – CW*, II, 368; *LFP – CW*, II, 369.
113. *FB – CW*, II, 209.

114. *TLH – CW*, I, 426.
115. *FB – CW*, II, 210.
116. *LFP – CW*, II, 310.
117. *LFP – CW*, II, 280; *LFP – CW*, II, 311.
118. For examples of Christ 'riding on clouds', see *FB – CW*, II, 214; *NYG – CW*, II, 140. Examples of Christ rising up include: *FB – CW*, II, 196; *NYG – CW*, II, 135, 137; *NLR – CW*, II, 527, 536.
119. *FB – CW*, II, 222–23.
120. *LFP – CW*, II.
121. *FB – CW*, II, 206.
122. *FB – CW*, II, 210.

5 John Milton's Adam and the English nation

Introduction: 'a daring political gesture'

In his tract, *The Ready and Easy Way to Establish a Free Commonwealth* (1660), John Milton reflects on the imminent demise of the English Commonwealth:

> Where is this goodly tower of a Common-wealth which the English boasted they would build, to overshadow kings and be another Rome in the west? The foundation indeed they laid gallantly, but fell into a worse confusion, not of tongues, but of factions, then those at the tower of *Babel*; and have left no memorial of their work behind them remaining, but in the common laughter of *Europe*.[1]

This image depicts the political context of the works that are to be the primary focus of this chapter: the end of the mid-seventeenth-century republican experiment and restoration of the Stuart monarchy. It represents Milton's initial high hopes for his nation (it was to be 'another Rome'), suggests the moral decline of its people from gallant action to petty factions and, perhaps too, an injury to the poet's pride as an Englishman, his country now at risk of becoming the laughing stock of Europe.[2] Milton had been closely engaged and implicated in the political upheavals of the 1640s and 1650s as a writer of political treatises and polemic and as Secretary for Foreign Tongues to Cromwell's Council of State. In his own time he was internationally renowned (or reviled) as a fierce defender of the English nation's right to execute their reigning monarch and of the republican model that was to take his place.[3] Like Winstanley's, Milton's later works have often been interpreted in the light of political disappointment by modern scholars. According to Christopher Hill, Milton was one of those prominent thinkers who struggled in this period to come to terms with 'the experience of defeat' of the 1660s.[4] In a climate of 'outcry against God's justice' a number of them (including Isaac Pennington, John Reeve, William Sedgwick, John Bunyan and John Dryden) sought to provide justification. The impact on Milton of this 'experience of defeat' has been variously interpreted, but his declared intention in *Paradise Lost* is to 'justify the ways of God to men'. It is significant for this study that, at this particular juncture in the history of the English state, he chose to do so through the story of Adam.

While *Paradise Lost* is the main focus for this study of Milton's Adam and his politics, other works from this period of Milton's writing will be referred to in support, in particular, *The Ready and Easy Way to Establish a Free Commonwealth* (quoted above), a text which advocates the adoption of a new constitutional model as a last ditch attempt to preserve the commonwealth in the face of the growing momentum of the movement for the king's return, and *De Doctrina Christiana*, Milton's lengthy Latin treatise on Christian doctrine firmly rooted in detailed Biblical study. Epic poem, political pamphlet and theological treatise, these works represent different genres of the author's oeuvre all written within a short time of each other.[5] *The Ready and Easy Way* was published in April 1660, *De Doctrina Christiana* was finished between 1658 and 1660, and *Paradise Lost* was probably begun in 1657–58 and published in 1667.[6] They are the works of Milton's maturity, a time of life characterised by political disappointment, of personal sorrow with the loss of his wife Katherine and their child in 1658 and of his coming to terms with the cruel affliction of his blindness – in his epic he describes himself as 'fall'n on evil days'.[7] The context of writing has encouraged scholars to analyse these texts for clues as to the state of Milton's political and religious thought at this time in his life and in the history of his nation, and the evidence has been variously interpreted, for breaks or continuity with his earlier writings.

In the interpretive history of *Paradise Lost* itself there have been both spiritual and political readings. There is a long-standing romantic interpretation of *Paradise Lost*, voiced by Blake and Coleridge, as the disillusioned poet's retreat from religion, politics and society to the living spirit and light within him. In writing this poem Milton 'avenged himself on the world by enriching it with this record of his own transcendent ideal'.[8] Blair Worden is a more recent exponent of a quietist understanding of *Paradise Lost*; with this poem, he argues, Milton no longer aspires to intervene in the government of his nation but 'withdraws from politics into faith' and 'eternal verities'.[9] Kenneth Borris observes how his politics 'shifted from enthusiastic effort to realise an ideal nation perfected through religious reform, to faith rather in a paradise within as the supranatural kingdom of God'.[10] A more activist view of Milton and his politics is expressed by Barbara Lewalski. For her the publication of *Paradise Lost* constitutes a 'daring political gesture'; it involves its readers in 'thinking through the ideological and polemic controversies of the recent war, engaging them to think again, and think rightly, about monarchy, tyranny, rebellion, liberty, hierarchy and republicanism'.[11] David Loewenstein describes the poem as 'polemically alive in the adverse milieu of Restoration England' as it 'constantly challenges its engaged readers by showing them how to discern the treacherous ambiguities and contradictions of political rhetoric and behavior, including their more revolutionary manifestations'.[12]

Milton presents his readers with a number of interpretive challenges in his poem, an analysis of its political messages being one.[13] Unlike Dante, he does not people the various spheres of his cosmology with contemporary figures and so those who seek to find in *Paradise Lost* commentary on the politics of his day must deal with resemblance and analogy.[14] Occasionally person-for-person correspondences have been identified including 'romantic attempts to link his God with Charles I as monarchs and Satan with Cromwell and Milton as revolutionaries'.[15] Suggested parallels with seventeenth-century reality and debate are made all the more convincing by echoes with Milton's prose works. At the level of satire, for example, there are parallels between the swarming hundreds and thousands of Satan's Councel of Hell, forced by supernatural means to reduce in size in order to fit like so many bees into the assembly hall, and Milton's criticism in *The Ready and Easy Way* of Harrington's electoral schemes where he argued the proposed popular assembly upward of a thousand would be 'unwieldie with their own bulk, unable in so great a number to mature their constitutions as they ought ... only now and then to hold up a forest of fingers'.[16] There are parallels between Satan's objections to the acts of submission expected for the newly elevated Son, 'knee-tribute', 'prostration vile', and Milton's statement in *The Ready and Easy Way* that a returning monarch would 'pageant himself up and down in progress among the perpetual bowings and cringing of an abject people on either side deifying and adoring him'.[17] Parallels can also be found with descriptions of the Father's kingship. In Book IV Satan accuses Gabriel of 'having practis'd distances to cringe' to God in Heaven; rather than deny it, Gabriel retorts, 'who more than thou / Once fawn'd and cring'd and servilely adore'd / Heav'n's awful Monarch?'[18] Further linguistic links are evident in comparison between the imagery and rhetorical assurance in the question asked in the political pamphlet, 'Is it such an unspeakable joy to serve, such a felicity to wear a yoke?' and Satan's words:

> But what if better counsels might erect
> Our minds and teach us to cast off this Yoke?
> Will ye submit your necks, and chuse to bend
> The supple knee? Ye will not, if I trust
> To know ye right, or if ye know yourselves
> Natives and Sons of Heav'n.[19]

The story of the rebellious angels has been particularly fruitful for these comparisons with recent and contemporary politics, for the rebels were provoked to revolt by the absolutism of the Father, his unexplained elevation of the Son to Lordship above all others and his demands for unquestioning obedience to His command.[20] To hear in Milton's poem republican values being voiced by Satan and find a Stuart-style pomp and demand for unquestioning obedience surrounding the kingship of God is disorienting for the reader.[21] As Stevie Davies expressed it, we are presented with 'England's defender of the regicide, whose epic concerns a rebellion against the monarchy of heaven together with a defense of that monarchy'.[22] Those who do not interpret these seeming contradictions as the poet's disillusionment with the cause to which he had devoted so much of his energy, and to politics in general, have sought other reasons for the paradox: Milton was opposed to tyranny rather than monarchy itself; Milton made a distinction between the political order of Earth and that of Heaven, which we should not seek to emulate; the poem offers a debate about kingship in which a distinction is drawn between the majesty of being 'king' and the virtue entailed in being 'kingly'.[23]

In addition to the vivid portrayals of statecraft and political conflict in Heaven and Hell, *Paradise Lost* offers other resemblances to contemporary affairs, most evidently in Archangel Michael's presentation to Adam in the final two books of the poem. Here Adam is afforded a vision of the unfolding of human history (primarily Biblical history but also the history of the Church) from that first act of disobedience in the garden. Particular correspondences can be made such as the parallel between Charles I and the politically ambitious and overbearing Nimrod, bringer of strife.[24] The continual backsliding, lapsing into faction and strife, of the people of Israel through their history, even when, as on their return from Babylon, they appeared to have won freedoms and attained a state of virtuous equilibrium, is a close parallel with the 'relapsing' English of *The Ready and Easy Way* 'treading back with lost labour all our happy steps'.[25] In this vision of human history the solitary just man stands out – Enoch, Noah, Abraham, Moses, Joshua, Christ. Milton may have seen himself as one of this company. Earlier in the poem he described his circumstances in similar terms to theirs as 'On evil days though fall'n, and evil tongues; / In darkness, and with dangers compassed round, / And solitude'.[26] Enoch's activity amidst 'factious opposition' reflects his own: 'In wise deport, spake much of right and wrong, / Of justice, of religion, truth and peace, / And judgement from above'.[27] In many ways Michael's history is a reprise of themes of national decline, of promise and disappointment from some of Milton's prose (*Of Reformation, History of Britain, Ready and Easy Way*); in *De Doctrina Christiana* he presents fallen history as a process of sin recapitulating itself through subsequent generations. In his study of Milton's history, Loewenstein finds the picture in *Paradise Lost* to be at its most grim, a cycle of decline broken only by the promised apocalyptic coming of Christ's kingdom at the end of days and resolution of all things when time will 'stand fixed'.[28] Even acknowledgement of this 'happy end' does not remove his suspicion that for Milton a tragic sense of history wins out over hope:

> The passages of historical decline, especially Michael's final narrative, are simply rendered too powerfully to be completely counteracted by the references to Christian typology and redemption.[29]

The confusions and contradictions inherent in the discourses of republicanism and monarchy in his Heaven and Hell have been noted, as has the tragic bent of Michael's presentation of history. The remainder of this chapter, however, will argue that Milton's outlook on human affairs and the earthly future of human society contained more optimism than these imply, and it will do this by giving a central place to Adam in the interpretation of the poem and of its intent. It is a temptation for modern readers to focus on the more obvious examples of political structures and disagreements portrayed in the story of the angels' rebellion – monarchy and political assembly – so that the republican versus absolutist positions put forward by the characters in this part of the narrative have been the focus and material of much debate about the poet's political thought. It could be argued that by drawing attention away from other parts of the narrative, they have made it easy to miss the political significance of the figure of Milton's Adam; they forget the common tendency of the time to return to Adam as our original so as better to understand the nature of man and the purposes God has for him as the foundation and validation of human society and political order.

In *Paradise Lost* Milton was not just reading off Adam's story from Genesis, so he could not ground his argument on a close and exact exegesis of the Biblical text as did Filmer and Locke; his telling involved ornamentation of the original, filling in the narrative gaps as a kind of Christian midrash. He could be accused of reading back into Adam what he has already concluded in other political texts, of giving his ideas a pseudo-Adamic authority. Against this, his *De Doctrina Christiana* gives ample evidence that his fictional embellishments of the story and the emphases he gives within the telling of Adam's story are based on his own detailed study and interpretation of Biblical teaching. The significance given to natural law, the concepts of man's natural liberty and sociability, his place and his agency in the story of Fall and Redemption, the activity of God in man's story are all founded on Scripture and so have the status of foundational truths that should underlie human association and activity. Extra-scriptural details, for example the nuanced portrayal of the relationship between Adam and Eve, the reported responses of Adam to the archangels' teachings, include patterns of thinking and behaviour that illustrate in observance or breach these fundamental principles and their implications.

In Books XI and XII it is easy again for attention to be diverted away from Adam to focus on the pageant of history. The content of that history may be of educative benefit to Milton's audience as well as to Michael's, but Adam in his reactions to the content is himself an object lesson. We can learn about Milton's political sense by focusing attention less on what Adam sees than on Adam himself as he sees it and as he grows in wisdom and understanding. Although the story being told may appear to be trapped in a cycle of decline, the responses of Adam, from his initial emotional reactions and occasional misreading of what he sees to the 'sum / Of wisdom' he has attained by the end of the presentation, show progress and promise hope for the future in this world.[30]

Adam as new dispensation

Paradise Lost is the story of two falls rather than one. It sets up a different time scale; the world is created and Adam arrives in the middle rather than at the beginning of the story. Milton's theology prepared the way for this different concept of time that exists before Creation. He saw no reason things invisible should not have been created before things visible, heaven and the angels before the first day of the Genesis creation story.[31] He used the Aristotelian notion that time is a measure of motion to argue the creation of the angels and rebellion of a number of them at specific, quantifiable times before the foundation of the world, an argument echoed by Raphael as he relates the story of this first fall to Adam:

> For Time, though in Eternitie, appli'd
> To motion, measures all things durable
> By present, past, and future.[32]

Milton's adoption of this double time frame has a major impact on Adam's significance in the scheme of things.

In Book V of *Paradise Lost*, the reader is shown how, in this time before Creation, the conflicting proclamations, protestations and political stances of the heavenly protagonists result in fierce battles, the defeat of Satan's forces and their terrible banishment. The language used to describe the opposing political and military camps possesses the epic grandeur that Milton must have intended to develop in his initial planned Arthurian epic that he put aside in favour of this Biblical theme.[33] The contrast in political rhetoric of the two sides amounts to very little when the opposing armies are amassed for battle or review. Whether he writes of the heavenly hosts of angels or of Satan's demonic forces, the language is the same.[34] There are direct linguistic correspondences between Milton's accounts of the two armies ('imperial', 'ensigns', 'standards', 'emblazoned', 'glittering', 'ten thousand', 'immeasureable' for 'innumerable') and common themes of authority, might, ceremony, number, adornment, colour and material richness.

Despite Adam's heroic epithet 'great', there is a stark contrast between these scenes of grandeur and our first ancestor's natural simplicity as he sets out to meet his angelic guest in the same Book V:

> Meanwhile our primitive great sire, to meet
> His godlike guest walks forth, without more train
> Accompanied than with his own complete
> Perfections; in himself was all his state,
> More solemn than the tedious pomp that waits
> On princes, with their rich retinue long
> Of horses led and grooms besmeared with gold
> Dazzles the crowd, and sets them all agape.[35]

This scene is preceded by Eve's housewifely preparations for the visitor and succeeded by a meal laid out on 'grassy turf', the diners seated on 'mossy seats'.[36] There is within this one book (as within the poem as a whole) a marked move between genres, here between the heroic and the bucolic, even domestic. Through this language Milton is signalling something different and something new. The first appearance of the human couple, as seen through Satan's eyes in Book IV, contrasts with the banners, ensigns, glitter and bluster of his infernal domain.[37] False pretensions are stripped away and the natural, unashamed nakedness of the pair stressed to such a degree that some commentators found it to be a source of scandal.[38] Satan was indeed shocked by the sight, but his reaction that made him stand transfixed 'in gaze' with 'failed speech', was one of wonder at the lovely yet strange and disconcerting vision.[39] The words he utters when he at length recovers power of speech indicate another reason for the strength of his reaction:

> 'O hell! What do my eyes with grief behold!
> Into our room of bliss thus high advanced
> Creatures of another mold, earth-born perhaps,
> Not Spirits, yet to heav'nly Spirits bright
> Little inferior; whom my thoughts pursue
> With wonder, and could love, so lively shines
> In them divine resemblance, and such grace
> The hand that formed them on their shape hath poured.[40]

In his wondering words Satan points to the real significance of this new creation. The primal couple are not only a new species ('creatures of another mold'), a contribution to God's teeming world, but they are designed as a replacement, a new order to fill the gap produced by failures in the old. Satan also observes that in their formation ('so lively shines / in them divine resemblance'), the couple signals a new relationship between Creator and created, the latter bearing a privileged position of favour. Earlier in the poem Satan's henchman Beelzebub explains that this new race is 'favoured more / Of him who rules above'.[41]

There are numerous places in Milton's poem where he rehearses this image of the creation of mankind as a new dispensation, of humankind as both bearing a privileged position of favour with the Almighty and also bearing His hopes of a reformed order. While the angels are commanded to bend their knee or else be cast out into utter darkness, God's first words to Adam tell him to rise:

> ... One came, methought, of shape divine,
> And said, 'Thy mansion wants thee, Adam, rise'.[42]

Adam records how God 'by the hand took me raised' and again how, when he, overcome with awe, fell in adoration at God's feet, 'He reared me'.[43]

Man was the Creator's 'new delight', and Adam and Eve were to found a 'new happy race of men / to serve him better: wise in all his ways'; a 'better race' to bring into the space left vacant by the 'spirits malign'.[44] Their increase was not to be numerical only, but, if they but proved faithful, they could ascend 'by degrees of merit' to the level of the angels and 'earth be changed to heaven and heaven to earth'.[45]

Beyond these detailed references in the text, the movement of the narrative shows how in Milton's scheme the battle of heaven is relegated to the historical background, and the relationship between God and man becomes central. It defines all others, so that Satan's prime purpose is now to subvert that relationship; the role of the angels is subordinated to the needs of their human charges, to the conveying of messages between God and his latest creation, to teaching, protecting, guiding and correcting them. In *De Doctrina Christiana*, Milton writes that the angels' ministry 'relates especially to believers'.[46] In *Paradise Lost*, even the story of the Son whose elevation provoked the heavenly rebellion becomes subsumed into that of mankind's salvation through his extraordinary act of generosity, offering himself as a ransom for man. The chronology of two falls means that the creation of man is not just a beginning but can also be seen as a response to the events of the previous age. Adam is given a dual role in the unfolding narrative of God's relationship with his creation and man's relationship with God. He is the cause of a fall from grace and exile from paradisiacal bliss, and the source of hope and instrument of the reformation of God's creation after the conflict and turmoil of the earlier and more dramatic fall of the rebellious angels. By portraying Adam as the cause of one fall and answer to the other, Milton is able to present a view of 'our primitive great sire' that is both Augustinian and humanist; that understands man to be contaminated and inclined to sin yet possessed of nobility, moral courage and reason. Through this double interpretation Milton's Adam at the same time foreshadows and explains the English nation's fall from the heights of republican liberty and offers it a model of renewal.

Adam in Eden

What has been said about Adam's status as 'high advanced' by God and 'the creator's new delight and favour' shows a state that has been established by God's decree. The subordination of the other creatures to the needs of man, whether the angels who are to serve and guide or beasts who are to be under man's dominion, reinforces the power of that decree. The superabundance of God's present gifts to man 'who at his hand / Have nothing merited' and even more of his future promise that eventually their bodies 'may at last turn all to spirit' and 'winged ascend / Ethereal' to dwell in 'heav'nly paradises', speaks of His Grace.[47] Such advancements are beyond mankind's possible deserving but are only attainable if man remains true to his calling and works to please God, as Raphael tells Adam, 'If ye be found obedient, and retain / Unalterably firm his love entire'.[48] Raphael informs his listener that God has left it in man's power to persevere in the goodness that God requires of him and will ensure his happiness and has left it to his will to choose so to persevere.[49] In this exposition the archangel is touching upon man's natural state as created for it is through his natural faculties that man might open himself to the superabundant blessings of God's Grace.

Milton's descriptions of Eden present a kind of fictional ethnography, echoing in some respects travellers' accounts of the peoples of America. He shows the same interest in details as Roger Williams, for example, in his careful accounts of Eve's preparation of food, of the cultivation of the land the first couple inhabit, of the customs of marriage, the nature of their discourse and customs of hospitality. Several of the same themes are explored, such as the emphasis on nakedness and modesty contrasted with pomp and shame, or the idea that these unlettered people are able to read off the mightiness of God from the 'Book of Nature' that surrounds them.[50] Through the study of life in Milton's Eden, as through the study of Indian societies, the discerning reader might obtain valuable insights into the nature, possibilities and purposes of mankind that have implications for the organisation and governance of human society. In *Paradise Lost* the reader is looking at something that is both primeval as the state of the first man and woman and also something new that replaces the grandeur and the warring of the pre-creation history that preceded it.

The naturalness of the Edenic state presented in *Paradise Lost* is emphasised, and authority where it exists is generally exercised with a light touch. There is very little positive law, the only positive command being that given by God concerning the forbidden fruit; 'From us no other service than to keep / This one, this easy charge'.[51] Even Adam and Eve's own dominion over the birds and beasts is so far from burdensome that the animals appear to spend their time, 'frisking', 'sporting', 'playing' and 'gamboling'.[52] In their activities and decisions the human couple is guided by natural law accessed by reason, as Eve explains to the serpent, 'our reason is our law'; it is the 'sanctity of reason' with which, Raphael tells Adam, they unlike their fellow creatures, are endued.[53] This reason is, he explains, most often 'discursive' reason worked out through discourse, contrasting with the 'intuitive' reason of the angels – and it is proved to be not infallible. When Eve makes her fateful decision to separate herself from Adam in Book IX to work in another part of the garden where she will later encounter the serpent, it was made on the basis of her reasoning, which won out over counter reasons given by Adam. Elsewhere in his writing Milton makes a strong link between 'reason' and 'conscience' as the faculties that enable man to discern right from wrong.[54]

In *De Doctrina Christiana* Milton explores the theme of natural law. It is 'the unwritten law ... the law of nature given to the first man'.[55] In essence though not in form it is the same law that was written down for Moses and in the Gospels; as natural law it has been implanted into the whole of mankind, accessible to gentiles and to the ancients as well as to Jews and Christians.[56] For Milton, sin's foundation is a perversion of that law: 'All committing sin also commit anomy, and sin is anomy.'[57] In his political works Milton indicates that the fact of the Fall has brought some changes to man's natural state, not least by necessitating the kind of formal governance not required in Eden. In *The Tenure of Kings and Magistrates* (1649), he is emphatic that 'no man who knows aught, can be so stupid as to deny that all men naturally were born free' and that they lived so until Adam's transgression led to wrong-doing and violence between men.[58] In *Paradise Lost* he writes of 'reason in man obscured, or not obeyed' but nevertheless, he insists a glimmering of that natural law remains in man ('a remnant or a kind of light persists in the hearts of all mortals'); in his poem God speaks of those who respond to 'my umpire Conscience'.[59] Milton's preference for natural law over positive law as an arbiter for human affairs is evident in *The Ready and Easy Way* when he writes of a parliament 'not bound by any statute of preceding parliaments, but by the law of nature only, which is the only law of laws truly and properly to all mankind fundamental' as opposed to 'mere positive laws'.[60]

Another aspect of life in Eden is its sociability. This sociability entails the kind of compatibility that enables fruitful rational discourse. On the day of his creation, Adam, surrounded by the newly created brute beasts, expresses to God his wish for a more compatible companion with whom to share his paradisiacal existence. He asks, 'Among unequals what society?' and requests 'fellowship ... fit to participate / All rational delight', someone with whom he can converse.[61] Without such a companion he would not be free to exercise the 'discursive reason' of which Raphael talks, which is to be the basis for his distinguishing right action. Milton's Adam requires for his fulfilment a more equal relationship than that of superior to inferior entailed in God's granting of dominion to him. There is a strong contrast between this interpretation of Adam and Filmer's emphasis on Adam's 'power Monarchicall' from the moment of his creation. The two models have very different implications for political society. Milton's model accords with the image of the nation in his 1644 treatise of liberty, *Areopagitica*, 'subtle and sinewy to discourse' strengthened by the disputing, reasoning and arguing so that it is enabled to fight off degeneration and decay and stand strong in the face of its enemies.[62] Filmer finds strength in the unquestioned obedience of the people to their undisputed sovereign.

In his reporting of this conversation between Adam and God, Milton makes a significant departure from the Genesis story. In the original it is God who decides that it is not good for man to be alone and who acts on this by creating Eve. In *Paradise Lost*, Adam himself decides that he needs a companion and informs God of his need. God, all-knowing, was well aware of Adam's need but determined that Adam should use his reason to recognise it himself and his freedom to ask, 'Expressing well the spirit within thee free'.[63] It is a demonstration of man's liberty to choose his own form of society. Liberty is a principle that is dear to Milton's political project; it is the impending loss of liberty that he fears in *The Ready and Easy Way*.[64] Liberty also defines Adam's state in Milton's Eden. It is explored in relation to the Fall in particular, and the discussion on the issue in Book III of *Paradise Lost* closely mirrors Milton's exposition of his position on the doctrine in *De Doctrina Christiana*. In both he acknowledges the tension between the concept of man's free will and those of God's pre-ordaining or of His foreknowledge of the event. In both texts Milton seeks a resolution that maintains man's freedom of will and action, one where Adam was created 'sufficient to have stood, though free to fall'.[65] In Book III he puts into the Father's mouth an explicit repudiation of the determinist accounts of predestination.[66] God indicates that, although Adam's fall is foreknown by Him, Adam will, like the rebellious angels, fall through his own choosing, unable justly to accuse his Maker for his fate.[67] The same position is outlined in Milton's theological treatise:

> In this way [God] knew that Adam would, of his own accord, fall. Thus it was certain that he would fall, but it was not necessary, because he fell of his own accord and that is irreconcilable with necessity.[68]

It is a question not just of God's justice but of the meaningfulness of man's obedience, for without choice, Raphael asks Adam, 'how / Can hearts not free be tried whether they serve / Willingly or no'.[69] There is a parallel between this argument and that in Book IX when Adam after some discussion reluctantly agrees that Eve should work alone in another part of the garden trusting to her free exercise of reason to guard her against the wiles of their foe, 'for thy stay, not free, absents thee more'.[70]

This focus on liberty, on choice and agency contributes to the restlessness in Milton's paradise. Although he paints a picture of pastoral delight that angels are pleased to visit and where Satan himself confesses he would like to linger, it is not a static world nor is it a place of leisure. A tireless labourer himself in the world of ideas, Milton portrays Eden as a site of intensive, though pleasurable, labour. The labour may be intellectual. Adam manifests a burning desire to know more about the world in which he finds himself, about worlds beyond this world and above all about the God who created him and all he sees. Indeed his first utterance is an interpretive question as he asks of the sun, the hills, rivers and woods and all living creatures:

> Tell, if ye saw, how came I thus, how here?
> Not of myself, by some great Maker then,
> In goodness and in power re-eminent,
> Tell me, how may I know him, how adore.
> From whom I have that thus I move and live
> And feel that I am happier than I know?[71]

Those questions that cannot be answered by studying nature, the 'Book of God' before him, he asks Raphael to answer.[72] This desire for knowledge is more than intellectual curiosity. Adam seeks to know so that he may adore and hopes that, 'In contemplation of created things / By steps we may ascend to God'.[73] The labour may be psychological; the relationship between Adam and Eve is one that is being negotiated through the poem. Book IX in particular contains a sensitive portrait of a marriage as the first man and woman try to work out their degrees of independence from each other, what authority Adam has as husband over his wife, how far they can trust each other apart or constrain each other by being always together. The labour is most obviously physical as each day Adam and Eve set to work taming the garden that threatens to run wild without their constant care.

In each of these areas of work, however, there are possibilities of failure or dangers of misdirection. The gardening task proves almost too much for the two of them unaided:

> ... what we by day
> Lop overgrown, or prune, or prop, or bind
> One night or two with wanton growth derides,
> Tending to wilde.[74]

It is when Eve decides to reorganise the activity by working in another area of the garden from Adam that she is exposed to the deceitfulness of Satan. Raphael warns Adam that he should contain his thirst for knowledge, 'be lowly wise: / Think only what concerns thee and thy being' and a form of intellectual pride, a wish to 'grow mature in knowledge as the gods who all things know' is bound up in Eve's eating of the forbidden fruit.[75] It is because Adam's love for Eve tends towards idolatry that he too, fearful of separation from her, partakes in the act of disobedience. These risks and temptations are essential to Milton's paradise and inseparable from the liberty of man's created state. His depiction of the garden in *Paradise Lost* is consistent with his comment in *Areopagitica* that had God not given Adam the freedom to transgress he would have been 'a mere artificial Adam, such an Adam as he is in the motions'.[76] Man's merit and his reward are dependent on his ability to resist these temptations; it is through obedience, not just through knowledge, that Adam and Eve could eventually reach the heavenly paradises promised.[77] This is a message reinforced in Milton's sequel *Paradise Regained* when Christ, the second Adam, commenced the task to repair the first Adam's fault by standing firm in the face of Satan's tests. Such thinking lies behind Milton's antipathy towards utopian models of society such as those offered by Francis Bacon and Thomas More; in *Areopagitica* he wrote:

> To sequester out of the world into Atlantic and Utopian polities which never can be drawn into use, will not mend our condition; but to ordain wisdom wisely as in this world of evil, in the midst whereof God hath placed us unavoidably.[78]

156 John Milton's Adam and the English nation

To be constantly striving for what is true and ever alert to what is false is the mode of being, whether in Eden or in the fallen world. In *De Doctrina* Milton declares 'God offers all his rewards not to those who are thoughtless and credulous, but to those who labour constantly and seek tirelessly after truth'.[79]

Adam the regenerate

The story is well known: Adam was not wise, he did succumb to temptation and he fell. The final three books of *Paradise Lost* deal with the continuation of that story and the consequences of that fall. This chapter began with consideration of the (for Milton) context of political disappointment in which *Paradise Lost* was completed and suggestions that the failure of the republican experiment into which he had invested so much hope and energy led to his comprehensive disillusionment with worldly affairs and the course of human history or to a retreat into faith and 'eternal verities'. The first of these responses is a counsel of despair discernible in Michael's words:

> ... So shall the world go on,
> To good malignant, to bad men benign,
> Under her own weight groaning.[80]

The second contains comfort, again found in Michael's presentation to Adam, '[thou] shalt possess / A paradise within thee, happier far'.[81] There are reminiscences in this phrase of Winstanley's internalising of the garden, but (as with Winstanley) the hope in fact extends beyond private, individual assurance. Michael speaks of changes on a cosmic scale when all the misery Adam has seen in the pageant of history yet to happen is resolved in Christ's second coming:

> ... thy Saviour and thy Lord,
> Last in the clouds from heav'n to be revealed
> In the glory of the Father, to dissolve
> Satan with his perverted world; then raise
> From the conflagrant mass, purged and refined,
> New heav'ns, new earth, ages of endless date
> Founded in righteousness and peace and love,
> To bring forth fruits, joy and eternal bliss.[82]

The historical cycle of disappointment and the resolution of all the perverted world into eternal bliss tend towards stasis of either despair or joy. The second state of being is an interruption of rather than a progression from the first. In his references to the Final Days in *Paradise Lost*, Milton uses a spiritual typology that entails a collapsing of time and person. In Book III, in the Father's conversation with the Son, he employs the Pauline typology whereby Christ is the second Adam who, in Adam's place, restores what he has lost through the Fall.

> ... be thou in Adam's room
> The head of all mankind, though Adam's son.
> As in him perish all men, so in thee
> As from a second root shall be restored
> As many as are restored, without thee, none.[83]

In his study of Puritan allegory, Thomas Luxon argues that typological interpretations of events lead to an emptying of history; if the single or literal sense of an historical event is the fulfilment it signifies, then its meaning is collapsed into that fulfilment, that moment of triumph.[84] By this logic the meaning of Adam and his story is taken up into Christ's redemptive act as in the lines quoted above and has no separate existence apart from the second Adam's 'victory triumphing through the air / Over his foes and thine', his coming with glory and power to dissolve, to judge and to herald the final union of earth and heaven, 'ages of endless date'.[85] To use Augustine's distinctions, 'corporal and temporal' disappear in the 'eternal and spiritual' of which they have ever only been the signifiers. In the completion is a conflation of all types and of the historical relationship between the types that also gave them some degree of separation from each other, and a point of stability, of stasis, is reached.[86]

Yet Milton's poem does not conclude with this triumphant fulfilment outside time but retains the reality of the present moment, its urgency and temporality. At the end of his instruction, Adam is led down from the hill 'for the hour precise / exacts our parting hence ... we may no longer stay.'[87] Eve too catches this sense of urgency: 'But now lead on; / in me is no delay', and it is a 'hast'ning Angel' who takes 'Our ling'ring parents, and to th'eastern gate / Led them direct, and down the cliff as fast / to the subjected plain'.[88] In the closing lines, as it looks forward to what will immediately follow, the poem retains its sense of time as Adam is told he will yet live 'for many days', and of space: 'The world was all before them, where to choose / Their place of rest'.[89] These final lines, too, convey a sense of possibility (the world before them, the ability to choose) that is different from the paralysis of guilt and despair that strong elements in Michael's projected history could have induced.[90]

In her article on typology in *Samson Agonistes*, Lynn Sadler reacts against a view of Milton's history as static or of his typology as one that subsumes particularities of time, event and action into spiritual absolute.[91] She traces a form of typology in Milton's later works that is in fact closer to the second, historical, typology identified by Reventlow in which people find parallels in the Bible to their own experiences:[92]

> A Miltonic type is an exemplar not the symbol of a spiritual absolute but the pattern of an action ... the pattern we are to reproduce in our circumstances.[93]

158   John Milton's Adam and the English nation

These parallels are educative, because they suggest actions and are therefore of direct application to the 'things at hand' and 'that which lies before us in daily life' that Raphael tells Adam should be his focus.[94] Attention is directed towards this world and man's own place within it. Adam in fact has multiple roles in the typology of these last books. He is the first Adam, the type for whom the second Adam Christ is the spiritual antitype into which his story will be absorbed; as someone of great promise who has fallen, he is the first of many historical types with whom Milton's contemporaries at the demise of the republican experiment might identify; as someone who in the poem receives and reacts to these lessons from history, he is a pattern of action for the individuals (or nation) to whom the poem is addressed. In the final books of *Paradise Lost* close attention to the responses of Adam and Eve to what they have done and to their unfolding awareness of the consequences of their act provides a model for regeneration. Adam and Eve, even as they leave the garden, already bear the hallmarks of the regenerate, supplying a promise to the sinner of regeneration in the timescales of this world, each man in his own day, without waiting for the trumpets to sound on Judgment Day.[95]

In his analysis of man's renovation in *De Doctrina Christiana*, Milton draws on mainstream Protestant theology but makes subtle changes that place more emphasis than many Reformed theologians on the agency of man in the process.[96] Although God's grace is essential, 'our own effort is always required'.[97] He ascribes the processes of Justification (imputing our sins to Christ and his merits to us) and Adoption (by the Father as His heirs) to God alone but intimates that Justification follows and depends on Regeneration; it is thus contingent on the human penitence and faith that lead to Regeneration.[98] Milton sets out several stages of repentance: recognition of sin, contrition, confession, abandonment of evil and conversion to good.[99] These stages are evident in Milton's poetic rendering of Adam and Eve's story. A crucial turning point in that story and significant move towards regeneration can be observed in Book X, when Adam and Eve shift from blame of each other to confession, self-reproach and repentance. The book ends with their prostrating themselves before the Father in genuine contrition confessing their faults:

> … both confessed
> Humbly their faults, and pardon begged, with tears
> Watering the ground, and with their sighs the air
> Frequenting, sent from hearts contrite, in sign
> Of sorrow unfeigned, and humiliation meek.[100]

The couple displays penitence; for regeneration, the addition of faith is required. The process continues with Michael's education of Adam, and the impact of this education can be seen in Adam's changing responses to the lessons he is receiving, a gradual increase in his understanding, in his faith in

God's purposes, and in his resolution to do good. In Book XI, the reader can see that Adam still has much to learn. His earlier reactions to the scenes from Biblical history express negative emotions of horror and dismay; 'Horrid to think, how horrible to feel!', 'O miserable mankind, to what fall / Degraded, to what wretched end reserved'.[101] When presented with the 'daughters of men' of Genesis 6 he shows himself still susceptible to temptation (an echo of the idolisation of Eve that led to his fall) misinterpreting the bevy of fair women with their 'wanton dress' and 'soft amorous ditties' as a 'better ... vision' of 'hope' portending 'peaceful days'.[102] When Raphael warns, 'Judge not what is best / By pleasure', Adam's immediate reaction manifests a lack of self-knowledge; blaming woman as the source of man's woe, he is corrected by Raphael who turns the fault, 'effeminate slackness', on to man himself and teaches the remedy, the use of wisdom.[103] Adam's progress is charted through his responses into Book XII where the story of God's chosen people opens his eyes and eases his heart with evidence of God's unmerited favour to his children.[104] His faith in God's providence is sealed and initial misery transformed to an excess of joy ('Adam with such joy / Surcharged as had like grief been dewed in tears') with the promise of Christ's coming and overcoming Satan and his works.[105] He then proceeds to learn that he must add works to his faith, following Christ's example of obedience and love. He absorbs Michael's lesson that regeneration is ultimately achieved through the performance of deeds answerable to one's own right understanding and right reason and will leave the garden in a regenerate state, 'greatly in peace of thought':[106]

> Henceforth I learn that to obey is best,
> And love with fear the only God, to walk
> As in his presence, ever to observe
> His providence, and on him sole depend.[107]

The emphasis on process and regeneration in these books casts a different light on the examples of sin, violence and decadence in the history presented there. Rather than being a counsel of despair they are a provocation to the acts of penitence required to move forward steadfast in determination, to act rightly so that God's purposes for mankind are achieved. They serve a purpose not dissimilar to Eliot's requirement that his praying Indians should acknowledge darkness and depravity in their former lives as part of their journey to Christian truth. This understanding positions Milton's millenarian thinking at this time as a 'prophetic' eschatology (again similar to the eschatology underlying Eliot's Indian mission) where man is involved over time and in many small ways ('by small / Accomplishing great things') in preparing the Kingdom.[108] This theme is picked up in the poem's sequel, *Paradise Regained* where, though the coming of his kingdom in the final days is prophesied, the portrayal of Christ, second Adam, remains on a human scale.[109] He tells his tempter that his time is not yet come.[110] The focus is on his pattern of human living through the right exercise of reason, obedience to God and growing understanding. *Paradise Lost* and *Paradise Regained* taken together constitute an education in the virtues and values that make man, object of God's 'delight and favour', worthy of the place of honour that God initially decreed for him.

Adam 'the honour and instruction of my own country'

An Adam-centred perspective on *Paradise Lost* has presented Adam as God's new dispensation, a focus of hope and expectation for a new world to replace the troubles of the old order; Adam's state in Eden guided by natural law accessed through observation and discursive reason, his natural liberty and sociability, the necessity for labour and vigilance; Adam as a pattern of the regenerate sinner. It is easy to argue for the relevance of all these Adams to Milton's own time and nation. To do so is to take seriously Milton's initial aims for his great epic poem and to hold that in essentials they did not change between his initial conception of this his life's work and legacy and its realisation in *Paradise Lost*. In his 1644 Tractate on Education Milton articulated his belief in the power of poetry to elevate the readers; to 'show them what glorious and magnificent use might be made of poetry both in divine and human things'.[111] His discussion of his great project in *The Reason of Church Government* (published in 1642) shows that his ideas had been germinating for many years. His ambition was to follow the poets and chroniclers of ancient times; as they, through their eloquence, had brought greatness and renown to their nations, so he would become the 'interpreter and relater of the best and sagest things among mine own citizens'.[112] By doing so he intended 'to imbreed and cherish in a great people the seeds of virtue and public civility, to allay the perturbations of the mind and set the affections in the right tune'.[113] The dual, but related, aims were thus 'the honour and instruction of my own country'.[114]

Milton's initial thoughts were to write an epic about King Arthur. Later he transferred his attention to King Alfred as a possible hero for the piece. The fact that he eventually set aside these home-grown British and Saxon heroes in favour of Adam is not proof of shift of interest away from England and English affairs. Milton's nationality had for long been a defining element of his identity. The title pages of his two treatises defending his nation against criticism for regicide proudly display this identity, 'John Milton, Englishman'.[115] Although in his later years he found himself on the margins of his country's affairs, the continued importance of that identity was evident in his concern expressed in *The Ready and Easy Way* about the reputation of 'the whole English name' in Europe.[116] Rather than loss of interest, the choice of Adam could be interpreted as a concern to dig deeper, to return to the beginning, as others of his contemporaries had done, for the original (foundations and model) of political society in his own land. The double interpretation of Adam in *Paradise Lost* as both the new and 'better race' and the fallible man under the tutelage of the angels, combines the 'honour and instruction' that Milton intended for the English nation. It would not be difficult for an English audience, especially of Milton's persuasion, to read their own story into that of Adam.

Several of Milton's prose works had already honoured his country by giving her special status among her neighbours. Like Adam, the country had been so honoured by God's decree, and like Adam, there was a sense that England had been chosen to start a new order after the decadence or turmoil that had gone before. The new age England was to herald in is variously understood, but essentially it is concerned with liberty religious and political, which in Milton's thinking are closely interwoven. In *Of Reformation* Milton writes of the main event of the Reformation with Wycliffe's role in mind; England had had 'this grace and honour from God, to be the first that should set up a standard for the recovery of lost truth, and blow the first evangelic trumpet to the nations'.[117] In *Areopagitica,* England is the starting place for a reformation of the Reformation:

> God is decreeing to begin some new and great period in His Church, even to the reforming of Reformation itself. What does He then but reveal Himself to His servants, and, as His manner is, first to His Englishmen?[118]

In *The Ready and Easy Way* Milton describes an 'extolled and magnified' nation that, with the aid of providence, has won a victory over tyranny as well as superstition setting it on course to become a new Rome.[119] In this pamphlet he uses the language of the epic when he writes of a 'nation valorous and courageous' of 'noble words and actions' that has 'fought so gloriously for liberty'.[120] Milton had hoped that the new order that follows this victory, his 'firm and free commonwealth', would be built on different foundations from the reliance on force of arms and military might that precede it.[121] Painfully conscious of the loss of life involved, 'the blood of so many thousand faithful and valiant Englishmen' that had been spent, he was concerned that his compatriots would not have to 'fight over again all that we have fought'.[122] There are close parallels with the new dispensation brought in with Adam's creation in *Paradise Lost* to replace the turbulence of the pre-creation history recorded there. The poem's interpretation and depiction of Adam in Paradise is appropriate for its time of writing providing hope for change after the battles and factions, the worldly pride and decadence of civil war, commonwealth and restoration and legitimisation for a social order based on virtue instead.

Areopagitica contains the striking image of the nation as epic hero, 'a noble and puissant Nation raising herself like a strong man after sleep and shaking her invincible locks'.[123] It also presents another model of English heroism based on study, on argumentation and searching after truth, which persists in Milton's thinking through to the description of Adam's Edenic state in *Paradise Lost*. When he writes of the natural character of the English people he describes a nation that is 'pliant and so prone to seek after knowledge', a nation 'not slow and dull, but of a quick, ingenious and piercing spirit, acute to invent, subtle and sinewy to discourse, not beneath the reach of any point, the highest that human capacity can soar to'.[124] The closeness of this ideal to that of Adam in the garden has already been noted; the inclination to knowledge and 'discursive reason' is the same, the readiness for hard work and the potential to rise higher.

Like Adam, the state of the English nation is not one of rest but one where constant labour and vigilance is needed.[125] Their national character means the English are 'sufficient to have stood', but they are also 'free to fall'. Throughout his political writings Milton held the providential status and virtuous character of the English in tension with examples of their falling away from this ideal. His *History of Britain* tells this story.[126] In *Of Reformation* he wonders how England once, by God's grace, first in the reformation of Christendom, 'should now be last and most unsettled in the enjoyment of that peace, whereof she taught the way to others'.[127] This tension is particularly evident in *The Ready and Easy Way*, where Milton portrays a nation in grave danger of slipping from the promised heights of a free commonwealth to the servility and debasement, the moral degeneration of monarchical rule.[128] He asks how that valorous and courageous nation could be so 'heartless and unwise'; how that extolled and magnified nation could 'creep back so poorly to their once abjured and detested thraldom of kingship'.[129] Milton uses uncompromising language for the condition and behaviour of his countrymen, 'a strange, degenerate contagion', 'ingrateful backsliding', 'ruinous proceedings', 'epidemic madness'; for the consequences of their actions, 'slavery', 'bondage', 'debauchery'; and for the scoffing reactions of those who observe their fall, 'scorn and derision'.[130] With these words he provokes his readers to guilt and shame and to an acknowledgement of the serious consequences of what they were doing. In its forcefulness the instruction he is giving to his countrymen matches that of Michael to Adam; the lesson of man's instability in the face of evil and lack of perseverance in virtue and liberty is the same.

While, in Milton's perspective, the English nation's providential status, its natural character and achievement in overthrowing the superstitions of the Church and the tyranny of the monarchy make it worthy of honour, its fickleness and inclination to fall make it as needful of instruction. He links this fickleness to England's character as an island nation; 'good education and acquisit wisdom ought to correct the fluxible fault if any there be of our watry situation'.[131] *The Ready and Easy Way* not only instructs but also establishes education as the key to the restoration of an English nation that is fast sliding away from its God-ordained and hard-won freedom. The emphasis on education's power to instil right understanding and values make the processes of this restoration very similar to the regeneration of Adam in *Paradise Lost*; the regeneration of Adam is a pattern for the regeneration of a nation. By the time he was writing *The Ready and Easy Way* and *Paradise Lost,* it seems Milton was not expecting an immediate regeneration of that nation. He envisaged a steady, step-by-step process involving the careful preparation of the people to fit them individually for this regenerate state and extend the benefits of their learning throughout the population. He recommends the establishment of schools and academies where children may acquire 'a noble education' in grammar and all liberal arts.[132] In his *Tractate on Education* Milton argues that the end of education is to restore in humankind that which it lost in Adam and Eve, 'to repair the ruins of our first parents by regaining to know God aright'.[133] From the schools and academies proposed in *The Ready and Easy Way,* right knowledge, civility and religion would spread throughout the nation and transform it:

> This would soon spread much more knowledge and civility, yea, religion, through all the parts of the land, by communicating the natural heart of government and culture more distributively to all extreme parts, which now lie numb and neglected; would soon make the whole nation more industrious, more ingenious at home, more potent, more honourable abroad.[134]

The political structures that Milton recommends in *The Ready and Easy Way* suggest a nation in a condition of tutelage. There are parallels here with the conclusion Winstanley drew after *his* expectations of revolutionary change were disappointed, that the English people were still in a stage of dependence. In its adjustment of expectations *The Ready and Easy Way* could be viewed as Milton's *Platform.* In his tract Milton expresses the view that the populace are unready for active involvement in government; he is wary of 'licentious and unbridled democracy'.[135] Instead his commonwealth is to be governed by a worthy minority, a general council 'of ablest men' sitting for life, with certain responsibilities (educational, legislative and judicial) devolved to the counties. Elections to this chamber are not to be committed to 'all the noise and shouting of a rude multitude' but to a carefully selected 'rightly qualified' group.[136] The model is pragmatic, adapted to the population as it now is rather than to his vision of what it might be. It is not the sum of Milton's political aspirations, however, but a staging post towards a greater liberty when the population is ready. The dependency of form of government on the character of the people is restated with greater clarity in Milton's *Brief Notes upon a Late Sermon,* published soon after *The Ready and Easy Way.* Here he suggests that the English might not yet be worthy of a free commonwealth and entertains the idea that they should as a temporary arrangement choose one man, with a proven record in the struggle against tyranny, to rule.[137] Free commonwealths are fittest, he argues, for 'civil, virtuous, and industrious, nations, abounding with prudent men worthy to govern'.[138] As he has already stated in his earlier work,

164   John Milton's Adam and the English nation

education is the key to the formation of the kind of citizens such commonwealths require:

> To make the people fittest to choose, and the chosen fittest to govern, will be to mend our corrupt and faulty education, to teach the people faith, not without virtue, temperance, modesty, sobriety, parsimony, justice; not to admire wealth or honour; to hate turbulence and ambition; to place every one his private welfare and happiness in the public peace, liberty and safety.[139]

In his attempt to sway the thinking of his countrymen Milton may warn of the dire consequences of their return to bondage, but ultimately the political message he gives in his late works – that the essential condition for man's liberty is not the structure of the government but the character of the man – is one of hope in the political climate in which he is writing. It gives each reader a course of action, 'add / Deeds to thy knowledge answerable, add faith, / Add virtue, patience, temperance, add love', and a sense of agency 'by small / Accomplishing great things'.[140] The virtuous life of each man contributes to the renovation of the whole. The story of Adam is uniquely appropriate to Milton's message. As father of each man and father of all men his history is both particular and universal; it reinforces the coupling of private and public interests embodied in the quote above. If good governance and public welfare is to be founded on the quality of the men they include, then a return to Adam is a reminder of what the state of man is and what it could ideally be. His story of Fall and (in Milton's telling) of regeneration encompasses the experiences of the individual reader and the nation and proposes ways forward for both.

Notes

1. *REW – PW*, 224.
2. Milton's reference was to republican Rome rather than the Empire of Papacy.
3. Lewalski, *Life*, Chapters 8–10.
4. Hill wrote a book on this theme; Christopher Hill, *The Experience of Defeat: Milton and Some Contemporaries* (Harmondsworth: Penguin, 1985).
5. Several commentators have drawn attention to the plurality of genres to be found within *Paradise Lost*, e.g. Barbara Lewalski, *Paradise Lost and the Rhetoric of Literary Forms* (Princeton, NJ: Princeton University Press, 1985).
6. Lewalski, *Life*.
7. PL, VII, 25. Lewalski discusses the impact of his second wife's loss on Milton in her analysis of his sonnet 'Mee thought I saw my late espoused saint …' – Lewalski *op. cit.*, 355–56.
8. William Blake, *The Marriage of Heaven and Hell* 1790; Samuel Taylor Coleridge, 'Lecture on Milton and the *Paradise Lost*' March 4, 1817 Lecture X in *Literary Remains,* (London, 1817).
9. Blair Worden, 'Milton's republicanism and the Tyranny of Heaven' in *Machiavelli and Republicanism* edited by Gisela Block, Quentin Skinner and Maurizio Viroli (Cambridge: Cambridge University Press, 1993), 225–45, p. 244.

10. Kenneth Borris, *Allegory and Epic in English Renaissance Literature: Heroic Form in Sidney, Spenser and Milton* (Cambridge: Cambridge University Press, 2000), 238.
11. Lewalski, *Life*, 442.
12. Loewenstein, *Representing Revolution*, 203.
13. See Dayton Haskins *Milton's Burden of Interpretation* (Philadelphia: University of Pennsylvania Press, 1994) where this is presented as Milton's understanding of the task of the Christian.
14. In his critique of the political activist interpretations of the author of *Paradise Lost*, W. Walker notes the recurring use of 'parallels', 'reflections', 'resemblances', 'echoes', 'similarities', and 'analogies' in studies of the poem. Walker, W. 'Resemblance and Reference in Recent Criticism on *Paradise Lost*,' *Milton Quarterly* 40 (2006): 189–206.
15. See Joan Bennett's criticism of these parallels: Joan Bennett, *Reviving Liberty: Radical Christian Humanism in Milton's Great Poems* (Cambridge, MA: Harvard University Press, 1989), 33.
16. *PL*, II, 776f.; *REW – PW*, 232.
17. *PL*, V, 779–82; *REW – PW*, 226.
18. *PL*, IV, 945; 958–60.
19. *PL*, V, 785–90.
20. *PL*, V.
21. As in the command that all angels should, on pain of exile, bow their knees to the son without offering reasons for this elevation to Lordship over all *PL*, V, 600–15. Satan is not consistent in his political speech and can voice both republican and monarchist sentiments, Loewenstein, *Representing Revolution*, 217–18.
22. Stevie Davies, *Images of Kingship in Paradise Lost. Milton's Politics and Christian Liberty* (Missouri & London: University of Missouri Press, 1983), 3.
23. For the first of these three positions see Robert Thomas Fallon, *Divided Empire: Milton's Political Imagery* (University Park: Pennsylvania State University Press, 1995), 32–33; for the second, Lewalski, *Life*, 466 and Peter Herman, *Destabilizing Milton "Paradise Lost" and the Poetics of Incertitude* (Basingstoke: Palgrave MacMillan, 2008) 84; for the third, Michael Bryson 'His Tyranny Who Reigns': The Biblical Roots of Divine Kingship and Milton's Rejection of 'Heav'n's King', in *Milton Studies*, edited by Albert C. Labriola (Pittsburgh: University of Pittsburgh Press, 2004), 43, 111–44.
24. *PL*, XII, 24–63.
25. *PL*, XII, 350; *REW – PW*, 223–24.
26. *PL*, VII, 26–28.
27. *PL*, XI, 666–68.
28. *PL*, XII, 555.
29. David Loewenstein, *Milton and the Drama of History* (Cambridge: Cambridge University Press, 1990), 123; 'Both in one faith unanimous though sad / With cause for evils past, yet much more cheered / With meditation on the happy end' *PL*, XII, 603–605.
30. For Adam's emotional reactions see, 'Horrid to think, how horrible to feel' – *PL*, XI, 465; for Adam's misreading see his wrong assumptions about the 'bevy of fair women' who appear in the pageant – *PL*, XI, 595f.
31. *DDC*, VII; based on the P account of Genesis.

32. *PL*, V, 580–82. This passage is based on Aristotle's explanation; 'It is plain that time is a measure of motion according to its beforeness and afterness, and is continuous (because time is continuous)'. – Aristotle, *The Physics*, trans. Philip H. Wicksteed and Francis M. Cornford, 2 vols. (London: William Heinemann, 1929), 1:394, section 220a, lines 25–7: see Russell M. Hillier, 'Spatial Allegory and Creation Old and New in Milton's Hexaemeral Narrative', *Studies in English Literature, 1500–1900* 49, no 1, (Winter 2009): 121–43.
33. Lewalski, *Life*, 117–18.
34. *PL*, V, 583f; *PL*, I, 531f; *PL*, V, 535f.
35. *PL*, V, 350–57.
36. *PL*, V, 391–92.
37. *PL*, IV, 288.
38. See Norbrook on T. S. Eliot's reaction, David Norbrook, *Writing the English Republic: Poetry, Rhetoric and Politics, 1627–1660* (Cambridge: Cambridge University Press, 1999), 481.
39. *PL*, IV, 356.
40. *PL*, IV, 358–65.
41. *PL*, II, 352–53.
42. *PL*, V, 607–15; *PL*, VIII, 296.
43. *PL*, VIII, 300; *PL*, VIII, 316.
44. *PL*, IV, 106; *PL*, III, 679–80; *PL*, VII, 189; *PL*, VII, 154.
45. *PL*, VII, 157–60.
46. *DDC*, IX.
47. *PL*, IV, 417–18; *PL*, V, 497–50.
48. *PL*, V, 501–502.
49. *PL*, V, 520f.
50. *Key*, 122 'Almost all naked, yet not one / Thought want of clothes disgrace'; *Key*, 67 'The Sunne and Moone, and Starres and seasons of the yeere doe preach a God to all the sonnes of men, that they which know no letters, doe yet read an eternall Power and Godhead in these'. Compare with 'for heave'n / Is as the Book of God before ye set – *PL*, VIII, 66–67.
51. *PL*, IV, 420–21.
52. *PL*, IV, 340f.
53. *PL*, IX, 654; *PL*, VII, 507–508.
54. His treatise *Areopagitica* 1644 demonstrates the importance of freedom of reason and of conscience in Milton's conception of human society.
55. *DDC*, XXVI, 516.
56. 'Since humanity was made in God's image, and had the whole law of nature born with them [*totam naturae legem ita secum natam*], and had it implanted within them, they were not lacking a precept to hold them to that law' (*DDC* Chapter XV: 114).
57. 1 Jn. 3:4.
58. *TKM – PW*, 191.
59. *PL*, XII, 86; *DDC*, XVI, 100; *PL*, III, 195.
60. *REW – PW*, 221.
61. *PL*, VIII, 389–91.
62. *AR – PW*, 176, 179.
63. *PL*, VIII, 440.
64. In *The Ready and Easy Way* Milton makes it clear that he is concerned with both political and religious liberty (the latter being more important for him),

which he sees as closely interrelated; 'This liberty of conscience, which above all other things ought to be to all men dearest and most precious, no government more inclinable not to favour only, but to protect, than a free commonwealth' – *REW* – *PW*, 239.

65. *PL*, III, 99.
66. *PL*, III, 114.
67. *PL*, III, 111f.
68. *PL*, III, 165.
69. *PL*, V, 531–33.
70. *PL*, IX, 372.
71. *PL*, VIII, 277–82.
72. *PL*, VIII, 66–67.
73. *PL*, V, 510–11.
74. *PL*, IX, 209–12.
75. *PL*, IX, 209–12, 803.
76. *AR* – *PW*, 163.
77. *PL*, V, 501.
78. *AR* – *PW*, 163.
79. *DDC*, VI, 120.
80. *PL*, XII, 537–39.
81. *PL*, XII, 586–87.
82. *PL*, XII, 544f.
83. *PL*, III, 285–89.
84. Luxon, *Literal Figures*, 35.
85. *PL*, XII, 452–53, 548.
86. Luxon employs Augustine's distinction – Luxon, *op. cit.*, 35–36.
87. *PL*, XII, 589.
88. *PL*, XII, 614–15, 637f.
89. *PL*, XII, 602, 646–47.
90. Haskins, *Milton's Burden*, 235. Neither the Bible nor *Paradise Lost* attempts to represent divine knowledge of Adam and Eve's eventual fate – the question of their salvation is left open.
91. Lynn Veach Sadler, 'Regeneration and Typology: Samson Agonistes and Its Relation to De Doctrina Christiana, Paradise Lost, and Paradise Regained', *Studies in English Literature, 1500–1900* ... Vol. 12, No. 1, (Winter 1972): 141–56.
92. See Chapter 1.
93. Sadler, *op. cit.* 144.
94. *PL*, VIII, 199, 193–94.
95. See also Sadler, *op. cit.* 144.
96. *DDC*, XXII–XXV.
97. *DDC*, XXI, 480. See Lewalski, *Life*, 433–34 for discussion.
98. Milton notes that they do not necessarily lead to regeneration as they may be temporary and natural – *DDC*, XVIII.
99. *DDC*, XIX.
100. *PL*, X, 1100–1104.
101. *PL*, XI, 465, 500–501.
102. *PL*, XI, 599–600. The reference is to Gen. 6:2–4.
103. *PL*, XI, 632–36.
104. *PL*, XII, 274.

168 *John Milton's Adam and the English nation*

105. *PL*, XII, 372f.
106. *PL*, XII, 581–82, XII, 558. Eve is to partake of this regenerate state as Michael commissions Adam to pass on to her the knowledge and insights he has acquired – *PL*, XII, 597f.
107. *PL*, XII, 561–64.
108. *PL*, XII, 566–67; This refers to Wilson's distinction between 'prophetic' and 'apocalyptic eschatologies, Wilson, *Prophet in Parliament*.
109. *PL*, IV, 146.
110. *PL*, III, 396.
111. *TE*, 8. This tractate was couched as a letter to Samuel Hartlib who was involved in various projects for educational reform. For Milton's relationship with the Hartlib circle see Lewalski, *Life*, 172f.
112. *RCG – PW*, 354.
113. *RCG – PW*, 354.
114. *RCG – PW*, 352.
115. *A Defence of the People of England, in Answer to Salmasius's Defence of the King* (1654) and *The Second Defence of the People of England, against an Anonymous Libel Entitled The Royal Blood Crying to Heaven for Vengeance on the English Parricides* (1654) (both originally written in Latin).
116. *REW – PW*, 224.
117. *RE – PW*, 6.
118. *AR – PW*, 177.
119. *REW – PW*, 237, 223, 224.
120. *REW – PW*, 227.
121. *REW – PW*, 223.
122. *REW – PW*, 224.
123. *AR*, 179.
124. *AR*, 177, 176.
125. This is in keeping with his theology that sees the regenerate state as one that does not necessarily persevere but has to be maintained through right actions and thought.
126. Published 1670.
127. *RE – PW*, 6.
128. *REW – PW*, 225–26.
129. *REW – PW*, 227, 223.
130. *REW – PW*, 224, 224, 244, 244, 224, 227, 226, 224.
131. *REW – PW*, 231.
132. *REW – PW*, 241.
133. *TE*, 4.
134. *REW – PW*, 241–42.
135. *REW – PW*, 232.
136. *REW – PW*, 233.
137. It seems Milton had General Monck in mind.
138. John Milton, 'Brief Notes upon a Late Sermon, Titled, The Fear of God and the King' in *The Prose Works of John Milton*, edited by Rufus Wilmot Griswold (Philadelphia: John W. Moore, 1847), Vol. 2. in *Online Library of Liberty* <http://oll.libertyfund.org/title/1210/78232> [accessed 4 November 2012].
139. *REW – PW*, 233.
140. *PL*, XII, 581–83, 565–67.

6 John Locke, Adam and the original of power

Introduction: short-term events and universal principles

Describing the subject of this chapter, Hans Aarsleff wrote: 'John Locke is the most influential philosopher of modern times ... his influence in the history of thought, on the way we think about ourselves and our relations to the world we live in, to God, nature and society, has been immense'.[1] According to Aarsleff (and with reference to the theme of this book) one of the many ways in which Locke has changed our thinking and provided foundations for the modern world is by freeing us from the 'timeless stasis' of Adamic patriarchalism and offering process and progress in a civil society based on freedom and contractual obligation. Locke's giant reputation means that he, more than any of the other authors discussed in this book, is of vital interest to all three of Pocock's categories – political scientists, political philosophers and political historians. This position is not without its tensions, as claims about the modernity or the universal relevance of his thought encounter evidence of the close relationship of his ideas with the intricacies of late Stuart politics and the influence of his religion on his writing.[2] From the 1950s, Locke scholars of the 'Cambridge School', prominent among them Peter Laslett, have presented his political writings, in particular his *Two Treatises of Government*, as texts-in-context, taking their historical character as fundamental to their interpretation and tracing their origins and the author's intentions to the immediate concerns of late Stuart politics; this is the so-called 'historicization' of John Locke.[3] The view of the universalism of Locke's work is weighed against the image of Locke as an actor on the stage of post-restoration politics, a henchman of Lord Shaftesbury working with the early Whigs during their struggles to control the arbitrary exercise of the royal prerogative amidst concerns about the French-leaning and 'Papist' tendencies of Charles II and open 'Papism' of his brother James II. Locke's association with Shaftesbury's party was so close, in the view of the authorities, that he was forced to spend the years between 1683 and 1689 in political exile and only returned once the successful and bloodless invasion of William of Orange and flight of James II radically changed the political climate. After the new political settlement Locke and his friends, whom he called his 'college', continued to play an active and highly visible role in lobbying, policy-development and drafting legislation into the 1690s.[4] The question for these scholars of Locke is how far are his political works bound by the concerns of seventeenth-century England, or how far do they transcend that context? Either way Locke's political theory has been interpreted according to varying timescales: the short term of the event (Charles II dissolves parliament; William of Orange lands in Brixham harbour); the longer term trends and rhythms of a society readapting itself through a progression of ages (Reformation, Enlightenment); the extremely long term that is almost timeless, speaking as it does of the human condition.

Laslett used the methods of the Cambridge School (parallels between historical circumstance and content, examination of documentary evidence, particularly letters and records of Locke's reading) to develop his theory, now commonly accepted, that Locke's *Two Treatises of Government* were written between 1679 and 1683.[5] This places them at the time of the Exclusion Crisis when Charles II was facing pressure from the Whiggish faction under Shaftesbury, to exclude his Roman Catholic brother James from succession to the throne. It was Charles's irritation with this faction that led to his exercise of the royal prerogative in the dissolution of parliament in 1681. John Dunn describes the *Treatises* as an 'Exclusion tract', and Richard Ashcraft echoes this understanding of the text as being addressed to a particular political situation when he describes the writing of the *Two Treatises* as a political action, an interpretation that begins with Locke's conclusion that 'it is lawful for the people … to *resist* their King (T II.xix.232: 437)'.[6] Political events move on in succession, and Locke's own justification for the publication of his work in 1690, as set out in his preface, links its reception to another historical event. He hopes his discourse will be 'sufficient to establish the Throne of our Great Restorer, Our present King William; to make good his title, in the Consent of the People'.[7] Interpreted in this timescale of historical events, Locke becomes one voice among many (now largely forgotten) in a contemporary debate. His friend James Tyrell was another of these. The publisher's preface to Tyrell's justification for the 1688 act of resistance, *A Brief Enquiry into the Ancient Constitution and Government of England*, signals this plurality of publications: 'There being many Treatises already published upon the subjects handled in this ensuing discourse, you may think it needless to trouble the World with more of this kind'. He goes on to justify the publication of yet another treatise on this subject, however, by reference to the pressing concerns of the current political context and constitutional struggle making a detailed consideration of the relative rights of king and people particularly urgent.[8] The tension between fundamental rights and liberties and the monarch's prerogative, that characterised the political polemic of the 1680s into which Locke was writing, had been a common theme threading through the succession of events that advanced the narrative of Stuart history from the beginning of the century through the trials of Charles I's reign, the descent into war, the establishment of Commonwealth and Protectorate and the restoration of the hereditary monarchy. The controversies of the 1680s prompted the resurrection and publication of texts (radical and conservative) that had engaged with the political and constitutional controversies of the previous generation, among them Philip Hunton's argument for limited mixed monarchy, *Treatise of Monarchie* (written 1643 and republished in 1689) and, most significantly for Locke, Robert Filmer's *Patriarcha* (written in the years leading up to the civil war and published as Tory propaganda in the 1679).[9] Locke possessed copies of both authors' texts. Filmer's writing is the chief butt of criticism in Locke's *Treatises* and Tyrell's *Patriarcha non Monarcha* written at roughly the same time.

Locke's political works are not just the polemic of (the here-and-now of) contemporary politics, however, but the engagement of the scholar who reacts to the dilemmas and complexities of the present moment by making links to his wider learning and deeper reflections.[10] He is, after all, author of the *Essay Concerning Human Understanding* and other works that explore the very foundations and limitations of human knowledge and comprehension. The interplay of timescales, the combination of short-term events and universal principles is something scholars have noted in Locke's work. Laslett sees it as an intellectual tour de force, 'Only a man of such endowment as an abstract thinker could have transformed the issues of a predominantly historical, highly parochial political controversy of this sort into a general political theory'.[11] The stature of Locke as thinker and the continued recognition of his influence on political theory require us to acknowledge his ability to turn contemporary concerns into universal principles, but this move between temporalities is not only the exercise of his skills, it is also characteristic of the political thinking of his time and of the questions that were being asked. Disordered times require big questions, as Locke makes clear in his *First Treatise*:

> The great question which in all Ages has disturbed Mankind, and brought on them the greatest part of those Mischiefs which have ruin'd Cities, depopulated Countries, and disordered the Peace of the World, has been, Not whether there be Power in the World, nor whence it came, but *who should have it*. The settling of this point being of no smaller moment than the security of Princes, and the peace and welfare of their Estates and Kingdoms, a Reformer of Politicks, one would think, should lay this sure and be very clear in it. For if this remain disputable, all the rest will be to very little purpose; and the skill used in dressing up Power with all the Splendor and Temptation Absoluteness can add to it, without shewing *who has a Right to have it*, will serve only to give greater edge to Man's Natural Ambition, which of itself is but too keen. What can this do but set Men on the more eagerly to scramble, and so lay a sure and lasting Foundation of endless Contention and Disorder, instead of that Peace and Tranquillity, which is the business of Government, and the end of Humane Society?[12]

This passage presents a stark picture of the tumultuous condition of mankind. Although Locke writes of 'all Ages' in this passage, the more immediate backdrop that gives urgency to the search for political reform is the 'contention and disorder' of the sixteenth- and seventeenth-century European religious and civil wars, as well as the recent turmoil of English politics. For the peace of estates and kingdoms it is imperative to know to whom power rightly belongs. This is a universal question, albeit prompted by particular circumstances, not interested merely in what works and what does not, but in legitimacy.[13] This search for legitimacy takes the argument back to the origins and foundations of society and, for Locke and his contemporaries, to the relationship between the divine and the human legitimisation of power. Algernon Sidney's answer to Filmer (his *Discourse concerning Government*) argued that those like himself who held radical views of political liberty (views for which he was later tried and executed) were concerned that their models be 'well grounded' in 'the will of God':

> Those who most delight in the glorious liberty of the sons of God, do not only subject themselves to him but are most regular observers of the just ordinances of man, made by the consent of such as are concerned according to the will of God.[14]

Some of Locke's later champions have been reluctant to acknowledge such a grounding for his political theory and, in their hesitations, have been able to take comfort from those of his contemporaries who, noting the unorthodoxy of various of his philosophical and theological positions, accused him of 'tendency to scepticism', and of 'socinianism'.[15] George Kateb, for example, eager to claim Locke as a modern, writes of his 'unequalled contribution to the process of secularism in general and political secularism in particular' and only regrets that, due to the dominant religious culture, which (he claims) put serious constraints on the freedom of expression of intellectuals at that time, Locke's writings show hesitations and concessions.[16] Kateb accuses him of 'backtracking' towards the end of his life, perhaps with his theological writings, *The Reasonableness of Christianity* and his *Paraphrase and Notes of the Epistle of St Paul*. Writing earlier, John Dunn had been prepared to take Locke's expressions of Christian belief more at their face value.[17] He did not doubt the genuine religiousness of Locke and claimed that the *Two Treatises of Government* is a work 'saturated with Christian assumptions'.[18] Dunn notes Locke's Puritan upbringing, his belief in the fallenness of mankind and the reality of the afterlife, which, he concludes, separate him from the modern liberal project; one 'cannot conceive of constructing an analysis of any issue in contemporary [i.e. present day] political theory around the affirmation or negation of anything which Locke says about political matter'.[19] Ultimately, Dunn argues from his own position of secularity, Locke fails because the rationality of human existence that he spent so much of his life attempting to vindicate was dependent on the truths of religion.[20] For Dunn, Locke's thought was severely restricted by his inability to break free from Adam. There is almost bitterness in the tone:

> Freedom of thought was necessary to make intelligible to all men the crudest of practical syllogisms. The human mind was to be made free in order that men might grasp more clearly their ineluctable confinement in the harness in which, ever since the delinquencies of the first ancestor, God had set human beings in the world.[21]

Jeremy Waldron's 2002 study, *God, Locke and Equality*, by contrast respects both the historical origins and the continuing relevance of religious reference in Locke's thought. He criticises the assumptions of secular theorists, such as Dunn, who, having created a crude caricature of what religious arguments are like, too readily dismissed them as irrelevant to public life. Waldron sees his own project, the analysis and elaboration of Locke's religious case for equality, as a chance to enrich our sense of what it is to make a religious argument in politics.[22] Locke was looking for a 'deeper principle', one requiring 'an argument that transcended particular times and particular places and which would have to be grounded in something general in human nature and something permanent in its significance for creatures like us'.[23]

This chapter follows Locke's search for that something permanent, his recourse 'to the original' in his search and interpretation of what that original entailed. In a letter, Locke wrote that 'true politicks ... [is] a Part of Moral Philosophie' and involves some consideration of 'the natural rights of men and the original and foundations of society and the duties resulting from hence'.[24] Locke, too, could not present his understanding of the underlying principles of political society until he had clarified his position on the significance of Adam and his reading of the first chapters of Genesis. From this he proceeded to show how his understanding of men's liberty and equality was in fact based on his interpretation of God's purpose for mankind in the most basic terms of the preservation of his finest creature. It is for this reason that a reading of his theological works, in particular the treatise *The Reasonableness of Christianity* (1695), which also begins with Adam, has direct relevance to the interpretation of his political thought. Although the *Two Treatises* were written in an earlier period of Locke's life and political career, their revision and publication in 1690 mean that they are not too far removed from the writings of Locke's later years for the interrelation between them and his theological treatise to throw light on the condition of his thinking on the foundations of political society at the end of this tumultuous century. There are different emphases reflecting the different purposes of the texts, but the moral basis for living, as an individual or in society, is a theme common to both, and in both cases the relationship between the exercise of reason and the obligation to obey divine command is crucial.

Locke's method applied to Adam

In the preface to his observations on Aristotle's politics, Filmer wrote, 'A Natural Freedom of Mankind cannot be supposed without the denial of the Creation of Adam'. This statement constitutes a two-pronged attack, both denying the existence of natural freedom, the foundation of the political theory of those who sought to limit the monarch's power, and questioning the faith in the Bible of those who subscribed to this theory. Locke rallies to the defence of both the principle of freedom and his own credentials as a Bible-believing Christian and sets out to prove, in his *First Treatise of Government* that the two elements of Filmer's statement are not mutually exclusive but on the contrary:

> I find no difficulty to suppose the *Freedom of Mankind*, though I have always believed the *Creation of Adam*.[25]

He objects to Filmer's attempt to mobilise the weight of Scripture and Christian doctrine in support of a natural inequality of men and the granting to particular individuals of a divinely ordained authority over their fellows; he employs his own Biblical knowledge, his wit and force of argument to refute these claims. Typically, when responding to the arguments of his opponents, Locke engages in a detailed point-by-point refutation of each of their contentions. In his *First Treatise* he sets about a comprehensive dismantling of Filmer's theory, identifying discrepancies in his methods, faults of logic, inconsistencies in his arguments, partiality in his selection of texts, over-interpretation of his evidence, all of which lead to the claim that his writings 'warp the Sacred Rule of the Word of God, to make it comply with his present occasion'.[26] The methods he employs in refutation of Filmer may have had some influence on the outcome of his argument giving particular prominence to certain elements such as disputes about the rights of fathers and the inheritance of power, but it would be wrong to suppose that Locke did not have his own interest in Adam unprompted by Filmer's preoccupation with the same. The fact that he began his theological treatise with an exploration of what 'we lost by Adam' indicates the importance to him of engaging with this figure, even if that engagement involves a clearing away (in 'under labourer' mode) of some traditional interpretations of Adam's status and role.[27]

Locke does not dispute Adam's historical existence as the first ancestor or the truth of his transgression and fall from a paradisiacal state of bliss – in both his political and his theological works he holds to this belief – but the combined force of his discussions on this subject casts doubt on two common contemporary understandings of the ways Adam has determined the human condition. For Locke traditional understandings of the meaning of a Biblical passage, though worthy of consideration, do not carry a necessary authority: any interpretation must be carefully justified in the text itself.[28] The first understanding on which he casts doubt emphasises ways in which each man and all men are bound up with Adam so that Adam's story is man's story and his state of being is man's state of being. It might present Adam as analogy, pattern or type of man or of some aspect of man, whether Milton's regenerate Adam as model of hope for his nation or Winstanley's A-dam as the dark side of each man's internal struggle between good and bad. It might be Adam as representative of mankind, the one who incorporates us all in his fall and fallen condition, a concept shared by all of our authors so far. The second understanding includes Filmer's model. It emphasises the ways in which Adam is separate and distinct from other men; his unique creation, his unique status as patriarch and as lord. Both understandings are undermined in Locke's writing by his fairly consistent principle that Adam should not be taken to stand for anyone else, whether for every man or for monarch.

In *The Reasonableness of Christianity* and in his *Paraphrases* of Paul's epistles, Locke acknowledges the apostle's typological interpretation of Adam's relationship with Christ (the Second Adam) that has given the former such enhanced significance in Christian cosmology, but he is himself wary of types and analogies as ways of understanding or presenting the force of Biblical narrative.[29] God, he believes, expresses his meaning directly and clearly to men, not 'crossing the Rules of language in use amongst them' and is careful when He humbles Himself to speak to them, not 'to lose his design in speaking' so they do not understand.[30] Locke is critical of arguments that make (unjustified) analogical or typological leaps from the plain words of the Scripture to a particular theory of society or government. He writes of Filmer's argument for the divine ordination of absolute monarchy from the subjection of Adam to Eve in Genesis:

> Let the words *Rule* and *Subject* be but found in the Text or Margent, and it immediately signifies the duty of a Subject to his Prince, the Relation is changed, and though God says *Husband* Sir Robert will have it *King*; *Adam* has presently *Absolute Monarchical Power* over *Eve*, and not only *Eve*, but *all that should come of her*, though the Scripture says not a word of it, nor our *A*. a word to prove it. But *Adam* must for all that be an Absolute Monarch and so down to the end of the chapter.[31]

Here Locke is not just finding a tool to dismiss Filmer's arguments but is expressing his accustomed approach to the interpretation of scripture as 'the plain direct meaning of the words and phrases' – plain enough for the day-labourer and dairy-maid to understand – and his general disapproval of the saying of one thing to signify another.[32] In his philosophical writing he often clarifies his statements with illustrative metaphors, but he insists that metaphorical expressions should only be used to support or 'set off' real and solid truth and should 'by no means be set in its place, or taken for it'; otherwise, he warns, 'we rather fancy than know' and 'content ourselves with what our imaginations, not things themselves, furnish us with'.[33] His position precludes the kind of Biblical reading that identifies types for our present and future state of being. Locke makes a distinction between references to Adam and references to the human species in the creation narratives. Where Genesis speaks of 'man', as in 'God made man in His own image' (Gen. 1:26), and of 'them' as when God blessed 'them' and granted dominion to 'them' over all living things (Gen. 1:28), all those who make up the species rather than Adam in particular are intended.[34] God's dealings with men, the creation and donation are direct rather than through Adam:

> *They* then were to have Dominion. Who? Even those who were to have the *Image* of God, the Individuals of that Species of *Man* that he was going to make, for that *Them* should signifie *Adam* singly, exclusive of the rest, that should be in the World with him, is against both Scripture and all Reason.[35]

Locke's position is not just linguistic and exegetical but is shaped by his philosophical stand on the foundations of human character and human knowledge, developed through study of human behaviour, through extensive reading of travel literature and attentive observation of the children in the families with whom he lived. Like Roger Williams with his detailed ethnographies of the Indians among whom *he* had lived, Locke adopted a scientific method (what Aarsleff describes as a 'comparative anthropology')[36] for the understanding of his fellow man. In his discussion of paternal authority and in his argument for its temporary character, Locke draws on observations of animal as well as human behaviour.[37] One outcome of his studies is a particularism that works against the idea that we are all one with Adam. Both his political and his educational treatises emphasise the individual variety of temperament and character among human beings, the different inclinations, different constitutions, native propensities, prevalences of the constitution; their 'original tempers', 'natural genius and constitution.'[38] In *Some thoughts concerning Education* he states that 'all that exists is particular'; in *Conduct of Understanding* he explains that even equalities of education cannot iron out this 'inequality of parts', 'the woods of America as well as the schools of Athens, produce men of several abilities in the same kind'.[39] With such variety it becomes more difficult to look at Adam and say 'this is how man is'.

Another aspect of Locke's thought that diminishes our inheritance from Adam (existing perhaps in some tension with the concept of native propensities and natural genius) is his opposition to innatism, whether innate knowledge or innate sinfulness transmitted through the generations. In *Some Thoughts concerning Education* he goes against contemporary orthodoxy when he claims that instances of bad behaviour all too frequently observed in young children are the result of conditioning rather than of any innate tendency to sin. He characterises 'children's delight in mischief and causing pain as a foreign and introduced disposition' and writes: 'I desire to know what vice can be named which parents and those about children do not season them with and drop into 'em the seeds as soon as they are able to receive them'.[40] Locke's denial of the innateness of ideas, the corner stone of the philosophical project in his *Essay concerning Human Understanding*, makes him resistant to any concept of inherited knowledge from Adam. According to the philosopher, ideas and notions are not born in us, but God has 'fitted men' with 'faculties and means to discover, receive and retain truths'.[41] These truths are received via sensations of the external world and not resurrected from an implanted, pre-lapsarian knowledge inherited from Adam. Locke's discourse on language in Chapter III of the *Essay* goes further to deny even the givenness of the knowledge by which (according to tradition) Adam himself knew the world and was able to name all God's creatures; it rather traces the origins of words to the formulations of ignorant people trying to sort, classify and make sense of the world according to their needs. This approach to the development of language is at a far remove from the efforts of some of his contemporaries (including Roger Williams) to find traces of Hebrew in the language of the American Indians. For Locke all men ever since Adam have had the same liberty in the formulation of words for new ideas.[42] They have this liberty not because Adam had it, but because they too are men.

It was not only Locke's theory of language or his conviction of the plain truth of the Scripture that led him to reject the idea that Adam could stand for man in general; he also found morally repugnant the idea that one man could be bound without consent by the actions of another and share in the consequences of their actions as though those actions were their own. At the beginning of *The Reasonableness of Christianity* he raises the question of how all of Adam's posterity should be doomed to punishment by the transgression of one whom 'no one had authorised to transact for him, or be his representative'.[43] At this point Locke was admittedly presenting the extreme views of those who reject the role of Adam so far as to take away from Jesus any status as saviour, and he is careful to distance himself from this view. However, he proceeds to make clear that he does not believe Adam has sinned as a representative of humanity, and so his act cannot be binding on his successors. It is a question of justice. 'Everyone's sin', he claims, 'is charged upon himself alone', and he uses the words of the New Testament to support his view: 'none are truly punished, but for their own deeds'.[44] This principle is not only revealed in the Scripture; for Locke, it has the status of a Law of Nature – it is 'the eternal and established law of right and wrong', of which 'no one precept or rule is abrogated or repealed; nor indeed can be, whilst God is an holy, just, and righteous God, and man a rational creature'.[45] His argument suggests that, like Grotius, he understands the Creator Himself to be bound by the natural law and the standards of right and wrong that He has set for His creatures. In *The Reasonableness of Christianity* he claims that if God had put men in a state of misery through no fault of their own it would be 'hard to reconcile with the notice we have of justice; and much more with the goodness and other attributes of the supreme Being, which he has declared of himself'.[46] As natural law is linked to reason, so rational argumentation is part of Locke's method; theories can be proved or disproved through the application of the kind of common sense evident in the following statement:

> Much less can the righteous God be supposed, as punishment of one sin, wherewith he is displeased, to put man under the necessity of sinning continually, and so multiplying provocation.[47]

Locke's treatment of the figure of Eve in his *First Treatise* is an example of his combination of textual exegesis and the application of eternal measures of right and wrong known through reason. For Filmer God's subjugation of Eve to Adam (a punishment laid on Eve) is one foundation for the absolute monarch and subject relationship on which his political theory rests. Filmer describes it as 'the original grant of government'.[48] Locke counters Filmer with a two-stage argument. First he uses analysis of the text to claim that God's words do not constitute a grant to Adam but a punishment directed at Eve and so, if Eve were to be understood in a representative role, this would apply to women only. He then employs the principle of justice to remove any suggestion that Eve was acting for others than herself or that the force of punishment is binding on anyone other than the wrongdoer. Locke brings together the two parts of God's curse laid upon Eve to argue that:

> There is here no Law to oblige a Woman to such a Subjection, if the Circumstances either of her Condition or Contract with her Husband should exempt her from it, then there is, that she should bring forth her Children in Sorrow and Pain, if there could be found a remedy for it.[49]

In so far as God's words apply to women other than Eve, they predict what a woman's lot will be rather than bind all womankind to Eve's act and the attendant punishment.

What we have lost by Adam[50]

His denial of a transmission of Adam and Eve's sinfulness through all generations of men was one of the grounds on which Locke was accused of Socinianism by contemporaries.[51] In a tract attacking *The Reasonableness of Christianity*, his critic John Edwards described him as 'all over socinianized' and therefore guilty of atheism.[52] The culmination of Edwards's argument was that a denial of original sin lessens the salvific significance of Christ – if not from sin then from what is he saving us? In effect Locke was accused of undermining the story of man that has Adam's transgression as its beginning and redemption through Christ as its end. Locke had evidently not come to his conclusions on this question without a struggle. In a 1692 letter he declared that a practising member of the Church of England (such as himself) whose Church professed this doctrine in no uncertain terms (in the Thirty Nine Articles and in the liturgy), could 'raise himself such difficulties concerning the doctrine of original sin, as may puzzle him though he be a man of study' and might 'question 'whether it may be truly said that God imputes the first sin of Adam to his posterity?"[53] He answered this dilemma by identifying in his treatise what the fundamentals of the Christian faith are and arguing that the doctrine of original sin is not one.

Locke was careful to distance his theology from the concept of inherited sinfulness, from inherited guilt or inherited punishment; however, in *The Reasonableness of Christianity* he conceded that Adam's act did have some significance beyond his own story, not the fall of mankind into a state of sin, but the loss of the state of immortality that was paradise. As Adam and Eve were expelled from paradise so all who would be born from them would be born out of paradise and therefore would be born mortal.[54] In this interpretation of the event Locke had the support of the story as told in Genesis: God set the penalty for Adam eating the forbidden fruit as death rather than guilt and eternal torment for all his posterity.[55] St Paul's pronouncement 'by one man sin entered into the world, and death by sin', presented more of a problem given Locke's conviction that Paul's words were divinely inspired.[56] In his *Paraphrases* of Paul's epistles, Locke ingeniously expanded on the original to give an interpretation that accords with his rejection of the doctrine of original sin. He used arguments based on Paul's style and delight in the beauty and force of antithesis; he explained how the apostle had put by a 'noe very unusual metonymie the causes for the effect (viz) the sin of eating the forbidden fruit for the effect of it on Adam viz Mortality, and in him on all his posterity', and offers the following paraphrase as a truer representation of the apostle's meaning:

> As by the act of one man Adam, the father of us all, sin entered into the world, and death, which was the punishment annexed to the offence of eating the forbidden fruit enterd by that sin for that Adam's posterity thereby might become mortal.[57]

Thus the sin that entered was just Adam's and the consequence of that sin was a general mortality for his posterity rather than a general sinfulness.

Edwards's criticism of Locke's stand on original sin raised another problem, less important perhaps to Edwards, who was more concerned about religious heterodoxy, but nevertheless of significance to this study's interest in political thought. In Locke's vindication of *The Reasonableness of Christianity* he reports the criticism of his thesis on the basis that 'the corruption and degeneracy of human nature, with the true original of it (the defection of our first parents,) the propagation of sin and mortality, is one of the great heads of Christian doctrine'.[58] There was a strong trend in political thinking at this time that it was this fallen condition, this very 'corruption and degeneracy', that necessitated government. Locke, a close observer of human behaviour, has no doubt that there is sinfulness in the world. He recognises fallibility in mankind; 'all men are liable to error', we are told in his *Essay*, 'and most men are in many points, by Passion or Interest, under Temptation to it'.[59] In *The Reasonableness of Christianity* he writes of the 'corruption of manners and principles' and in *The Second Treatise* of 'the corruption and vitiousness of degenerate men'.[60] It is this condition, he argues, that prompted the formation of men into smaller associations and polities for the protection of themselves and their properties. The language of 'degeneracy' echoes that of those who hold most firmly to the corrupting effect of the Fall on all mankind; however, we have seen elsewhere in Locke's writing his contestation of post-lapsarian transmission of sin. It is not so much sin transmitted via Adam but failure to use to the full the light of reason with which God had endowed them, that causes men to err. Consistent with his emphasis on external as opposed to innate influences, Locke indicates that the condition that necessitates a coming together into a political unity is not the condition of man in terms of his essential character but rather the conditions in which he lives. In theological writings Locke makes a distinction between paradise as context for living and the world beyond paradise in which all men other than the original couple were born. In a journal entry in 1693 (*Homo Ante et Post Lapsum*), Locke describes paradise in the following terms:

> Man was made mortal put into possession of the whole world where in the full use of creatures there was scarce room for any irregular desires but instinct and reason carried him the same way and being neither capable of covitousnesse or ambition when he had already the free use of all things he could scarce sin.[61]

Man's propensity to sinfulness is determined by context; he could scarcely sin in paradise when all was free for his use except for the one fruit forbidden by God's 'probationary law'.[62] In the extra-paradisiacal context of mortality man experiences a greater vulnerability to death as he is 'excluded from that which could cure any distemper ... and renew his age'. *The Reasonableness of Christianity* also contrasts the conditions of living *ante* and *post lapsum*; the former environment is a place of 'tranquillity' and 'bliss' as well as immortality; the latter contains 'drudgery' and 'sorrow'.[63] Locke writes of the 'toil, anxiety, and frailties of this mortal life'.[64] The emphasis on hard work as a necessary response to this context of mortality suggests a link between the post-lapsarian conditions of living and the origins of the polity in Locke's scheme. In his *Second Treatise of Government* he explains stage by stage how the need to preserve the self from death is the original cause for association in political society. Man needs meat and drink for his preservation, and labour is required to secure these.[65] Originally all the earth was given to men in common, but each man has a property in his own person, so the labour of his body and work of his hands are rightly his; thus, if he removes something, or some parcel of land from what is held in common so that he has 'mixed his *Labour*' with it, then it becomes his own property.[66] Once men began to mark out property as their own, jealousies arose. It is for the preservation of their property (understood in both senses as their persons and their possessions) and for protection from the invasion of others that men agree to unite themselves into commonwealths and put themselves under a government.[67]

There is a difference in the flavour of Locke's treatment of property in his theological and political works. In his theological writings Locke presents labour in negative terms, part of the curse of mortality. In *The Reasonableness of Christianity* he uses God's uncompromising words from Genesis 3:17–19 to characterise the mortal condition and the toil it entails: 'Cursed is the ground for thy sake: in sorrow shalt thou eat of it all the days of thy life; in the sweat of thy face shalt thou eat bread, till thou return into the ground'.[68] In *Homo Ante et Post Lapsum* he portrays property and labour as the outcomes of this curse and the cause of discord in human society:

> When private possessions and labour, which now the curse of the earth had made necessary, by degrees made a distinction of conditions, it gave room for covetousness, pride and ambition, which by fashion and example spread the corruption which has so prevailed over mankind.[69]

His references to 'fashion' and 'example' in this note reiterate his position that human corruption is not universal and innate but learnt.

This view of labour is strikingly different from that of Milton, for whom labour is the positive activity of paradise and the means to its restoration. It also differs from that of Locke's own political writings where labour is presented in more positive terms and where he shows himself to be as much in favour of hard work as the poet. In the *Second Treatise of Government* he links labour not only to man's need for sustenance but also to God's command in Genesis 1.28 to subdue the earth:

> God, when he gave the World in common to all Mankind, commanded Man also to labour, and the penury of his Condition required it of him. God and his Reason commanded him to subdue the Earth, *i.e.* improve it for the benefit of Life, and therein lay out something upon it that was his own, his labour.[70]

The imperative to work is both God's positive law and the natural law known to man through his reason. The inclusion of this pre-lapsarian command weakens the link between the Fall and labour in Locke's scheme. It is indicative of the distance of paradisiacal themes from the world that interests Locke in his political writings that the labour that seems a curse in his discussions of the Fall is praised for its benefits in his *Second Treatise*.[71] These benefits are set out in material rather than spiritual terms. Locke calculates the added value given to a piece of land by cultivation, the difference between the value of an acre planted with tobacco or sugar, wheat or barley, and one held in common without any husbandry, and reflects on the comforts of life that are earned through industry; bread, wine, cloth and silk are preferable to acorns, water, leaves and skins as resources for living.[72] The reference to the difference between the lives of American Indians and those of the Europeans is clear. This is the pragmatic voice of the man who would later become a founder member of the Board of Trade and as such architect of the old colonial system.[73] His theory of labour and its outcomes does not have the same concern with the grand narrative of redemption and salvation as the 'good employment' of Eliot's Indians, the heroics of Milton's Englishmen seeking God's truth in their studies, or the eschatological hope of Winstanley's diggers.[74] Daniel Judah Elazar wrote of Locke's model: 'No longer a community of the faithful engaged in the Lord's work, civil society was to be a commercial association of individuals engaged in private enterprise'.[75] It is a model that has led to the association of Locke with the rise of capitalism.[76] This commercialism is tempered with a civic morality whereby all have responsibility for the well-being of each other and no one should take to himself so much property that he leaves any of his fellow men destitute.[77] Locke's model was not devoid of reference to God, however, and his morality was bound up with the need to please Him. Nevertheless, he shows little interest in a millennial dawn in his scheme of things. In many ways Locke's society is most similar to the morally and civilly good society advocated by Williams for the present moment of interlude and calm in the grand drama of salvation.

Had Locke been more interested in Adam as story he might have given greater moment to the loss of immortality as the consequence of Adam's act of disobedience, as so much of his theorising of human society hangs on the fact of man's vulnerability to death. Natural Law consists of the right and obligation to preserve the self and mankind in general.[78] Adam's act, by imposing mortality upon himself and his successors, could be viewed as both breaking that law and establishing the law (dependent as it is on the possibility of death) at the same time. Locke, however, does not show much interest in the drama of the event but moves in another direction in *The Reasonableness of Christianity* to play down the magnitude of the change entailed in this post-lapsarian state of mortality. Concerned that his readers might understand mortality as a punishment meted out by an unjust God on all men for the sin committed by one, Locke explains that immortality was not a due that Adam or any of his descendants could claim as their right, but a free gift from God (a *donum superadditum*), which not to receive is not to be punished.[79] Locke makes it clear that Adam's fall does not deny to any of his descendants the possibility of attaining immortality and bliss, for 'those who have lived in exact conformity to the law of God are out of reach of death', though in practice no one has achieved this state of perfection.[80] Although the context of man's existence may have changed from one where death was a threatened punishment for just one particular act (the eating of the forbidden fruit) to one where death is an ever-present reality, Adam's transgression does not appear to have resulted in a new state of being. It could be conceded that men's vulnerability to death after Adam's Fall is the same as Adam's before the Fall as it was an inability to live in exact conformity to God's law that lost him his immortality. He may have had far fewer temptations, but the first man was arguably more susceptible to the specific temptation that existed for him (the eating of a piece of fruit) than many of his descendants would have been given the same prohibition. We learn in the *Second Treatise of Government* that 'the Law that was to govern *Adam*, was the same that was to govern all his Posterity'.[81] It was the law of reason (that was also the law of nature) directed at the preservation of self and the other human beings who were to follow.[82] Although he was created in full possession of his reason, Adam's exercise of reason, like that of other men, was not infallible. He made a basic and common error by letting his better judgement be overruled by his appetite and reasoning wrongly where his best interests lay. It appears then that, though the context may have been far removed, Adam's act of disobedience was not qualitatively different from sinful deeds committed by individual descendants of his.

Locke's answer to the question 'What have we lost by Adam?' would thus seem to be 'Not very much'. In his scheme the event and the story of Adam's Fall are not the determining factors for the condition of man that others have made them out to be. In *The Reasonableness of Christianity*, Locke explains that it is the purity of God rather than the fallenness of Adam that makes it so difficult for men to obey all of God's commands and so ensure that ultimate preservation of self that is eternal life; 'It was such a law as the purity of God's nature required, and must be the law of such a creature as man'.[83] Had the law not been so hard, God would have created rational beings but not required them to use their reason; the result would have been 'disorder, confusion and wickedness in his creatures'. Each man's relationship to the law and the law-maker is thus direct, not mediated through Adam – the only acknowledged mediator in this relationship is Christ. The difficulty of keeping God's law by reason alone is the context for his saving grace, 'considering the frailty of man'.[84] Christ offers an alternative route through the law of faith to eternal life, a law that requires honest effort to fulfil God's commands while allowing for error. In his theological treatise Locke undertakes a careful examination of the Gospels to identify the plain and intelligible fundamentals of the faith by which a man might be saved. In his account of the day of judgement his interest is predominantly in which individuals will and which will not enter Christ's Kingdom (and on what criteria) rather than in a triumphant and glorious overthrow of the old order.[85] In his political works, on the other hand, the focus is on the observance of that law of nature and law of reason sufficient for the security of person and property within a worldly context of human interaction. The emphasis is less on the difficulty of the law, more on the consequences for man's political freedom and earthly well-being of its contravention; loss of liberty rather than that of eternal life is the primary concern. In Filmer's theory, the chief object of Locke's criticism in these works, this liberty is threatened not so much by Adam's fallen as by his elevated state.

What Adam has lost by Locke

Filmer (like Locke) does not accord great significance to the Fall in his political theory. He is not interested in any merging of Adam's story and condition with those of men in general; rather, his argument is based on the distinctiveness of Adam; for Filmer, Adam's unique creation, his paternal authority and God's gift of dominion to him alone raise him, and his immediate heirs, above the rest of mankind. In his *First Treatise* Locke tackles each of these three elements of distinctiveness with line-by-line and word-by-word refutations of Filmer's arguments, the details of which it is unnecessary to rehearse in this chapter. It is in some respects a clearing of the ground for Locke's construction of his thesis in the *Second Treatise*, so he can begin Book II with the claim that he has 'clearly made out, it is impossible that the Rulers now on Earth, should make any benefit, or derive any the least shadow of authority from that, which is held to be the Fountain of all Power, *Adam's Private Dominion and Paternal Jurisdiction*', and go on to state that the purpose of this second part is to 'find out another rise of Government, another Original of Political Power'.[86] However, this is not a liberation of political thinking from a 'timeless stasis' of Adamic patriarchalism to make way for a modern progressive civil society.[87] The arguments of both treatises, the repetition and development of themes (the diverse character and origins of political societies across the world and in history; the limits paternal authority; the obligations of man to God as his creator) present a different understanding of Adam's relationship to the rest of mankind that has implications for the significance of Adam as well as for the nature of man and that ends up with man no less bound to his Maker than he was when Adam was held to have the decisive role. The process involves a minimisation of the differentiation between Adam and the rest of the human race that underpins Filmer's thesis while avoiding the suggestion that Adam thereby becomes everyman. Rather Locke counters arguments from Adam's distinctiveness by suggesting that he was not a representative of all men but a man much like any other.

In his *Treatises of Government* Locke does not deny the uniqueness of Adam's creation straight from the hand of God 'without Intervention of Parents or the pre-existence of any of the same Species to beget him', but he reduces its significance first by questioning the assumption that Adam has the right to rule all those whose creation was less direct, then more importantly by emphasising that all men are created by God.[88] He reduces the role of parents, particularly the father, by arguing that the act of begetting is not an act of creation as it is not purposeful. Procreation is not foremost in the father's mind at that time; indeed the begetting of a new human being is often an unwanted consequence of a thoughtless gratification of desire.[89] Furthermore, parents lack the intimate knowledge of the inner workings of their children (and, more poignantly, the knowledge of how to restore them to health should these workings fail) that they would have were they indeed the creators.[90] This knowledge is God's alone, and so parents beget children 'not as their own workmanship, but the Workmanship of their Maker, the Almighty, to whom they were to be accountable for them'.[91] By this logic the difference between Adam's origins and those of the rest of mankind is not as great as Filmer implies, and arguments from this difference to sovereignty over others are weakened. The concept of man as God's workmanship comes to play a crucial role in Locke's interpretation of the aims of political society and the regulation of men's relations within it.

Recognition of God's own workmanship in each human being diminishes the natural authority of the father, and thus the authority that Adam might have as first father over his descendants. According to Locke, the child does not belong to the parent, and a father's power over his children is indirect, a delegated responsibility for their education and well-being to cover their period of minority when they lack the resources to pursue their true interests and secure their own preservation. The dominion parents have over their children during their years of dependency 'is but a help to the weakness and imperfection of their Nonage' and not a limitation of their freedom for 'to turn [the child] loose to an unrestrain'd Liberty, before he has Reason to guide him, is not allowing him the priviledge of his Nature, to be free; but to thrust him out among Brutes, and abandon him to a state as wretched, and as much beneath that of a man as theirs'.[92] Any parental power that the father has in practice is inseparably linked to nourishment and education and not at all to the act of generation, for if a father gives up the care of his children to another he then loses power over them.[93] In return the child has obligations to honour his parents once he has grown in gratitude to the degree to which they have nurtured and tended him, involving him in 'all actions of relief, assistance and comfort of those, by whose means he entered into being, and has been made capable of any enjoyments of life'.[94] For Locke the family is then based on (no more than) a model of contractual and mutual obligations similar to the model of the political realm in his thought; it is a temporary rather than a binding relationship for as long as it is in the interests of the parties involved.

Locke finds no natural reason that Adam, as first created and first father, should have lasting dominion over other men. Filmer's third proof, that Adam was granted dominion by God's appointment giving him authority by decree rather than by nature, Locke opposes with a combination of Scripture proof and reason. He cites Filmer's faulty interpretation of the noun 'man' and pronouns 'them' and 'they' in the Genesis text, argues from the

Bible that dominion was given to the whole species of men, that this was the case when God gave dominion jointly to Adam and Eve (the only members of the species at the time) and again, after the Flood, to Noah and all members of his family. Not willing to concede that God's positive law can contradict natural law, he reasons that for God to do otherwise than give all things in common would entail a denial of the law of nature, which binds each man to his own preservation. God, having told men to 'increase and multiply' would not then have made them dependent for their subsistence on the will of a man who had the power to destroy them, by withholding their rights to food and clothing should he so wish.[95] Empirically based arguments are used as Locke musters his knowledge of different human societies and their histories to demolish Filmer's thesis. At the simplest level he disputes the right of any contemporary ruler to claim power through inheritance from Adam by employing the argument of interruption; it is not possible to trace an unbroken succession back to the first sovereign of the world. Even if Filmer were not mistaken (and Locke clearly thinks he was) about Adam's right to an absolute supreme authority that could be transmitted genealogically to future kings and governors, what Locke calls 'all this ado about Adam's Fatherhood, the greatness of its Power, and the necessity of its supposal' could be 'of no use to the Government of Mankind now in the World' when it cannot be known to whom that power currently by right belongs, and so 'we must seek some other Original of Power for the Government of Politys then this of *Adam*, or else there will be none at all in the World'.[96]

Although Locke has no doubt that Adam was indeed an historical figure, his arguments in the *Treatises* serve to diminish his historical significance, whether in a story of the corruption and regeneration of man or in a Bible-based genealogy of the human race. Knowledge of other nations and civilisations with their own narratives is employed to demonstrate the limits of traditional conceptualisations of human history based on Biblical chronology and any concept of descent of sovereignty through Adam, Noah and the lordship of Noah's sons. Locke's interpretation of mankind and of human society is not limited to those nations that 'believe the Bible'. When Filmer claims that 'most of the civillest Nations of the Earth, labour to fetch their Original from some of the Sons or Nephews of Noah', he counters with:

> I fear the *Chineses*, a very great and civil People, as well as several other People of the *East, West, North* and *South*, trouble not themselves about this matter.[97]

At the other end of the scale from this 'very great and civil People', Locke also observes that America 'is still a Pattern of the first Ages in *Asia* and *Europe*' and that there are many parts of the land where there is no government at all.[98] With civilised nations that find alternative origins for their forms of governance and other peoples that appear to be at different stages of political development or to have missed out on government at all, it is difficult to uphold the theory of a universal rolling out of political society from the lordship of Adam. The story fragments and resolves itself into a series of particular histories. The different circumstances in which different peoples find themselves mean they take different routes to political society and select different forms of governance. The conditions of life in the Americas are used to explain the particular forms of political organisation or absence of them in these parts of the world. Locke argues that the vastness of the American wilderness means it is much easier for men there to work a piece of land and make it their own without the fear of encroachment on each other's property that is a prime motivator for coming together into political society.[99] Quoting Josephus Acosta's history of the Indies, Locke notes how different peoples in those parts of the world might form temporary groupings and choose captains for themselves according to whether or not they are threatened by war with their neighbours.[100] Distance from the 'Conquering Swords' of the Peruvian or Mexican empires seems to be a key factor here.[101] He concedes that historically political societies have often begun with the concentration of authority into the hands of one man, often into the hands of the father of the family group, but he argues that this was not *jure divino* but because, in simpler societies, innocent of the ambition and luxury of later ages, such a figure might be trusted to put the common good before his own.[102] The logic of Filmer's genealogical model of patriarchalism leads to only one possible divinely decreed form of government, the absolute sovereignty of Adam's heirs – it is a unifying model.[103] Locke's particularism, his acknowledgement of the influence of context and circumstance, means that for him (as for Williams) political society begins with individuals joining together and setting up 'what form of Government they thought fit', be it a democracy, an oligarchy, an hereditary or elective monarchy.[104]

The original

Locke acknowledged that the big question of his age and all ages is who should have power. In his *Treatise* his declared aim is to find this out. Filmer's answer to the same question is soundly rejected; Locke seeks the original of political power not in Adam but in the natural state of men. Chapter 2 of the *Second Treatise* details the different characteristics of this state, the most significant of these being man's natural liberty and his natural equality:

> To understand Political Power right, and derive it from its Original, we must consider what State all Men are naturally in, and that is, a *State of perfect Freedom* to order their Actions, and dispose of their Possessions, and persons as they think fit, within the bounds of the Law of Nature, without asking leave, or depending upon the Will of any other Man. A *State* also *of Equality*, wherein all the Power and Jurisdiction is reciprocal, no one having more than another.[105]

Within this state men are governed not by human law but by the law of nature, which is the law of reason. They are also subject to the invasions of individuals who choose to break that law and so they have the natural right ('the Executive Power of the Law of Nature') to punish the offender and seek reparation for injury.[106] It is, Locke acknowledges, a state that has great inconveniences, not just the depredations of these offenders but the likelihood that men will be carried too far in their revenge and the punishment of those against whom they have a grievance. Civil government becomes desirable to protect lives and property and to restrain the partiality and violence of men.[107] It is achieved by groups of men consenting to give up their natural liberty and executive power and make one body politic under one government.[108] Man's natural state is described in terms that put him in a particular relationship with other men. His freedom is a freedom from others, his equality an equality with others, his rights are rights to preserve and defend himself against the incursions of others. Rather than looking back to Adam as the solitary origin of the human condition, Locke finds the original of political power in a plurality of human beings.

Although he argued that all human society began in this way – as in his celebrated phrase, 'in the beginning all the World was *America*' – Locke admitted in his *Second Treatise* that there are in fact very few recorded accounts in history of men living together in a state of nature; the inconveniences of this state are so great that no sooner do men group together than they tend to form a political society.[109] This and Locke's readiness to argue from empirically grounded knowledge of human activity raise the question as to why he felt he had to look beyond examples of actual political societies to a less readily identifiable state of nature. Why did he not adopt Bodin's inductive method, comparing states, identifying what they had in common, where they differed and drawing conclusions about human society from these?[110] There are indeed similarities in the two writer's outlooks; they had the same interest in the varied influences of environmental factors and sense of the mutability of the human world and of the individual states of which it is constituted. Nevertheless, Locke had his reasons for wanting to trace the original. His interest in the people's rights of resistance to an overweening power meant that he needed a point of reference outside the framework of the political state.

Locke's search did not take him back to the garden or to the dawning of time. He was curious about historical societies, as he was about contemporary geographically distant societies, for the insights they afforded into a diversity of human experience and behaviour, but he was not interested in historical determinism, whether the genealogical inheritance from Adam, the rolling out of human history from Adam's transgression or the efforts of some contemporaries to fit the far-flung nations of the earth into a universal Biblical chronology. His concern was more with man's state than with his story. The ahistorical character of his interpretation of man's original state of nature is evident in the examples he used to show that, though this state of nature is not a current reality in most of societies across the world, it is present as a constant alternative. His perception that there are still some peoples in the Americas to whom this state applies has been mentioned. In his *Second Treatise* Locke offers several other occasions in which the relationship between men can be described in this way because, in the context in which they find themselves, they have not been joined to each other in a contract or elected any third party the power to regulate their dealings. He uses an illustration of two men who find themselves together on a desert island and of a Swiss and an Indian who encounter each other in the woods of America.[111] The rulers of individual nations too are in a state of nature vis-à-vis each other, with no sovereign authority to arbitrate between them.[112] The movement from the state of nature into civil society is not a one-off event in the history of a people; rather, he suggests, men can move to and fro between 'the loose State of Nature' and 'Politick society' according to circumstance and choice.[113] If the polity is going astray, in particular if the members' lives are no longer secure and their liberties are being encroached upon, a reversion to a state of nature and original liberty is an opportunity to readjust, to rebalance and, by mutual consent, return to a state of governance where the foundational principle of the preservation of self and property is upheld. Chapter XIX of the *Second Treatise* is concerned with the different conditions that require such dissolution of government and temporary recourse to a government-less state preliminary to the appointment of a new government of the people's choice. The circumstances he describes for this reversion to a natural state are very pertinent to the late Stuart politics in which he was engaged. They include cases where the sovereign sets up own will in place of laws declared by the legislative, where he hinders the legislative from meeting in due time or acting freely, where he alters the elections or election process, where he encroaches upon people's property and exercises absolute power over the lives, liberties and estates of the people; where he uses force, treasure or offices to corrupt the people's representatives.[114] Locke argues that the inconveniences of such conditions are worse than in the state of nature and the 'remedy farther off and more difficult'.[115] In this final chapter and culmination of his treatises, Locke does exactly what he said he would and returns to the original to determine the legitimate exercise of power for his day. At the same time he has provided a powerful justification for the events of the 1689 Revolution.

Locke sought a political stability based on eternal principles and maintained through timely readjustment and realignment should the actions of any of the key players threaten the equilibrium of the settlement. In the *First Treatise* Locke emphasised that stability was dependent on legitimacy, without which the polity would be plunged into 'endless contention and disorder'.[116] By the end of his *Two Treatises* it is evident that Locke's answer to the question, 'Who has the right?' is the one (or the body) to whom power is granted by agreement of the people. Power is legitimated by, and continues to rest upon, the people's consent. Earlier in this chapter Sidney was quoted as saying that the people's right to delegate their own power to another should be grounded in the will of God. This grounding would give the political system the ideological weight of a transcendent moral force, such as that claimed by the covenantal communities of New England, for example, where God is viewed as a third party in any political settlement or indeed in Filmer's model where political power is granted by divine decree.

While he did not doubt Adam's creation or his identity as our first ancestor, Locke effectively uncoupled men's current condition from his story. The fact of Creation and the relationship that it sets up between God and man is nevertheless essential to Locke's scheme; his political theory did not constitute a withdrawal of God from the affairs of men. Locke's emphasis on contracts and compacts between men as the founding acts of civil society has enabled secular readings of his *Second Treatise* in particular. Elazar characterises Locke's system in this way 'if individuals could not love their neighbours covenantally as fellow Christians they could at least love their neighbours contractually as potential consumers and business partners'.[117] Locke himself, however, acknowledged the influence of the divine law-giver in these dealings. It is an influence exercised above all through the guidance of man's reason, which, in Locke's thinking, is none other than 'the voice of God in him'.[118] He uses St Paul in *The Reasonableness of Christianity* to correlate that voice with conscience and reason's activity with the work of God's law written in men's hearts.[119] In the *First Treatise* he explains that it is God who directs man, through his senses and his reason, towards whatever is serviceable for the preservation of his being. In the *Second Treatise*, he argues that in the state of nature, it is God's measure of right and wrong (knowable through reason) that each man is to use to judge the actions of another and punish his or her transgressions.[120] He also suggests that faced with the inconveniences and insecurity of the natural state, men are led by this same reasoning to consent to the establishment of a political society. God has a presence of sorts in the societal compact between men; Locke writes of 'reason which God hath given to be the Rule betwixt Man and Man, and the common bond whereby humane kind is united into one fellowship and societie'.[121] For men to go against this reason and act in a way detrimental to that preservation of self is to go against God's command. As Locke writes in *The Reasonableness of Christianity*:

> To disobey God in any of his commands, (and 'tis he that commands what reason does,) is direct rebellion; which, if dispensed with at any point, government and order are at an end; and there can be no bounds set to the lawless exorbitancy of unconfined man.[122]

Although Locke tended to reserve the term 'covenant' for covenants of faith (to Abraham) and grace (through Christ to Christians) in the context of salvation, this quotation suggests a threefold covenantal relationship: man with magistrate with God. Indeed, if God is not part of the covenant then it cannot hold. This is the understanding at the root of the refusal of toleration to atheists in his *Letter concerning Toleration:*

> Those are not at all to be tolerated who deny the Being of a God. Promises, Covenants, and Oaths, which are the Bonds of Humane Society, can have no hold upon an Atheist. The taking away of God, tho but even in thought, dissolves all.[123]

In Locke's scheme God does not just guide the process of men coming together but, in a combination of gift and command, supplies them with the powerful motive for their association. In *The Reasonableness of Christianity* Locke declares that not only immortality but life itself is a free gift from God to men out of His goodness and not their deserving:

> Nay, if God afford them a Temporary Mortal Life, 'tis his Gift, they owe it to his Bounty, they could not claim it as their Right, nor does he injure them when he takes it from them.[124]

The idea that a man's life is not his own by right but is in the gift of his Maker is expressed in the *Treatises* in Locke's discussion of a father's power over his children. It is developed in the concept of each man being God's workmanship.[125] As such he is made to last during God's and not his own or any other man's pleasure.[126] The concept has implications for men's relations with each other; not having arbitrary power over his own life, a man cannot give another man power over it, to protect or destroy at will.[127] In turn a man is bound, as far as he can without harm to himself, to preserve the lives of other men.[128] Although men cannot claim life as a right from their Maker, their duty to preserve that life bountifully given means they now have rights vis-à-vis each other. The fact that the facilitation of human ends and facilitation of divine ends so exactly correspond means there is a convergence of human rights and duties owed to God.

The significance of man as God's workmanship extends beyond a code of conduct, to provide the underlying legitimacy for the whole of Locke's political model based as it is on men's strong desire for self-preservation. This very desire, he argues, is subservient to God's design 'that Man should live and abide for some time upon the Face of the Earth, and not that so curious and wonderful a piece of Workmanship by its own Negligence, or want of Necessities, should perish'.[129] Locke's words suggest, importantly, not a 'first cause' deism, but God's continuing pleasure in this wonderful piece of workmanship and concern that it should abide. Ultimately, what underpins the whole process of the formation and regulation of the polity is not that man has a natural inclination towards his self-preservation but that God wills and decrees it. Its foundation is a relationship that echoes the keen personal interest and direction evident in God's dealings with the new creation of man as described in the first chapters of Genesis.

192   John Locke, Adam and the original of power

For Locke the right to govern rests on the consent of the people. The origins of the people's power are traced to a state of nature where men are led by divine imperative embedded in reason to seek their own preservation and that of mankind. The legitimation of that desire as the principle for human action and political association is found in God's will. Locke's polity is thus both ideological and pragmatic as men are commanded by God, through their reason, to work out what is the best form of government in their circumstances to serve their self-interest and thereby to fulfil the purposes of their Maker present in their creation. As with Filmer's model, the beginnings of Locke's theory of the polity can be traced to the activity of Creation, but in his case it is an on-going activity repeated for each and every new man rather than a single historic event. The creation of each human being in our world is given the same significance as the creation of Adam in the garden.

Notes

1. Hans Aarsleff, 'Locke's influence' in *The Cambridge Companion to Locke*, edited by Vere Chappell (Cambridge: Cambridge University Press 1994), 253.
2. An illustration of such claims for Locke's modernity and universal relevance is Van Der Pijl Kees's discussion of 'Lockean liberalisation' in western societies: 'So that it is possible to write of 2006 interpretation of modern European politics resistance of statist to 'Lockean embrace' liberalisation of Anglophone civil society v state' Van Der Pijl, Kees 'A Lockean Europe?' *New Left Review*, 37 (2006): 9–37.
3. This development was resourced by the Bodleian Library's acquisition of the Lovelace Collection of Locke's papers.
    Laslett's edition was the key turning point: *John Locke, Two Treatises of Government*, edited by Peter Laslett (Cambridge: Cambridge University Press, 1960); also John Dunn, *The Political Thought of John Locke: An Historical Account of the Argument of the 'Two Treatises of Government'* (Cambridge: Cambridge University Press, 1969).
4. Mark Knights, 'John Locke and Post-Revolutionary Politics: Electoral Reform and the Franchise' *Past and Present* 213, 1 (2011): 41–86, p. 42.
5. This is acknowledged by Knights: 'Once assumed to have been a justification of the revolution of 1688, his *Two Treatises* are now located amongst the radical Whig writings of the late 1670s or early 1680s' – Knights, *op. cit.*, 41.
6. Dunn, *Political Thought*, 51; Richard Ashcraft, 'Locke's political philosophy', in *The Cambridge Companion to Locke*, edited by Vere Chappell (Cambridge: Cambridge University Press, 1994), 226.
7. 2TG, Preface, 137.
8. James Tyrell, *A Brief Enquiry into the Ancient Constitution and Government of England as Well in Respect of the Administration, as Succession Thereof ... By a True Lover of His Country. (1695)* (EEBO Editions, Proquest, 2011).
9. There are references to Hunton in Locke when he repeats 'the old question' Hunton posed about who shall be the judge' of the excesses of the sovereign – 2TG, 379.
10. Having described Locke's *Treatises* as a political act Ashcraft recognises that in writing them Locke was attempting to realise several objectives, not only

offering justification for resistance to the actions of Charles II or James II but also, for example, supplying a solution to intellectual problems raised by the writings of Hugh Grotius or Samuel Pufendorf.
11. Laslett's introduction to his 1960 edition of the *Two Treatises of Government* (78), while Dunn finds incongruity 'there can be read in the Two Treatises, oddly side by side, both a systematic moral apologia for the political attitudes of the Exclusionists and a theological proclamation of the autonomous rights of all men in the conduct of politics' – Dunn, *Political Thought*, 51.
12. *1TG*, 106.
13. James Tully writes of the legitimation crisis of sixteenth- and seventeenth-century Europe and identifies the four problems that faced all major thinkers of the seventeenth century: the theoretical nature of government and political power, the relation of religion to politics, the practical art of governing and the types of knowledge involved in religion and in political theory and practice. James Tully, *An Approach to Political Philosophy: Locke in Contexts* (Cambridge: Cambridge University Texts, 1993), 9–10.
14. Algernon Sidney, *Discourses Concerning Government* vol. 2 (Edinburgh: G. Hamilton and J. Balfour, 1750), 6.
15. Stillingfleet, cited by Aarsleff, 'Locke's Influence', 263. Locke answers these accusations in two *Vindications of his Reasonableness of Christianity*, printed with *TRC*, 159f, 191f.
16. George Kateb, 'Locke and the Political Origins of Secularism' *Social Research: An International Quarterly* Volume 76, Number 4/ Winter (2009), 1001–1034, p. 1001; 'It is important to emphasise that for most of human history thinkers about religion, not just Locke, wrote or spoke with a caution bred of fear. We have to admit we will never know what some of them really thought' – Ibid., 1002.
17. Dunn, *Political Thought*.
18. Ibid., 99.
19. Later Dunn did concede some lasting influence to selected elements of Locke's political thought in John Dunn, 'What is Living and What is Dead in the Political Theory of John Locke', in *Locke. Vol. II*, edited by Dunn and Harris (Cheltenham: Edward Elgar Publishing, 1997).
20. Dunn, *Political Thought*, 263.
21. Ibid., 264.
22. Waldron, *God, Locke*, 20.
23. Ibid., 9.
24. Cited in Ashcraft, *Locke's Political Philosophy*, 235.
25. *1TG*, 151.
26. *1TG*, 184.
27. *TRC*, 4; Locke employs the term 'under labourer' to describe his method in his *Essay Concerning Human Understanding*.
28. Locke describes his exegetical method in the preface to his paraphrases to St Paul's epistles – *PN*, xiii–xiv.
29. Reference to the Adam – Christ typology can be found in *TRC*, 9, and Locke's paraphrases of St Paul's Epistles written towards the end of his life and published posthumously – *PN*, 174.
30. *1TG*, 173.
31. *1TG*, 175; A. refers to 'Author' means Filmer.
32. *TRC*, 5, 146.

33. *OCU*, Section 32, 209.
34. *1TG*, 161.
35. *1TG*, 161.
36. Aarsleff, 'Locke's Influence', 258.
37. *2TG*, 319–20.
38. John Locke, *The Works of John Locke in Ten Volumes Vol. 9* (London: W. Otridge and Son, 1812), 47f.
39. *OCU*, Section 2, 167.
40. *STCE*, Section 116, 91; *STCE*, Section 27, 37.
41. *ECHU*, I: IV, 57.
42. Aarsleff sees Locke as having played a crucial role in a shift in language theory from what he sees as the restrictions of 'Adamism'. Hans Aarsleff, *From Locke to Saussure: Essays in the Study of Language and Intellectual History* (Minneapolis: University of Minnesota Press, 1982).
43. *TRC*, 4.
44. *TRC*, 7–8. In this Locke shares Winstanley's view that 'when a man fals let him not blame a man that died 6000 years ago but blame himself' *NLR-CW*, I, 500.
45. *TRC*, 10, 112.
46. *TRC*, 8.
47. *TRC*, 6.
48. *1TG*, 171.
49. *1TG*, 173.
50. Locke begins *The Reasonableness of Christianity* with the question 'what the scriptures show we have lost by Adam'. To know this, he declares, is essential for understanding 'what we are restored to by Jesus Christ'. *TRC*, 4.
51. W. M. Spellmann, *John Locke and the Problem of Depravity* (Oxford: Clarendon Press, 1988), 104ff.
52. *TRC*, 152.
53. Locke's Third Letter (Works VI, 409–12), see John Marshall, *John Locke: Resistance, Religion and Responsibility* (Cambridge: Cambridge University Press, 1994), 327. Article IX of the Thirty Nine Articles concerns Original Sin.
54. *TRC*, 7.
55. *TRC*, 6.
56. Rom. 5:12; *PN*, xvi.
57. Paraphrase of Rom. 5:12, *PN*, 293.
58. *A Vindication of the Reasonableness of Christianity & From Mr Edwards's Reflections, A Second Vindication of the Reasonableness of Christianity*, in *TRC; TRC*, 169.
59. *ECHU*, IV, XX, 17.
60. *TRC*, 144; *2TG*, 352.
61. John Locke, *Locke: Political Essays* edited by Mark Goldie (Cambridge: Cambridge University Press, 1997) 320; see also Marshall, *John Locke*, 397.
62. In this journal note Locke is less rigid about the distinction between Adam the man and man as the human species. He applies the probationary law forbidding the fruit to man in general whereas in *The Reasonableness of Christianity* mention of God's positive law given to Adam about the fruit is immediately followed by the statement that some of God's laws are only intended for particular times, places and persons – TRC, 13.
63. *TRC*, 7.

64. *TRC*, 7.
65. *2TG*, 285–86.
66. *2TG*, 287–88.
67. *2TG*, 350–51.
68. *TRC*, 7.
69. John Locke, *Political Essays*, 321.
70. *2TG*, 291.
71. There may be a difference in time here, the theological writings referred to being written a few years later than the revision and publication of the *Treatises*, though the different foci and purposes of the works would account for this difference in treatment of a shared theme.
72. *2TG*, 296, 297.
73. The Board of Trade was founded in 1696; Laslett's introduction to his 1960 edition of *The Two Treatises of Government*, 39.
74. The educational writings of Milton and Locke show the contrast between their approaches, Locke interested in the social stability that comes with moral propriety ('a healthy mind in a healthy body' is his declared goal for young learners) while Milton's educational theory aims for the creation of heroes, 'brave men and worthy patriots'. *STCE*, 10; *TE*, 7.
75. Daniel Judah Elazar, *Covenant and Civil Society: The Constitutional Matrix of Modern Democracy* (New Brunswick, NJ: Transaction Publishers, 1998), 45.
76. Neil J. Mitchell 'John Locke and the Rise of Capitalism' in *History of Political Economy* Summer 1986 18(2): 291–305.
77. *1TG*, 170.
78. *2TG*, 271.
79. *TRC*, 7–8.
80. *TRC*, 10.
81. *2TG*, 305.
82. Of God's gift to man, he writes: 'He gave him reason, and with it a law that could not be otherwise than what reason should dictate: unless we should think that a reasonable creature should have an unreasonable law' – *TRC*, 157.
83. *TRC*, 11.
84. *TRC*, 157.
85. *TRC*, 109–14.
86. *2TG*, 267.
87. As in Aarsleff's understanding, Aarsleff, 'Locke's Influence'.
88. *1TG*, 151. This emphasis on God's role in the creation of *all* men has essential links to Locke's thesis whereby what one has made – i.e. mixed one's labour with – is one's own property.
89. *1TG*, 179.
90. *1TG*, 179.
91. *2TG*, 305.
92. *2TG*, 309.
93. *2TG*, 310–11.
94. *2TG*, 311–12.
95. *1TG*, 169.
96. *1TG*, 232, 203, 203.
97. *1TG*, 243.

98. *2TG*, 339, 335.
99. *2TG*, 293.
100. *2TG*, 335.
101. *2TG*, 337.
102. *2TG*, 341–43.
103. Locke declares that according to the logic of Filmer's model there can only be one rightful sovereign for all the peoples of the world – *1TG*, 217.
104. *2TG*, 337, 354.
105. *2TG*, 269.
106. *2TG*, 275, 272.
107. *2TG*, 276.
108. *2TG*, 332.
109. *2TG*, 334. For the statement that 'all the World was America', *2TG*, 301.
110. We know that Locke read Bodin as he recommended him as reading to his students at Oxford.
111. *2TG*, 277.
112. *2TG*, 277.
113. *2TG*, 406.
114. References to these cases can be found respectively in *2TG*, 408; *2TG*, 409 – a reference to Charles II's dissolution of parliament; *2TG*, 409 – a reference to Charles II and James II's attempts to alter parliamentary franchise by remodelling the charters of the borough; *2TG*, 412–13; *2TG*, 413 – a reference to James II's attempts to control the electorate.
115. *2TG*, 415.
116. *1TG*, 219.
117. Elazar, *Covenant and Civil Society*, 45.
118. *1TG*, 205.
119. *TRC*, 13. Citing Romans 2:13–14.
120. *2TG*, 298. This is in keeping with St Paul (Romans 2:14) as cited by Locke in *The Reasonableness of Christianity*; men's consciences bear witness to God's law within them 'and amongst themselves their thoughts accusing or excusing one another'. *TRC*, 13.
121. *2TG*, 382f.
122. *TRC*, 11.
123. *LCT*, 51.
124. *TRC*, 8.
125. *2TG*, 305, 271.
126. *2TG*, 271.
127. *2TG*, 323.
128. *2TG*, 271.
129. *1TG*, 205.

7 Eliot, Williams, Winstanley, Milton and Locke
Man's state and ongoing story

Recapitulation

The preceding four chapters have followed the Adamic threads through the writings of five focus authors. Although they have not exhausted the possible readings of Adam set out in Chapter 2, they have nevertheless provided illustrations of the complex interweaving of his plural significances in seventeenth-century political thought. This chapter involves a brief recapitulation of some of the main themes of these chapters in relation to the categories of state and story before taking the authors' stories forward to their conclusion, the interplay of different time frames impacting on the interpretation of that end.

In their writings about, and dealings with, the American Indians, Roger Williams and John Eliot (Chapter 3) give the figure of Adam a universal and universalising significance. His reach is extended to include the American Indians who, being descended from him, share in his natural state and fallen condition and, being included in his act of disobedience, are subject to its spiritual consequences. As the English too are part of the same story, it means that these different peoples become mirrors to each other, their customs and behaviours serving as each other's critiques and (in Eliot's understanding at least) the salvation of one advancing the salvation of the other. While both men believed in the story of the Fall and trusted in its eventual resolution with Christ, comparison of their works shows the difference between a story that has been interrupted by a period of waiting, of managing the day-to-day in the interim (Williams) and a continuously advancing story unfolding in the activities of humanity (Eliot). For the interim, man's natural state, and what persists of that which was 'good' in Creation, becomes the measure of the polity; it is based on moral and not spiritual distinctions for, while all men are sons of nature, the identity of those whom God has elected to be His sons by grace on the Last Day is knowable only to Him. The dynamism of the advancing story, on the other hand, gives eschatological significance to the actions of men and their politics; it looks to the transformation of the polity so that it becomes what God wants it to become and proactively sets the stage for Christ's coming in glory.

Chapter 4, by focusing on Winstanley alone, has shown an individual's creative (and occasionally confused) dialogue with the richness of the

Genesis story and its various traditions of interpretation. It reveals the flexibility of Adamic traditions (offering mystical, spiritual, historical and political interpretations) and their adaptability to a variety of circumstances and audiences. The contrast *between* Eliot and Williams is found *within* Winstanley as he moves from interest in Adam as story to interest in Adam as state. Like Eliot, he too was caught up in excitement of millennial expectations, and he too was led to adjust these expectations when his hopes failed to materialise. With his eschatological hopes deferred he, like Williams, proceeded to devote energy to a secular ordering of the polity for the meantime. Winstanley's different emphases have different implications for his politics. His tellings of the story of the first and second Adam deal with individual, universal and cosmic expectation and transformation, with the collapsing of the story (at all of these levels) into its final resolution and the absolutes of peace, equality, liberty and (because if these are secure no government is needed) of political anarchy. His mystical works and his digging experiment both indicate that by his calculation this ideal was soon to be realised; his other works express more limited (or delayed) ambitions. Where Adam as state was his theme, Winstanley presented him as both subject and sovereign. The subject was natural man in his created innocency, possessing simple childlike goodness but vulnerable to temptation (as the Adam of Genesis was) and therefore in need of the structures and guidance for citizens that Winstanley proposed in his *Platform*.[1] The sovereign is Adam as the father to whom his children naturally turn to ensure their safety, a pattern for the magistrate within Winstanley's commonwealth. The concept of man's state as good but fallible encouraged practical rather than ideal solutions to questions of government.

In *Paradise Lost*, Milton (Chapter 5) expanded on both Adam's state and his story. His descriptions of life in Eden, of the activity and relationship of Adam and Eve, embellish the original tales and fill out the pattern for the human behaviours and social structures they present. His descriptions of these carry echoes of Williams's accounts of Indian lives, the difference being that Milton inserts into his fictionalised account demonstrations of man's natural state (as interpreted by his theology), while Williams uses empirical observation to identify the persistence of this natural state in the behaviours of his Indians. In Milton's poem, Adam's conversations with angels constitute a process of 'emplotment' by which the first ancestors' experiences are placed within a wider narrative, extending back in time as well as forward into the future. They are given new significance as a result. In earlier chapters some tension has been suggested between the stability of Adam as state and the dynamism of Adam as story. Milton reduces the tension between them by presenting the natural conditions of Adam's life in Eden as part of the story. He does not interpret the paradisaical existence as the end for man decreed by God but sees it as a time of preparation for a higher state of being that can be obtained by diligent labour in obedience to God; there is a restlessness and positive ambition about it. This emphasis on movement forward towards a greater end means that human history can be viewed as a combination of advances and setbacks and difficulties viewed as barriers to be overcome in order to continue along the path divinely ordained for man. His *Ready and Easy Way* is a response to such a setback. In it he reduces his immediate ambitions for the English polity and, like Winstanley in his *Platform*, he sets out a careful description of how this less-than-perfect model might be managed. For Milton the Free Commonwealth is a stage along a journey to perfection. There are some commonalities here with other authors; for Milton and Eliot civic virtue, and for Winstanley a state of Gospel childlikeness, had to be achieved before the ushering in of the divinely ordained order on which they pinned their hopes. Milton's dynamic interpretation of both man's state and his story is able to encompass a providential role for his own nation, recognition of shortcomings and backslidings and possibilities of reform. Milton's Adam does not just serve as an explanation of the way things are, or as a justification for political change, but provides a clear pattern for man and nation in his pre-lapsarian state of activity and his post-lapsarian resolution to live a virtuous life and so attain greater things.

While, relative to the other authors, Locke (Chapter 6) gives Adam a reduced significance in his scheme, his political writing is still embedded within that seventeenth-century tradition of Adamic interpretation. Locke clearly accepts Adam as a historical figure and gives much space to the interpretation of his significance in his political treatises. He is very careful to stress that there is no contradiction between his political theory and belief in Adam's creation, but he does not afford the same prominence to Adam's story as a determining influence on the story of mankind. Locke progressively disconnects his theories of sovereignty and government from the narrative of Adam and from traditional views of the consequences of his fall. In his politics he tends to prefer stasis to dynamism provided personal liberty and property are secured; his interest is in stability, and he advocates political change only where it is needed to restore the terms of the compact and equilibrium between interests on which his polity is founded. Locke's political theory is based on man's natural state of being rather than his story. It is not teleological in the way of Eliot, Winstanley or Milton's political experiments or theoretical models. He is not setting up a temporary political order as a staging post to an as-yet-unfulfilled ideal. Locke is more like Williams in founding his polity on the natural state of man as created by God and his natural liberty, on natural law as knowable by reason and on the (divinely decreed) imperative of self-preservation. Provided those conditions are met, Locke, like Williams, is prepared to countenance a variety of forms of government based only and always on people's consent. Locke employed empirical evidence to illuminate man's natural state, yet there still exists a strong link with the experience of Adam; although we as humans do not derive our natural state from Adam, we do share it with him as fellow creatures of God. Ultimately, the state on which Locke built his scheme is man's state at Creation, and his theories of government can only be fully understood in this light. Locke's political model depends on his belief that like Adam all men (as individuals and as the human race) are God's workmanship; we do not belong to ourselves alone but to our Creator, are under His continuing direction and obligation to obey His command.

Interacting time frames

Key distinctions among the five authors' handling of Adamic themes revolve around questions of time and different time frames, human and sacred. Is the end of time imminent or to happen at some unknowable future date? Are the workings of the sacred time frame visible in the events of the human or will they break suddenly into earthly affairs? Should men look back in time and use the created state and fallen condition of Adam to regulate their affairs, or should they look forward to the resolution of the story with the coming of the Second Adam and direct their activities to this end? All of these questions are relevant to readings of the authors' work. The application of their theories to the experiences and pressing issues of their own times adds a more specific chronological context encouraging a historical reading bound by seventeenth-century horizons. In the centuries that followed the authors' own, their work has been brought into conversation with different historical eras introducing a series of new time-related questions: were the authors of their time, ahead of their time, let down by their own time, at the dawn of a new time? By some interpretations they have become part of the founding myths of various political systems (liberalism, communism, socialism, capitalism) and have themselves become the originals of a new 'modern' age.[2] The continual reshaping of the status and significance of each of these authors, and the way this relates to the experiences, preoccupations and philosophies of different ages, would make interesting studies but are beyond the scope of this book, which has set out from the beginning to examine their works within their own age.

Reading the authors within their seventeenth-century context acknowledges the contemporary interest of their writing, the directness of its address to contemporary figures (Williams to John Cotton and leaders of Massachusetts Bay colony, Eliot to the funders of his Indian enterprises, Winstanley to Fairfax and Cromwell), the engagement with the practical political circumstances of their day (Locke's detailing of the political misdemeanours of the Stuarts in his *Second Treatise of Government*, Milton's attempt, in his *Ready and Easy Way*, to find an alternative political solution in the midst of a constitutional crisis), the belief in the imminence of the transformation they expected (the 'now ... now ... now', 'in-our-time' expectation of Eliot and Winstanley). All five selected authors invested their intellectual and practical energies in the political reordering of their society, often at considerable cost and risk to themselves. Perhaps only Locke (with the Williamite settlement and constitutional monarchy of the later Stuarts) can be said to have seen the achievement of the political order he desired by the end of his life. The failure of the Digger experiment for Winstanley and of the republican experiment for Milton were undoubtedly occasions of deep disappointment for the two men, and some have read their writings from this period in this way.[3] That Winstanley's flurry of writing activity came to an end in 1652 has also been interpreted as the result of bitter disillusionment with the political sphere. Hill had Winstanley drifting into Quaker quietism – 'where else could he go after it became clear that Christ was not going to rise in Charles II's England?'[4] In this he likely overestimated both the quietism of Quakerism in this period and Winstanley's commitment to the movement.[5]

The New England authors also had cause for disenchantment. Roger Williams found the continual legal and boundary disputes of his colony of Providence Plantation and Rhode Island wearisome. In addition there were his heated debates with the Quakers who, in Williams's eyes, threatened chaos in their radical behaviour and beliefs and put his colony's founding principle, 'liberty of conscience' to the test. A further blow to his work were the Indian wars of 1675 and 1676 (King Philip's War), which wreaked havoc across the settlements of New England and tore apart the positive relations Williams had helped to build between the different nations.[6] For John Eliot, too, this war had a serious impact on his life's work, the Indian Praying Towns. The towns' inhabitants were caught between the two sides (Indian and English) and trusted by neither; ten of the fourteen towns were disbanded as a result.

Despite these multiple setbacks and disappointments the image of disillusionment and retreat is inadequate for the authors' responses to these events and their own circumstances. It has been argued in Chapters 4 and 5 that Winstanley and Milton's disappointments did not mean a loss of hope. As Christians they retained their faith that 'God is about the reformation of the world and he will go forward with his work', and they continued to find a role for themselves within his purposes. In her biography of the poet, Lewalski records the activity of Milton's final years, a busy-ness in keeping with his declaration in 1666, 'Let me not be useless whatever remains for me in this life'.[7] He had not given up on his project, though he may have revised its terms. In the very year of his death he published a second edition of *Paradise Lost* and the two new works *Paradise Regained* and *Samson Agonistes*. In this last work Milton reprises the argument of *The Ready and Easy Way* that it is never too late to reclaim one's freedom, but states that for this to happen there is needed a virtuous citizenry that understands what is at stake and values liberty. It has been described as 'a fit poetic climax to Milton's lifelong effort to help create such citizens'.[8] In contrast to Milton, Winstanley's publications dry up in his later years, but it appears he was active in another way. Local records show him taking on a number of citizenship duties, living out the role of overseer of community required in his *Platform*.[9] He appears to have held successive public offices, as Way-warden in the parish of Cobham in 1659, Overseer for the Poor in 1660,

Churchwarden in 1667–68, Chief Constable of Elmbridge in 1671, a degree of civic engagement that does not suggest someone defeated retiring to lick his wounds.[10] Both men thus remained active till the end of their lives in ways consistent with Milton's refusal to give up on the story that will end with man's regeneration and with Winstanley's understanding of how to live 'in the meantime', with the goodness yet fallibility that is the human state.

Neither did the New England authors give up hope in the face of their setbacks. Through all the difficulties of the Indian wars, Williams reminded his Massachusetts Bay contemporaries that 'our Candle [is] yet burning'. During that bloody conflict he wrote a letter to Connecticut's Governor Winthrop containing grim news about lives lost, but he ended it by asking, 'Why is our Candle yet burning but to ... [serve] God in serving the public in our generation?' That year he also wrote to Massachusetts Governor Leverett that while everyone was busy trying to keep their families from being murdered and homes from being burned, still the principal task remained, 'to listen to what the Eternal Speaketh to the whole ship (the Country, Colonies, Towns, ...) and each Private Cabin, family, person etc.'[11] Whatever the evils that afflict them God still speaks to His people and His people still have His work to do. Characteristically for his commitment to story, Eliot's expression of hope is somewhat different having a future orientation rather than present reassurance. Convinced that his own work contributed in some small way to God's plan for the world, he too showed trust in the face of the destruction of his Indian project:

> There is a cloud a dark cloud upon the work of the Gospel among the poor Indian. The Lord revive and prosper that work, and grant it may live when I am dead.[12]

Although Eliot and others may have had to reconcile themselves to the fact that they personally would not see the longed-for transformation of the world, yet they still trusted that the transformation would take place in the grand narrative of God's time.

The image of the disillusioned prophet is one that focuses on the smaller story of the personal biography of the writer, and it is the case with some of the authors that their political writings and activities are closely bound to a sense of a singular and personal calling and destiny. Milton's work is shot through with autobiographical detail. It is very likely he saw himself as one among the succession of isolated righteous men presented in various of his prose and poetical works (including the magisterial reformers in *Of Reformation* and Archangel Michael's pageant in *Paradise Lost*) who, through the ages have been brave enough to stand up against forces of oppression.[13] Williams's *Key* relates his own experience of exile. It seems he aspired to be one of the 'prophets in sackcloth' whom God had raised up to spread the gospel and guide his people in the wilderness, though their remit fell short of founding particular churches.[14] Winstanley was accused by contemporary Lawrence Clarkson of having his identity so bound up in his project that 'there was a self-love and vain-glory nursed in his heart that if possible, by digging to have gained people to him, by which his name might be great among the poor Commonalty of the Nation ...'.[15]

Such a heightened sense of personal calling and destiny could leave the individual vulnerable to crushing disappointment and disillusion should expectations not be met, but the continuation of hope observed in these authors stems from the fact that for them their personal stories are framed by another universal story that cannot but have a positive resolution. Whether they understand the present as a time of waiting for or acting towards that transformation, the surety that it will come counsels against despair. What is involved is a union of two temporalities similar to those identified in the literary theory of Jacques Ehrman when he wrote of a dialectic between the individual destiny marked by birth and death and collective destiny marked by the origin and end of humanity.[16] The second of these sequences matches the theme of this book, the origin and continuation of human society in Adam. A dialogue between individual and collective destiny is carried out in various ways through the selected authors' work; the relationship between inner restoration of the individual and the outer restoration of the whole of humanity (the rising up within and the coming of Christ's kingdom) in Winstanley's mystical writings; the interdependency in Eliot's scheme of global salvation, the spiritual health of his Praying Towns and the regeneration of each individual Indian (evidenced in personal testimonies); Milton's study of the personal story and psychology of the individual Adam, which becomes the story of the collective humankind; even Locke links the life of the individual to God's own time. The stories of the individual authors or of the individuals about whom they write are interpreted by them and demand to be understood by their readers, in their intersection and interaction with the collective temporal sequence of man's story of Creation, of Fall and Redemption.

Notes

1. This refers in particular to Adam in the Genesis j account (see Chapter 1 of this book).
2. Lee Ward describes Locke as 'one of the most influential architects of the modern world', the man who 'helped preside over the birth of modernity' in *John Locke and Modern Life* (Cambridge: Cambridge University Press, 2010), 3, 9. Indeed, in the days when the end of the Cold War was heralded as 'the end of history' Locke's liberalism was not only viewed as giving birth to a new modern age but as setting the seal. Thus Lee Ward wrote, 'if since the end of the Cold War we are all liberals then the suspicion is that in some sense we are all Lockean now'. Ibid., 9.
3. Stanley Fish interpreted the complexities of *Paradise Lost* as the work of an aged and disillusioned poet setting his admonitory traps for unwary readers so that they might learn through repetitions of the author's own self-deception, while

204 Eliot, Williams, Winstanley, Milton and Locke

George Schulman viewed *The Law of Freedom's Platform* as an expression of Winstanley's own disillusion. Stanley Fish *Surprised by Sin: The Reader in "Paradise Lost"* (New York: St. Martin's Press, 1967); Georg Schulman *Radicalism and Reverence: The Political Thought of Gerrard Winstanley* (Berkeley: University of California Press, 1989). 216.

4. Hill, *Religion*, 51.
5. James Alsop's study suggests that Winstanley's Quaker funeral may have been a sign of his wife's conviction more than his own. James Alsop, 'Gerard Winstanley: Religion and Respectability' in *Historical Journal* Vol. 28, No. 3 (Sept. 1985), 708.
6. For an account of Williams's difficult last years, see Gaustad, *Liberty*.
7. This comment was Milton's response to a suggestion made by an acquaintance, Peter Heimbach, that like old Simeon, the poet now desired nothing more than to be taken to his heavenly patria. See Lewalski, *Life*, 2000, 450.
8. Ibid., 536.
9. Although the details of this role and structures into which it fit differed in several significant ways including the role of the Church and place of property.
10. Alsop suggested that the lack of published work after 1652 may reflect not reluctant resignation in the face of hostile, reactionary governments, but rather a reflection of inner contentment. (Alsop, *Gerrard Winstanley*, 708).
11. Gaustad, *Liberty*, 189.
12. Cited in Convers Francis, *Life of John Eliot, the Apostle to the Indians* (Boston: Hilliard Gray, 1836), 335.
13. Lowenstein, *Drama of History*, 24.
14. Morgan, *Roger Williams*, 50f.
15. Lawrence Clarkson, *The Lost Sheep Found: or the Prodigal Returned to His Father's House* (London, 1660), 27.
16. Jacques Ehrman and Jay Caplan 'The Tragic/Utopian Meaning of History', in *Yale French Studies No. 58, In Memory of Jacques Ehrman: Inside Play Outside Game*, 1979, 16.

Bibliography

Aarsleff, Hans. *From Locke to Saussure: Essays in the Study of Language and Intellectual History*. Minneapolis, University of Minnesota Press, 1982.
———. 'Locke's Influence.' In *The Cambridge Companion to Locke*. Edited by Vere Chappell, 252–89. Cambridge: Cambridge University Press 1994.
Acosta, Ana M. *Reading Genesis in the Long Eighteenth Century: from Milton to Mary Shelley*. Aldershot: Ashgate, 2006.
Adams Jr., Charles Francis. *The New English Canaan of Thomas Morton: with Introductory Matter and Notes 1883*. IndyPublish, 2008.
Adamson, John, ed. *The English Civil War: Conflicts and Contexts 1640-49*. Basingstoke: Palgrave Macmillan, 2009.
———. 'Introduction: High Roads and Blind Alleys. The English Civil War and Its Historiography.' In *The English Civil War: Conflict and Contexts 1640-49*. Edited by John Adamson. Basingstoke: Palgrave Macmillan, 2009.
Almond, Philip C. *Adam and Eve in Seventeenth-Century Thought*. Cambridge: Cambridge University Press, 1999.
Alsop, James D. 'Gerard Winstanley: Religion and Respectability.' *Historical Journal* 28, 3 (Sept. 1983): 705–709.
Ames, William. *Conscience with the Power and Cases thereof*. trans. (London: s.n. 1639) in *Internet Archive* <http://archive.org/details/conscpo00ames> [accessed 4 November 2011].
Aquinas, Thomas. *The Summa Theologica of St. Thomas Aquinas*. Trans. by Fathers of the English Dominican Province rev. edn. London: Burns Oates and Washbourne, 1920, in *New Advent Online* <http://www.newadvent.org/summa/> [accessed 4 April 2012].
Ashcraft, Richard. 'Locke's Political Philosophy.' In *The Cambridge Companion to Locke*. Edited by Vere Chappell, 226–51. Cambridge: Cambridge University Press, 1994.
Auerbach, Eric. *Mimesis: The Representation of Reality in Western Literature*. Princeton: Princeton University Press, 1973.
Augustine. *City of God*. Edited by David Knowles. Harmondsworth: Penguin, 1972.
Axtell, James. *The Invasion within: The Contest of Cultures in Colonial North America*. New York: Oxford University Press, 1985.
Baker, Philip. 'Rhetoric, Reality and the Varieties of Civil War Radicalism.' In *The English Civil War: Conflict and Contexts 1640-49*. Edited by John Adamson. Basingstoke: Palgrave Macmillan, 2009.
Bamford, Francis, ed. *A Royalist's Notebook: The Commonplace Book of Sir John Oglander, Kt., of Nunwell, born 1585, died 1655*. London: Constable & Co., 1936.

Barry, John H. *Roger Williams and the Creation of the American Soul: Church, State and the Birth of Liberty*. New York: Viking, 2012.
Beach, James Mark. *Christ and the Covenant: Francis Turretin's Federal Theology as a Defense of the Doctrine of Grace*. Göttingen: Vandenhoeck and Ruprecht, 2007.
Bennett, Joan. *Reviving Liberty: Radical Christian Humanism in Milton's Great Poems*. Cambridge, MA: Harvard University Press, 1989.
Bernstein, Eduard. *Cromwell and Communism: Socialism and Democracy in the Great English Revolution*. London: Allen and Unwin, 1930.
Bizik, Amy Stewart. *"Sufficient to Have Stood though Free to Fall": The Parabolic Narrative of Free Will in Paradise Lost*. Dissertation University of Arizona, 2008.
Boehme, Jacob. *A Description of the Three Principles of the Divine Essence*. Trans. John Sparrow. London, 1648.
Boemus, Johannes. *The Fardle of Facions conteining the aunciente maners, customes and lawes, of the peoples enhabiting the two partes of the earth, called Affricke and Asie*. Trans. William Waterman. London: Ihon Kinstone and Henry Sutton, 1555.
Bohun, Edmund. *A Defence of Sir Robert Filmer, against the Mistakes and Misrepresentations of Algernon Sidney, Esq. in a Paper Delivered by Him to the Sheriffs upon the Scaffold on Tower-Hill, on Fryday December the 7th 1683 before His Execution There*. London: Kettily, 1684.
Borris, Kenneth. *Allegory and Epic in English Renaissance Literature: Heroic Form in Sidney, Spenser and Milton*. Cambridge: Cambridge University Press, 2000.
Braddick, Michael J., ed. *The British Atlantic World 1500–1800*. Basingstoke: Palgrave MacMillan, 2002.
Bradstock, Andrew. *Faith in the Revolution: The Political Theories of Münster and Winstanley*. London: SPCK, 1997.
Bremer, Francis J. *The Puritan Experiment: New England Society from Bradford to Edwards*, second edn. Hanover and London: University Press of New England, 1995.
——, ed., *Puritanism: Transatlantic Perspectives on a Seventeenth-Century Anglo-American Faith* Boston: Massachusetts Historical Society, 1993.
Breward, Ian, ed. *The Work of William Perkins*. Appleford, UK: Sutton Courtenay Press, 1970.
Brightman, Thomas. *Apocalypsis Apocalypseos or a Revelation of the Revelation*. Leyden, 1616.
Brinkley, R. F. *Coleridge in the Seventeenth Century*. Durham, NC: Duke University Press, 1955.
Brockunier, Robert F. and Samuel Hugh. *The Irrepressible Democrat, Roger Williams*. New York: The Ronald Press Company, 1940.
Bross, Kristina. *Dry Bones and Indian Sermons: Praying Indians in Colonial America*. Ithaca and London: Cornell University Press, 2004.
Brown, Andrew. *The Darwin Wars: The Scientific Battle for the Soul of Man*. London: Simon and Schuster 1999.
Brown, Colin. 'Campbell Interrupted Blair as He Spoke of His Faith: "We Don't Do God"' in *The Telegraph*, 4 May (2003) <http://www.telegraph.co.uk/news/uknews/1429109/Campbell-interrupted-Blair-as-he-spoke-of-his-faith-We-dont-do-God.html> [accessed 5 June 2015].

Bryson, Michael. '"His Tyranny Who Reigns": The Biblical Roots of Divine Kingship and Milton's Rejection of "Heav'n's King."' In *Milton Studies*. Edited by Albert C. Labriola, 43: 111–144. Pittsburgh: University of Pittsburgh Press, 2004.

Budziszewski, J. *Written on the Heart: The Case for Natural Law*. Downers Grove, IL: IVP Academic, 1997.

Burgess, John P. *The Problem of Scripture and Political Affairs as Reflected in the Puritan Revolution: Samuel Rutherford, Thomas Goodwin, Jon Goodwin and Gerrard Winstanley*. Unpublished DPhil thesis University of Chicago, 1986.

Byrd, James P. *The Challenges of Roger Williams: Religious Liberty, Violent Persecution and the Bible*. Georgia: Mercer University Press, 2002.

Catterall, Douglas. 'Interlopers in an Intercultural Zone? Early Scots Ventures in the Atlantic World 1630–1660.' In *Bridging the Early Modern Atlantic World: People, Products and Practices on the Move*. Edited by Caroline A. Williams. Farnham: Ashgate, 2009.

de Certeau, Michel. *The Writing of History*. New York: Columbia University Press, 1988.

Cesarini, J. Patrick. 'The Ambivalent Uses of Roger Williams's 'A Key into the Language of America.'*Early American Literature* 38:3 (2003): 469–94.

Chaplin, Joyce. *Subject Matter: Technology, the Body, and Science on the Anglo-American Frontier 1500–1676*. Cambridge, MA: Harvard University Press, 2001.

Chillingworth, William. *The Works of William Chillingworth M.A. of the University of Oxford*. London: D. Midwinter et al., 1742.

Clarkson, Lawrence. *The Lost Sheep Found: or the Prodigal Returned to His Father's House*. London 1660.

Coppin, Richard. *A Hint of the Glorious Mystery of Divine Teachings, between God, Christ, and the Saints*. London: Giles Calvert, 1649.

Corns, Thomas N. 'Radical pamphleteering.' In *The Cambridge Companion to Writing the Revolution*. Edited by N. H. Keeble, 71–86. Cambridge: Cambridge University Press, 2001.

Craik, Henry, ed. *English Prose Vol. III Seventeenth Century*. New York: MacMillan, 1916.

Cumberland, Richard. *A Treatise of the Laws of Nature*. Trans. with Introduction and Appendix by John Maxwell (1727). Edited by Jon Parkin. Indianapolis: Liberty Fund, 2005.

Cummings, Brian. *The Literary Culture of the Reformation: Grammar and Grace*. Oxford: Oxford University Press, 2002.

Cust, Richard, and Anne Hughes. *Conflict in Early Stuart England: Studies in Religion and Politics, 1603–1642*. London: Longman, 1989.

———, ed. *The English Civil War*. London: Arnold, 1997.

Daly, James. *Sir Robert Filmer and English Political Thought*. Toronto: University of Toronto Press, 1979.

Davies, Stevie. *Images of Kingship in Paradise Lost: Milton's Politics and Christian Liberty*. Missouri & London: University of Missouri Press, 1983.

Davis, J. C. 'Utopia and History.' *Australian Historical Studies* 13, 50 (1968): 165–76.

Devine, T.M. *The Scottish Nation: A Modern History*. London: Penguin, 2012.

Dunn, John, *The Political Thought of John Locke: An Historical Account of the Argument of the 'Two Treatises of Government.'* Cambridge: Cambridge University Press, 1969.

———. 'What Is Living and What Is Dead in the Political Theory of John Locke?' In *Interpreting Political Responsibility: Essays 1981–1989*. Edited by John Dunn. Princeton: Princeton University Press, 1990.

Dzelzainis, Martin. 'Ideas in Conflict: Political and Religious Thought during the English Revolution.' In *The Cambridge Companion to Writing of the English Revolution*. Edited by N. H. Keeble. Cambridge: Cambridge University Press, 2001.

Eames, Wilberforce, ed. *John Eliot and the Indians 1652–1657 Being Letters Addressed to Rev Jonathan Hamner of Barnstable, England*. Reprod. from Original Manuscripts in Possession of Theodore N. Vail. New York, 1915.

Edwards, Thomas. *The Third Part of Gangræna or a Catalogue and Discovery of Many of the Errours, Heresies, Blasphemies and Pernicious Practices of the Sectaries of the Time*. London, 1646.

Ehrmann, Jacques, and Jay Caplan. 'The Tragic Utopian Meaning of History.' *Yale French Studies No. 58, In Memory of Jacques Ehrmann: Inside Play Outside Game* (1979): 15–30.

Elazar, Daniel Judah. *Covenant and Civil Society: The Constitutional Matrix of Modern Democracy*. New Brunswick, NJ: Transaction Publishers, 1998.

Eliot, John. *A Brief Narrative of the Progress of the Gospel amongst the Indians in New England, in the Year 1670*. London: John Allen, 1670.

———. *The Christian Commonwealth or The Civil Policy or The Rising Kingdom of Jesus Christ*. London: Livewell Chapman, 1659.

———. *The Eliot Tracts: with Letters from John Eliot to Thomas Thorowgood and Richard Baxter*. Edited by Michael P. Clark. Westport, CT: Praeger Publishers, 2003.

———. *Further Account of the Progress of the Gospel amongst the Indians in New England, 1660*. Whitefish, MT: Kessinger Publishing, 2003.

———. *The Indian Grammar Begun*. Cambridge: Marmaduke Johnson, 1666.

———. *John Eliot and the Indians 1652–1657 Being Letters Addressed to Rev. John Hamner of Barnstable, England*. New York: The Adams and Grace Press, 1915.

———. *John Eliot's Indian Dialogues: A Study in Cultural Interaction*. Edited by Henry W. Bowden and James P. Ronda. Westport, CT: Greenwood Press, 1980.

Emen, Paul. 'The Theological Basis of Digger Communism,' *Church History* 23 (1954): 207–18.

D'Entreves, Alessandro Passerin. *Natural Law an Introduction to Legal Philosophy*. New Brunswick NJ: Transaction Publishers, 1994.

L'Estrange, Roger. *Americans No Jewes or Improbabilities that the Americans Are of that Race*. London, 1652.

Evans J.M. *Paradise Lost and the Genesis Tradition*. Oxford: Clarendon Press, 1968.

Fallon, Robert Thomas. *Divided Empire: Milton's Political Imagery*. University Park: Pennsylvania State University Press, 1995.

Filmer, Robert. *Sir Robert Filmer's Patriarcha and Other Writings*. Edited by Johann P. Somerville. Cambridge: Cambridge University Press, 1991.

Fish, Stanley. *Surprised by Sin: the Reader in "Paradise Lost."* New York: St. Martin's Press, 1967.

Fleming, James Dougal. *Milton's Secrecy: and Philosophical Hermeneutics*. Burlington VT: Ashgate, 2008.

Francis, Convers. *Life of John Eliot, Apostle to the Indians*. Boston: Hilliard Gray, 1836.

Furniss, Tom. 'Reading the Geneva Bible: notes toward an English revolution?' *Prose Studies: History, Theory, Criticism* 31, 1 (2009): 1–21.
Games, Alison. 'Migration,' In *The British Atlantic World 1500–1800*. Edited by David Armitage and Michael J. Braddick. Basingstoke: Palgrave MacMillan, 2002.
Gaustad, Edwin S. *Liberty of Conscience: Roger Williams in America*. Valley Forge: Judson Press, 1999.
Gee, Edward. *The Divine Right and Originall of the Civill Magistrate from God. Illustrated and Vindicated*. London, 1658.
Gibbs, Lee W. 'The Puritan Natural Law Theory of William Ames.' *Harvard Theological Review* 64, 1 (January 1971): 37–57.
Gibbons, B.J. *Gender in Mystical and Occult Thought: Behmenism and its Development in England*. Cambridge: Cambridge University Press, 1996.
Gilpin, W. Clark. *The Millenarian Piety of Roger Williams*. Chicago: University of Chicago Press, 1979.
Grabill, Stephen John. *Rediscovering the Natural Law in Reformed Theological Ethics*. Grand Rapids, Michigan: Wm. B. Eerdmans, 2006.
Grafton, Anthony. *New Worlds, Ancient Texts: The Power of Tradition and the Shock of Discovery*. Cambridge, MA: Belknap Press of Harvard University Press, 1992.
Gray, Kathryn N. *John Eliot and the Praying Indians of Massachusetts Bay: Communities and Connections in Puritan New England*. Lanham, MD: Bucknell University Press, 2013.
Gray, Robert. *A Good Speed to Virginia (1609)*. Proquest: EEBO editions, 2010.
Grotius, Hugo. *De Iure Praedae Commentarius: A Translation of the Original Manuscript of 1604* tr. Gwladys L. Williams. Oxford: Clarendon Press, 1950.
———. *The Rights of War and Peace*. Edited by Richard Tuck. Indianapolis: Liberty Fund, no date. <http://files.libertyfund.org/files/1425/1032-01_LFeBk.pdf> [accessed 4 November 2012].
Habermas, Jürgen. 'Religion in the Public Sphere.' *European Journal of Philosophy* 14, 1 (2006): 1–25.
Hale, Matthew. *The Primitive Origination of Mankind Considered and Examined According to the Light of Nature*. London: William Godbid, 1677.
Harris, Tim. *Restoration: Charles II and His Kingdom 1660–85*. London: Allen Lane, 2005.
Haskins, Dayton. *Milton's Burden of Interpretation*. Philadelphia: University of Pennsylvania Press, 1994.
Hawkes, David. *John Milton: A Hero of Our Time*. Berkeley: Counterpoint, 2009.
Herman, Peter. *Destabilizing Milton: 'Paradise Lost' and the Poetics of Incertitude*. Basingstoke: Palgrave MacMillan, 2008.
Heylyn, Peter. *Cosmographie: Containing the Chorography and History of the Whole World*. London, 1682.
Hill, Christopher. *The English Revolution 1640*. London: Lawrence & Wishart, 1940.
———. *The Experience of Defeat: Milton and Some Contemporaries*. Harmondsworth: Penguin, 1985.
———. *The Religion of Gerrard Winstanley*. Oxford: Past and Present Society, 1978.
———, ed. *Winstanley: The Law of Freedom and Other Writings*. Harmonsworth: Penguin Books, 1973.

———. *The World Turned Upside Down: Radical Ideas During the English Revolution*. Harmondsworth: Penguin, 1972.
Hillier, Russell M. 'Spatial Allegory and Creation Old and New in Milton's Hexaemeral Narrative.' *Studies in English Literature 1500–1900* 49, 1 (Winter 2009): 121–43.
Hirst, Derek. '"That Sober Liberty": Marvell's Cromwell in 1654.' In *The Golden and the Brazen World: Papers in Literature and History 1650–1800*. Edited by John Malcolm Wallace. Berkeley: University of California Press, 1985.
Hobbes, Thomas. *Behemoth or the Long Parliament*. Edited by Ferdinand Tönnies. Chicago: University of Chicago Press, 1990.
———. *Leviathan*. Edited by C. B. Macpherson. Harmondsworth: Penguin, 1968.
———. *On The Citizen (De Cive)*. Edited by Richard Tuck and Michael Silverthorne. Cambridge: Cambridge University Press, 1998.
Hodgen, Margaret T. *Early Anthropology in the 16th and 17th Century*. Philadelphia: University of Pennsylvania Press, 1971.
Holmes, Clive. *Seventeenth Century Lincolnshire (History of Lincolnshire)*. Lincs Local Hist. Soc, Hist. of Lin., 1980.
Holstun, James. *A Rational Millennium: Puritan Utopias of Seventeenth Century England and America*. Oxford: Oxford University Press, 1987.
———. 'Communism, George Hill and the Mir: Was Marx a Nineteenth Century Winstanleyan?' *Prose Studies: History, Theory, Criticism* 22, 2 (1999): 121–48.
Hopton, Andrew, ed. *Gerrard Winstanley: A Common Treasury*. London: Verso, 2011.
Hughes, Ann. 'The Meanings of Religious Polemic.' In *Puritanism: Transatlantic Perspectives on a Seventeenth-Century Anglo-American Faith*. Edited by Francis J. Bremer. Boston: Massachusetts Historical Society, 1993.
Hunton, Philip. *A Treatise of Monarchy*, rev. edn. London: E. Smith, 1689.
Jendrysik, Mark Stephen. *Explaining the English Revolution: Hobbes and His Contemporaries*. Idaho Falls, ID: Lexington Books, 2007.
Johnson, Robert. *Nova Britannia Offering Most Excellent Fruites by Planting in Virginia*. London: Samuel Macham, 1609.
Jones, Rufus M. *Spiritual Reformers in the 16th and 17th Centuries (1914)*. Whitefish, MT: Kessinger Publishing, 1998.
Juretic, George. 'Digger No Millenarian: The Revolutionizing of Gerrard Winstanley.' *Journal of the History of Ideas* 36 (1975): 263–80.
Kateb, George. 'Locke and the Political Origins of Secularism' *Social Research: An International Quarterly* 76, 4 (Winter 2009): 1001–34.
Keeble, N. H., ed. *The Cambridge Companion to Writing of the English Revolution*. Cambridge: Cambridge University Press, 2001.
Kees, Van Der Pijl 'A Lockean Europe?' *New Left Review* 37 (2006): 9–37.
Kellaway, William. *The New England Company 1649–1776 Missionary Society to the American Indians*. Glasgow: The University Press, 1961.
Kenyon, Timothy. *Communism and the Fall of Man: The Social Theories of Thomas More and Gerrard Winstanley*. PhD thesis, University of Warwick, 1981.
———. *Utopian Communism and Political Thought in Early Modern England*. London: Pinter Publishers, 1989.
Kirby W. J. Torrance. 'Richard Hooker's Discourse on Natural Law in the Context of The Magisterial Reformation1.' *Animus* 3 (1998) <http://www.mun.ca/animus/1998vol3/kirby3.htm#N_1_> [accessed 20 August 2011].

Kishlansky, Mark. *A Monarchy Transformed: Britain 1603–1714*. Harmondsworth: Penguin Books, 1996.
Knights, Mark. 'John Locke and Post-Revolutionary Politics: Electoral Reform and the Franchise.' *Past and Present* 213, 1 (2011): 41–86.
Knott, James. *The Sword of the Spirit: Puritan Responses to the Bible*. Chicago and London: University of Chicago Press, 1980.
Kupperman, Karen Ordahl. *Indians and English: Facing off in Early America*. Ithaca: Cornell University Press, 2000.
Lake, Peter. 'Calvinism and the English Church 1570–1653.' In *Reformation to Revolution: Politics and Religion in Early Modern England*. Edited by Margot Todd. London: Routledge, 1995.
Laslett, Peter. *Locke's Two Treatises of Government*. Cambridge: Cambridge University Press, 1960.
Lawrence, Michael Anthony. *Radicals in their Own Time: Four Hundred Years of Struggle for Liberty and Equal Justice in America*. Cambridge: Cambridge University Press, 2010.
Levin-Walman, Oren M. *Reconceiving Liberalism: Dilemmas of Contemporary Liberal Public Policy*. Pittsburgh: Pittsburgh University Press, 1996.
Lewalski, Barbara K. *The Life of John Milton: A Critical Biography*. Oxford: Blackwell, 2000.
———. *Paradise Lost and the Rhetoric of Literary Forms*. Princeton, NJ: Princeton University Press, 1985.
———. *Protestant Poetics and the Seventeenth Century Religious Lyric*. Princeton, NJ: Princeton University Press, 1979.
Locke, John. *An Essay concerning Human Understanding 1690*. Edited by P. Nidditch. Oxford; Oxford University Press, 1975.
———. *John Locke: Essays on the Law of Nature: The Latin Text with a Translation*. Edited by Wolfgang Von Leyden, rev. edn. Oxford: Clarendon Press, 2002.
———. *LCT–A Letter concerning Toleration*. Edited by James Tully. Indianapolis: Hackett Publishing, 1983.
———. *Locke: Political Essays*. Edited by Mark Goldie. Cambridge: Cambridge University Press, 1997.
———. *A Paraphrase and Notes on the Epistles of St. Paul*. London: Thomas Tegg, 1823.
———. *The Reasonableness of Christianity*. London: C and J Rivington, 1824.
———. *Representing Revolution in Milton and His Contemporaries: Religion, Politics and Polemics in Radical Puritanism*. Cambridge: Cambridge University Press, 2001.
———. *Some Thoughts concerning Education* and *Of the Conduct of Understanding*. Edited by Ruth W. Grant and Nathan Tarcov. Indianapolis: Hackett Publishing Company, 1996.
———. *Two Treatises of Government*. Edited by Peter Laslett. Cambridge: Cambridge University Press, 1960.
Loewenstein, David. *Milton and the Drama of History*. Cambridge: Cambridge University Press, 1990.
Lund, W. R. 'The Historical and Political Origins of Civil Society: Hobbes on Presumption and Certainty.' In *Thomas Hobbes Critical Assessments Vol. III: Politics and Law*. Edited by Preston T. King. London: Routledge, 1993.

Bibliography

Lutz, Christopher Stephen. *Reading Alastair MacIntyre's After Virtue*. London: Continuum, 2012.

Luxon, Thomas H. *Literal Figures: Puritan Allegory and the Reformation Crisis in Representation*. Chicago: University of Chicago Press, 1995.

MacIntyre, Alastair. *After Virtue: A Study in Morral Theory*. London: Duckworth and Co., 1981.

Maloney, Pat. 'Leaving the Garden of Eden: Linguistic and Political Authority in Thomas Hobbes,' *History of Political Thought* 18 (1997): 242–66.

Marshall, John. *John Locke: Resistance, Religion and Responsibility*. Cambridge: Cambridge University Press, 1994.

Mather, Cotton. *The Life and Death of the Reverend John Eliot*. London: John Dunton, 1694.

McGiffert, Michael. 'From Moses to Adam: The Making of the Covenant of Works.' *Sixteenth Century Journal* 19, 2 (1988): 131–55.

Mede, Joseph. *A Translation of Mede's Clavis Apocalyptica*, Trans. R. Bransby Cooper. London: J. G. and F. Rivington, 1833.

Mendelsohn, J. Andrew. 'Alchemy and Politics in England 1649–1665.' *Past and Present* 135, 1 (1992): 30–78.

Miller, Perry. *The New England Mind: The Seventeenth Century*. New York: MacMillan, 1939.

———. *Roger Williams: His Contribution to the American Tradition*. New York: Atheneum, 1953.

Milton, John. *A Brief History of Moscovia and of Other Less-Known Countries Lying Eastward of Russia as Far as Cathay, Gathered from the Writings of Several Eye-Witnesses*. Proquest: EEBO Editions, 2010.

———. *Complete Prose Works of John Milton*. Edited by Maurice Kelley. trans. John Carey. New Haven: Yale University Press, 1973.

———. John Milton, 'Brief Notes upon a Late Sermon, Titled, The Fear of God and the King' in *The Prose Works of John Milton* Edited by Rufus Wilmot Griswold (Philadelphia: John W. Moore, 1847). Vol. 2. in *Online Library of Liberty* <http://oll.libertyfund.org/title/1210/78232> [accessed 4 November 2012].

———. *Milton Poetical Works*. Edited by Douglas Bush. Oxford: Oxford University Press, 1966.

———. *Prose Writings* reprint. London: Dent, 1974.

———. *Tractate on Education* Vol III, Part 4 The Harvard Classics. New York: P.F.Collier and Son 1909–14; Bartleby.com 2001.

———. *A Treatise of Civil Power in Ecclesiastical Causes 1659* reprint. London: J. Johnson, 1790.

Mitchell, Neil J. 'John Locke and the Rise of Capitalism.' *History of Political Economy* 18, 2 (Summer 1986): 291–305.

Molesworth, William, ed. *The English Works of Thomas Hobbes, of Malmesbury vol. 6*. London: John Bohn, 1839.

Moots, Glenn A. *Politics Reformed: The Anglo-American Legacy of Covenant Theology*. Columbia: University of Missouri Press, 2010.

Morgan, Edmund S. *Roger Williams: The Church and State*, new edn. New York: W. W. North and Company, 2006.

Morrill, John. 'The Church in England 1642–1649.' In *Reactions to the English Civil War*. Edited by Morrill. London: Macmillan, 1982, chap. 4.

———. 'The Causes and Course of the British Civil Wars.' In *The Cambridge Companion to Writing of the English Revolution*. Edited by N. H. Keeble. Cambridge: Cambridge University Press, 2001.

———, ed. *Reactions to the English Civil War*. London: Macmillan, 1982.

———. *Revolt in the Provinces: the People of England and the Tragedies of War, 1630–1648*, rev. edn. New York: Longman, 1999.

Morrison, Dane. 'A Praying People: Massachusetts Acculturation and the Failure of the Puritan Mission 1600–1690.' *American Indian Studies*, vol. 2. New York: Peter Lang, 1995.

Morton, Thomas. *The New English Canaan of Thomas Morton: With Introductory Matter and Notes*. Edited by Charles Francis Adams Jr., 1883 reprint. IndyPublish, 2008.

Norbrook, David. *Writing the English Republic: Poetry, Rhetoric and Politics, 1627–1660*. Cambridge: Cambridge University Press, 1999.

Overall, John. *The Convocation Book of 1606: Commonly Called Bishop Overall's Convocation Book, Concerning the Government of God's Catholic Church and the Kingdoms of the Whole World*. Oxford: J. H. Parker, 1844.

Palladini, Fiammetta. 'Pufendorf Disciple of Hobbes: The Nature of Man and the State of Nature: The Doctrine of *Socialitas*.' *History of European Ideas* 34 (2008): 26–60.

Parker, Kim Ian. *The Biblical Politics of John Locke*. Waterloo: Wilfrid Laurier University Press, 2004.

Pelikan, Jaroslav, ed. *Luther's Works*. St. Louis, MO: Concordia, 1986.

Perkins, Anne. 'David Cameron "Does God" and Puts Faith on the Table.' *The Guardian*, 18 April, (2014) <http://www.theguardian.com/politics/2014/apr/18/david-cameron-god-faith> [accessed 5 June, 2015].

Perkins, William. *Workes, Vol. III*. Edited by J. Legate and C. Legge III. London, 1618.

———. *The Work of William Perkins* Edited by Ian Breward. Abingdon: Sutton Courtenay Press, 1970.

Pocock, J. G. A. *Politics, Language and Time: Essays on Political Thought and History*. New York: Atheneum, 1971.

Poole, Matthew. *Commentary on the Holy Bible: Vol. III Matthew to Revelation*. McLean, VA: MacDonald, 1985.

Prindle, David F. *The Politics of Evolution*. New York: Routledge, 2015.

Quin, David B., and Alison M. Quin, ed. *The English New England Voyages 1602–1608*. London: Hakluyt Society 2nd series no. 161, 1983.

Ralegh, Walter. *The History of the World*. London: Walter Burre, 1614. <https://archive.org/details/historyofworld00rale> [accessed 4 April 2012].

Read, David. *New World, Known World: Shaping Knowledge in Early Anglo-American Writing*. Columbia: University of Missouri Press, 2005.

Reventlow, Henning Graf. *The Authority of the Bible and the Rise of the Modern World*. Trans. John Bowden. London: SCM, 1984.

Ricoeur, Paul. *Fallible Man*. Trans. Charles A. Kelbley. Chicago: Henry Regnery, 1965.

———. *History and Truth*. Trans. Charles A. Kelbley. Evanston: Northwestern University Press, 1965.

———. *Time and Narrative: Volume 1*. Chicago and London: University of Chicago Press, 1984.

214 Bibliography

Ripper, Jason. *American Stories: Vol. II from 1865*. Abingdon: Routledge, 2015, 235.
Rose, Jacqueline. *Godly Kingship in Restoration England: The Politics of Royal Supremacy 1660–1688*. Cambridge: Cambridge University Press, 2011.
Russell, Conrad. *The Causes of the Civil War: The Ford Lectures Delivered in the University of Oxford 1987–1988*. Oxford: Clarendon Press, 1990.
Sabine, George, ed. *The Works of Gerrard Winstanley*. New York: Russell and Russell, 1965.
Sadler, Lynn Veach. 'Regeneration and Typology: Samson Agonistes and Its Relation to De Doctrina Christiana, Paradise Lost, and Paradise Regained.' *Studies in English Literature, 1500–1900* 12, 1 (Winter, 1972): 141–56.
Salkeld, John. *A Treatise of Paradise 1617*. Georgia: Emory University, 1968.
Saltmarsh, John. *Sparkles of Glory or Some Beams of the Morning Star: Wherein Are Many Discoveries as to Truth and Peace to the Establishment and Pure Enlargement of a Christian in Spirit and Truth 1647*. London: E. Huntington, High St Bloomsbury, 1811.
Scanlan, Thomas. *Colonial Writings and the New World 1583–1671: Allegories of Desire*. Cambridge: Cambridge University Press, 1999.
Schochet, Gordon. *The Authoritarian Family and Political Attitudes in 17th Century England: Patriarchalism in Political Thought*, new edn. New Brunswick: Transaction Inc., 1988.
———. *Patriarchalism in Political Thought*. Oxford: Blackwell, 1975.
Schulman, George. *Radicalism and Reverence: The Political Thought of Gerrard Winstanley*. Berkeley: University of California Press, 1989.
Schweitzer, Ivy. *The Work of Self-Representation: Lyric Poetry in Colonial New England*. Chapel Hill: University of North Carolina Press, 1991.
Seligman, Adam B. *Modernity's Wager: Authority, the Self, and Transcendance*. Princeton: Princeton University Press, 2000.
Sharpe, Kevin. *The Personal Rule of Charles I*. New Haven: Yale University Press, 1992.
Shawcross, John T. *John Milton: The Self and the World*. Lexington: The University Press of Kentucky, 2001.
Sheehan, Bernard. *Savagism and Civility: Indians and Englishmen in Colonial Virginia*. Cambridge: Cambridge University Press, 1980.
Sidney, Algernon. *Colonel Sidney's Speech Delivered to the Sheriff on the Scaffold December 7th 1683*. London, 1683.
———. *Discourses concerning Government*, vol. 2. Edinburgh: G. Hamilton and J. Balfour, 1750.
Simmons, A. John. *The Lockean Theory of Rights*. Princeton: University of Princeton Press, 1992.
Simut, Corneliu C. *The Doctrine of Salvation in the Sermons of Richard Hooker*. Berlin: Walter de Gruyter, 2005.
Smith, Nigel. *Perfection Proclaimed Language and Literature in English Radical Religion, 1640–1660*. Oxford: Clarendon Press, 1989.
Somerville, J. P. 'John Selden, the Law of Nature, and the Origins of Government.' *Historical Journal* 27, 2 (1984): 437–47.
Spellmann, W. M. *John Locke and the Problem of Depravity*. Oxford: Clarendon Press, 1988.
Steele, Margaret. 'The "Politick Christian": The Theological Background to the National Covenant.' In *The Scottish National Covenant in its British Context*

1638–1651, 31–67. Edited by John Morrill. Edinburgh: Edinburgh University Press, 1990.

Stout, Harry S. *The New England Soul: Preaching and Religious Culture in Colonial New England*. Oxford: Oxford University Press, 1986.

Strauss, Leo. *Natural Right and History*. Chicago: University of Chicago Press, 1965.

Symonds, William. *A Sermon Preached at Whitechapel in the presence of the Adventurers and Planters for Virginia (1609)*. New York: Theatrum Orbis Terrarum, 1968.

Teunissen, John J., and Evelyn J. Hinx, ed. 'Roger Williams, Thomas More, and the Narragansett Utopia,' *Early American Literature* 11, 3 (Winter 1976–1977): 281-95.

———. *Roger Williams: A Key into the Language of America*. Detroit: Wayne State Uni. Press, 1973.

Thiselton, Anthony C. *The Hermeneutics of Doctrine*. Grand Rapids, Michigan: Wm. B. Eerdmans Publishing Co., 2006.

Thornton, Helen. *State of Nature or Eden? Thomas Hobbes and His Contemporaries on the Natural Condition of Human Beings*. Rochester: University of Rochester Press, 2005.

Thorowgood, Thomas. *Jewes in America or Probabilities That Those Indians Are Judaical, Made More Probable by Some Additionals to Former Conjectures*. London: 2nd Edition, 1660.

Todd, Margo. *Christian Humanism and the Puritan Social Order*. Cambridge: Cambridge University Press, 1987.

———, ed. *Reformation to Revolution: Politics and Religion in Early Modern England*. London: Routledge, 1995.

Torrance Kirby, W. J. 'Richard Hooker's Discourse on Natural Law in the Context of the Magisterial Reformation1' *Animus* 3 (1998) <www.swgc.mun.ca/animus 30> [accessed 12 October 2011].

Trent, William P., and Benjamin W. Wells, ed. *Colonial Prose and Poetry. 1901. Vol. I. The Transplanting of Culture: 1607–1650*. New York: Thomas Y. Crowell & Co., 1901.

Trent, William Peterfield, John Erskine, Stuart P. Sherman, Carl van Doren, ed. *The Cambridge History of American Literature*. New York: G. P. Putnam's Sons, 1917 to 1921.

Trueman, Carl R. *John Owen: Reformed Catholic, Renaissance Man*. Aldershot: Ashgate Publishing Company, 2007.

Tuck, Richard. *Natural Rights Theories: Their Origin and Development*. Cambridge: Cambridge University Press, 1979.

Tully James. *An Approach to Political Philosophy: Locke in Contexts*. Cambridge: Cambridge University Press, 1993.

Turretin, Francis. *Institutes of Elenctic Theology (1679–85)*. Edited by James T Dennison, Jr. Phillipsburg, NJ: P&R Publishing, 1992–97.

Tyacke, Nicholas. 'Puritanism, Arminianism and Counter-Revolution.' In *Reformation to Revolution: Politics and Religion in Early Modern England*. Edited by Margot Todd. London: Routledge, 1995.

Tyrell, James. *A Brief Enquiry into the Ancient Constitution and Government of England as Well in Respect of the Administration, as Succession Thereof ... By a True Lover of His Country (1695)* (Proquest: EEBO Editions, 2011).

———. *A Brief Disquisition of the Law of Nature, According to the Principles and Method Laid down in the Reverend Dr. Cumberland's (Now Lord Bishop* of Peterborough's) *Latin Treatise on that Subject. As also His Confutations of Mr. Hobb's Principles, Put into Another Method. The Second Edition Corrected, and Somewhat Enlarged*. London: W. Rogers, 1701.

———. *De patriarcha non monarcha*. London: Richard Janeway, 1681.

Underdown, David. 'Popular Politics before the Civil War.' In *Reformation to Revolution: Politics and Religion in Early Modern England*. Edited by Margot Todd. London: Routledge, 1995.

———. *Revel, Riot and Rebellion: Popular Politics and Culture in England 1603–1660*. Oxford: Oxford University Press, 1987.

Vaughan, Alden T., ed. *The Puritan Tradition in America, 1620–1730*, rev. edn. Hanover and London: University Press of New England, 1972.

Waldron, Jeremy. *God, Locke and Equality: Christian Foundations in Locke's Political Thought*. Cambridge: Cambridge University Press, 2002.

Walker, W. 'Resemblance and Reference in Recent Criticism on *Paradise Lost*.' *Milton Quarterly* 40 (2006): 189–206.

Walsh, Lynda. *Scientists as Prophets: A Rhetorical Genealogy*. Oxford: Oxford University Press, 2013.

Walsham, Alexandra. *Providence in Early Modern England*. Oxford: Oxford University Press, 1999.

Ward, Lee. *John Locke and Modern Life*. Cambridge: Cambridge University Press, 2010.

———. *The Politics of Liberty in England and Revolutionary America*. Cambridge: Cambridge University Press, 2004.

Weir, David. *Early New England: a Covenanted Society*. Grand Rapids, MI: Wm. B. Eerdmans Publishing Co., 2005.

Werman, Golda. *Milton and Midrash*. Washington DC: Catholic University of America, 1995.

Westminster Assembly. *The Westminster Confession of Faith* (Westminster, 1647) online <http://www.churchofscotland.org.uk/__data/assets/pdf_file/0011/650/westminster_confession.pdf> [accessed 4 December, 2012].

Whateley, William. *Prototypes, or, The Primary Presidents out of the Booke of Genesis. Shewing, the Good and Bad Things They Did and Had. Practically Applied to our Information and Reformation*. London, 1640.

Wilding, Michael. *Dragon's Teeth: Literature in the English Revolution*. Oxford: Clarendon Press, 1987.

Williams, N. P. *The Ideas of the Fall and of Original Sin: A Historical and Critical Study*. London: Longmans, Green and Co., 1929.

Williams, Roger *The Bloudy Tenent of Persecution, for Cause of Conscience Discussed in a Conference between Truth and Peace*. London: J. Haddon, 1848.

———. *The Bloudy Tenent of Persecution for Cause of Conscience Discussed and Mr. Cotton's Letter Examined and Answered* (1848 edition reprinted). Edited by Edward Bean Underhill. Whitefish, MT: Kessinger Publishing, 2004.

———. *The Complete Writings of Roger Williams*. Edited by Perry Miller et al. New York: Russell and Russell, 1964.

———. *A Key into the Language of America*. London: Gregory, 1643.

———. *Letters of Roger Williams 1632–1682*. Edited by John Russell Bartlett. Providence: Narragansett Club, 1874.

Wills, Garry. 'The Day the Enlightenment went out.' *The New York Times* published November 4 (2004), <http://www.nytimes.com/2004/11/04/opinion/04wills.html?_r=0> [accessed 5 June 2015].

Wilson, John. *Prophet in Parliament: Puritanism during the Civil Wars 1640–1648*. Princeton: Princeton University Press, 1969.
Winstanley, Gerrard. *The Complete Works of Gerrard Winstanley*. Edited by Thomas N. Corns, Ann Hughes, David Loewenstein. Oxford: Oxford University Press, 2009.
Winthrop, John. *The Winthrop Papers* Edited by Allyn Bailey Forbes. Boston, MA: The Massachusetts Historical Society, 1944.
Woolhouse, Roger. *Locke: A Biography*. Cambridge: Cambridge University Press, 2007.
Wootton, David. 'From Rebellion to Revolution.' In *The English Civil War*, 340–56. Edited by Richard Cust and Anne Hughes. London: Arnold, 1997.
Worden, Blair. 'Milton's Republicanism and the Tyranny of Heaven.' In *Machiavelli and Republicanism*, 225–45. Edited by Gisela Block, Quentin Skinner and Maurizio Viroli. Cambridge: Cambridge University Press, 1993.
Xenos, Nicholas. 'The Neocon Con Game: Nihilism Revisited.' In *Confronting the New Conservatism: The Rise of the Right in America*. Edited by Michael Thompson, 225–46. New York: New York University Press, 2007.
Young, Alexander, ed. *Chronicles of the First Planters of the Colony of Massachusetts Bay 1623–1636*. Boston: Charles C. Little and James Brown, 1846.
Young, James P. *Reconsidering American Liberalism: The Troubled Odyssey of the Liberal Idea*. Boulder, CO: Westview Press, 1996.
Zahedieh, Nuala. 'Economy.' In *The British Atlantic World 1500–1800*. Edited by David Armitage and Michael J. Braddick, 51–68. Basingstoke: Palgrave MacMillan, 2002.
Zakai Avihu. 'Thomas Brightman and English Apocalyptic Tradition.' In *Menasseh Ben Israel and His World*. Edited by Yosef Kaplan, Henry Méchoulan and Richard H. Popkin, 31–44. Leiden: E. J. Brill, 1989.

Index

Abel 122
Abraham 18–19, 56, 90, 147, 190
Acosta, Josephus 187
Ainsworth, Henry 51
Alexander, William 58
America 55–6, 58–9, 85–119, 152, 176, 182, 186–89
American Indians *see* 'Indians'
Ames, William 59, 61
angels 10, 34n8, 146–52, 154, 161; Archangel Gabriel 146; Archangel Michael 147–48, 156–59, 162, 202; Archangel Raphael 149, 151–52, 154–55, 159
Anglicanism 29, 63 *see also* Church of England
anti-catholicism *see* anti-papism
anti-clericalism 15, 130
anti-papism 30, 66, 123, 169–70 *see also* Exclusion Crisis, Rye House Plot
apocalypse 17, 20–1, 24–5, 66–7, 120 *see also* eschatology
Aquinas, St Thomas 12, 46, 48, 59
Aristotle 24, 46, 48, 55, 149, 166n32
Arminianism 12, 29–30, 33, 40n118, 40n120
Arminius, Jacob 12
Augustine, St 11–12, 50, 56, 67, 151, 157

Baptists 33
Barclay, William 46
Bible: biblical exegesis 2–3, 6, 8–12, 14–18, 24, 43, 46, 66, 73, 174–76, 179, 183, 185–86; genres 20–1; Geneva Bible 13–15, 18, 21, 27; King James (Authorised Bible) 13, 31; Tyndale's Bible 18
Blackwood, Adam 46
Bodin, Jean 71, 73, 84n178, 188
Boehme, Jacob 69

Boemus, Iohan 71–2, 114n35
Bohun, Edmund 42
Bradshaw, John 63
Brightman, Thomas 66–7
Bruno, Giordano 73
Bunyan, John 19, 144

Cain 14, 18, 122
Calvin, John 12, 18, 43, 60–1, 125
Cambridge Assembly 33
Carey, Edmund 14
Carleill, Christopher 56, 93
Charles I 26–31, 62–3, 67, 124, 140n26, 146–47, 169
Charles II 26, 169–70, 196n114, 201
Chillingworth 17
Christ 11–12, 17, 20–1, 27, 57, 60, 65, 68, 70, 73, 86, 89, 101, 107, 109–11, 121–22, 124–26, 128, 130, 133–138, 147, 151, 156, 159, 177, 183, 190, 197, 203; Second Adam 70, 123, 129–31, 135, 155, 157–59, 175, 198, 200
Church: Church of England 30–1, 45, 67, 104 *see also* Anglicanism; church governance 1, 20, 31–3, 108, 118n131; church practices 12, 15, 85, 162; God's Church 13–14, 18, 67, 104–105, 109, 112 *see also* elect
Cicero 48, 55–6, 60
civility 55–7, 74, 93–102, 112, 186, 189
civil war 3, 5, 19, 22–5, 27–9, 31–3, 68, 116n70
Clarkson, Lawrence 203
Coke, Edward 37n76
commonwealth 5, 19, 26, 28, 68, 124, 127–28, 133–38, 144, 162–64, 169
communism 23–4, 120, 200
Congregationalism 32–3, 40n126, 41n130, 63

Index

conscience 13, 16, 31–2, 36n34, 61–3, 80n112, 81n117, 152, 166n54, 166n64, 190, 196n120, 201
contract 27, 46, 169, 185, 190
Coppin, Richard 70
Cotton, John 81n117, 87, 104, 108, 200
covenant 32–3, 56, 62–5, 81n125, 81n126, 81n127, 107–109, 190–91; Covenant of Faith 190; Covenant of Grace 63–4, 190; Covenant of Redemption 81n125; Covenant of Works 63–4; half-way covenant 81n126
creation 3–4, 6, 8–11, 13, 18, 24, 28, 43–4, 49, 51, 54, 61, 64–5, 87–90, 95, 100, 102, 106, 110–12, 121, 128–129, 132, 149, 151, 190, 192, 197, 199, 203
Cromwell, Oliver 5, 26, 32, 120–21, 127, 133, 141n92, 144, 146, 200
cultivation 25–6, 73, 102–103, 106, 152, 182 *see also* labour
Cumberland, Richard 49, 59

Daniel 20, 120
Dell, William 16, 69–70, 122
Deuteronomy 21
Diggers 5, 23, 121, 123–27, 140n26, 182, 198, 201
Digges, Dudley 45, 53
dispensationalism 66, 82n142
dominion: Adam's dominion 9–10, 25, 50, 55, 57, 65, 132–33, 176, 184–86
Dryden, John 144
Durham, James 18

Eden 4, 8, 50–1, 54, 56, 62, 87, 98–9, 131, 151–56, 160, 179, 181, 198 *see also* garden
education 160, 162–64, 168n111, 176, 195n74
Edwards, John 178–79
Edwards, Thomas 28
egalitarianism *see* equality
elect 12–14, 32, 63, 100–101, 103, 105, 197; *see also* pre-destinarianism, God's Church
Eliot, John 4–5, 13, 20–1, 25–7, 58, 62, 64, 68, 71, 73, 85–119, 123–24, 128, 136, 138, 159, 182, 197–203; *Brief Narratives* 87, 95, 103–4; *The Christian Commonwealth* 21–2, 86–7, 103, 107–109, 123–124, 128; *The Day Breaking if not the Sun Rising of the Gospell with the Indians of new England* 95; *A Further Narrative of the Progress of the Gospel amongst the Indians in New England* 71; *Indian Dialogues* 87–8, 91, 94–5, 103; *Strength out of Weaknesse* 108
Elizabeth I 66–7
Engagement Controversy 107
English nation 6, 19–20, 66–8, 103, 105, 108–110, 119n155, 120, 123–24, 133, 144, 153, 144–164, 197, 199
Enoch 147
equality 9, 22, 28, 49–50, 53–4, 111, 130, 153, 172–73, 187–88, 198
Esau 13, 18, 122, 136
eschatology 2, 11, 13, 65, 67, 74, 122, 197; apocalyptic eschatology 68–69, 109, 168n108; prophetic eschatology 68–9, 109, 121, 159, 168n108
Eve 6, 8–9, 11, 26, 54, 70, 78n69, 88, 95, 103, 148, 152, 154–55, 157–59, 168n106, 175, 178–79, 186, 198
Everard, John 122
Exclusion Crisis 30, 169
Exodus 108
Ezekiel 20, 88

Fairfax, Thomas 5, 120, 200
fall 3–4, 8, 10–13, 21, 24, 59–61, 64, 70, 87–90, 95, 98, 102, 107, 111–12, 121, 123, 129–32, 134, 138, 148–49, 151, 156, 163, 178–79, 181–82, 184, 200, 203
fallen condition 10–13, 31, 56, 68, 74, 95, 98, 100, 102, 109, 134, 137, 153, 179–83, 197
Familialists 120
fatherhood 20, 43, 45–6, 55, 136–37, 163, 174, 184–86, 190, 198 *see also* patriarchialism
Filmer, Robert 2, 5, 14, 26–8, 42–51, 54, 56–8, 60, 122, 136, 148, 153, 174–75, 178, 184, 186–87, 190; *The Anarchy of a Limited or Mixed Monarchy* 42; *Observations of Aristotle's Politics* 54; *Observations Concerning the Original of Government* 42, 49; *Patriarcha* 15, 20, 22, 30, 42, 48, 171
freedom *see* liberty

garden 87, 98–9, 102–107, 117n114, 133, 159, 188, 192 *see also* Eden
Gee, Edward 47
genealogy (descent from Adam) 3, 10, 13, 20, 43–51, 71, 74, 89–91, 186–87
Genesis 2–4, 8–12, 18, 24–6, 42–3, 48–9, 53, 71, 73, 87–90, 98, 111, 132, 148–49, 153, 159, 173, 175–76, 179, 181, 191, 197–98
Glorious Revolution *see* revolution (1689)
Goddard, Thomas 45
Goodwin, Thomas 66
grace 12, 59–60, 63, 65, 101, 108, 151, 158, 162, 183, 197 *see also* elect (as recipients of grace)
Grafton, Richard 72
Gray, Robert 55
Grotius, Hugo 49–52, 77–8n59, 177, 193n10

Hakluyt, Richard 56, 93
Hale, Matthew 72
Hampton Court Conference 31
Harrington, James 22, 28, 146
Hartlib, Samuel 168n111
Hayward, John 46
Heylyn, Peter 73, 84n183
Hobbes, Thomas 8, 25, 28, 30, 46, 49–51, 53–9, 68, 78n65, 122, 134; *De Cive* 58; *Leviathan* 2, 22, 47, 49, 55, 57–8, 68
Hooke, Thomas 68
Hooker, Richard 46, 49, 53, 60
Hunton, Philip 8, 28, 34n1, 44, 62, 171, 192n9
Hutchinson, Anne 6, 33

Independents (churches) 32–3, 63
'Indians' 4–6, 20–21, 26, 55–6, 58–9, 62, 64, 71–4, 85–119, 136, 152, 159, 176–77, 182, 197, 200–202; supposed Jewish ancestry 72–3, 89–91; Algonquians 89, 113n1, 115n46; Mauguaûogs 99, 104; Narragansett 2, 85, 88, 91–4, 96, 110–12, 117n97; Pequot 1, 99; Indian towns *see* praying towns; *see also* King Philip's War
interregnum *see* commonwealth
Ireton, Henry 22, 33
Ishmael 13, 18, 122
Isaac 18, 122

Jacob 18, 122, 136
James I 15, 22, 26, 31, 47, 67
James II 27, 30, 42, 169, 196n114
Jesus *see* Christ
Johnson, Robert 55, 59
Judas 130
Justification 158

King Philip's War 104, 201–202
kingship *see* monarchy

labour 10, 94, 97, 103, 154–55, 160–61, 180–82, 198; *see also* cultivation
La Peyrère, Isaac 73
Laud, Archbishop William 23, 30–1, 86
Leade, Jane 70
legitimacy (political) 12, 27, 134, 171–72, 189, 191–92, 193n13
Levellers 22–3, 28, 33, 107; Putney Debates 28
Leverett, John 202
Le Roy, Louis 55
liberalism 7n9; 22, 42–3, 47, 52, 85, 192n2, 200, 203n1
liberty 6, 22, 25, 28, 44, 46, 53–4, 58, 109, 111, 124, 130, 132, 148, 153–54, 160, 166n54, 166n64, 169, 172–74, 184–85, 187–89, 198–99
Locke, John 5, 13, 15, 17, 19, 21, 25–26, 28, 30, 43, 46–7, 49, 52, 53–4, 58, 71, 148, 169–192, 197, 199–200, 203; *Conduct of Understanding* 176; *Essay Concerning Human Understanding* 171, 177, 179–80; *Essays on the Law of Nature* 52; *Homo ante et post Lapsum* 180–81; *A Paraphrase and Notes on the Epistles of St Paul* 16, 21, 172, 175, 179; *The Reasonableness of Christianity* 2, 17, 21, 172–73, 175, 177–81, 183, 190–91; *Some Thoughts Concerning Education* 176; *Treatises of Government* 2, 20, 22, 27, 30, 42, 53–4, 169–192, 200
Luther, Martin 12, 35n30, 60

Magna Carta 23, 109
Marxism *see* communism
Massachusetts Bay Colony 5, 32–3, 67, 86, 94, 102, 104–105, 200, 202
Mather, Richard 97
Mede, Joseph 67, 122
midrash 21

migration 26; to New World 6, 19, 26, 67–8; reverse migration 6, 68, 82n152
millenarianism *see* millennial expectation
millennial expectation 3–4, 25, 27, 66, 68, 90, 95, 107, 109, 112, 118n126, 121–26, 129–33, 159, 182, 198, 200
Milton, Katherine 145, 164n7
Milton, John 1, 5–6, 13, 16–17, 19, 21, 25, 28–9, 62, 67, 71, 105, 144–64, 175, 181–82; *Areopagitica* 15–16, 153, 155, 161, 197–202; *Of Civil Power in Ecclesiastical Causes* 32; *De Doctrina Christiana* 145, 148, 151–52, 154, 156, 158; *History of Britain* 147, 162; *Of Prelatical Episcopacy* 15; *Paradise Lost* 2, 6, 54, 66, 103, 144–64, 198, 201–202; *Paradise Regained* 155, 158–60, 201; *The Ready and Easy Way to Establish a Free Commonwealth* 22, 62–3, 144–64, 198, 200; *Reason of Church Government urged against Prelatry* 20, 160; *Of Reformation* 147, 161–62, 202; *Samson Agonistes* 201; *The Tenure of Kings and Magistrates* 56, 153; *Tractate on Education* 163
monarchy 1, 5, 19, 22, 26, 28, 31, 39n100, 42–51, 57, 62, 66, 133–34, 146–48, 162, 171–72, 174–75, 178, 187
Monck, George 168n137
Montagu, Richard 31
Morton, Thomas 96, 98, 102, 117n115
Moses 9, 14, 18, 20, 61, 63–4, 88, 90, 108, 128, 138, 147, 152
mysticism 4, 17–18, 20, 69, 120–22, 198

native Americans *see* 'Indians'
natural law 4, 13, 23, 44, 46–66, 78n65, 122, 124, 148, 152–53, 160, 177–78, 181–83, 186, 188, 199
natural rights 4, 22, 24, 47–55, 109, 188, 191
nature (state of) 10–13, 24, 33, 44, 49, 56–8, 65–6, 68, 74, 87, 95, 98–9, 102, 106, 109–112, 117n114, 122, 124, 134, 152, 180–83, 187–90, 192, 197–200
Nishohku 95
Noah 11, 44, 55, 72, 74, 89, 147, 186
Norton, James 33

Oglander, John 25
Origen 18–19
original sin *see* sin
Overall, Bishop John 45–6, 56
Owen, John 64–5, 105

Pagitt, Ephraim 29
paradise *see* Eden
Parker, Henry 22
parliament 26–32, 63, 105, 107, 120, 122, 124, 127, 137, 153
patriarchialism 3–4, 9, 50, 56, 66, 136, 169, 175, 184, 187 *see also* fatherhood
Paul, St 4, 12, 17, 19–21, 43, 60–1, 70, 156, 179, 190, 196n120
Peneovot 88, 95
Perkins, William 16, 19, 36n50, 61
Peter, Hugh 93, 96
Pocock, Mary 6, 70
polygenism 73, 89, 114n27
Poole, Matthew 66, 140n23
post-lapsarian condition *see* fallen condition
praying towns 5, 58, 62, 86–7, 94–5, 103–4, 124, 136, 201–203
pre-Adamism 73, 89
pre-destination 12, 30–1, 154; *see also* the elect
pre-lapsarian condition *see* nature (state of)
preparation theology 64, 94, 101, 107–108, 124–25, 158–59
Presbyterianism 28, 31–3, 63, 68
preservation of person 24, 33, 53, 55, 111, 122, 133–34, 173, 183, 186, 188–89, 191–92
property 4, 22, 24–5, 33, 43, 50, 53, 111, 132–33, 181, 184, 187–89, 199
providence 5, 12, 24, 50, 66–7, 93, 109, 123–24, 161–62
Pufendorf, Samuel von 49, 54, 57, 193n10
Purchas, Samuel 71–2

Index 223

Quakers 16, 33, 201, 204n5

radicals 22–3, 25, 28–9, 67, 69, 201; 'elite radicalism' 27, *see also* Diggers, Levellers, Ranters
Ralegh, Walter 56, 72–73
Ranters 23
reason 3, 15–16, 23, 36n34, 48, 49, 59–61, 70, 80n112, 125, 140n40, 152, 183, 185, 188, 190, 192, 199
redemption 1, 3–4, 12–13, 63, 65, 68, 89, 108, 110, 130, 132, 147–48, 157, 178, 182, 203
Reformation 12, 15, 28–9, 31–3, 60, 63, 66–7, 118n132, 161, 169
republicanism 1, 22, 28, 146–48, 157, 201
restoration (eschatological) 4, 13, 112, 121, 123, 125, 130, 132, 181, 203
restoration (of monarchy) 5, 86, 144–45
Revelation 11, 20, 66, 108, 120, 126
revolution (1689) 5, 189
Rhode Island and Providence Plantations 5, 87, 96, 111, 201
Rollock, Robert 64
Rossier, James 96
Rous, Francis 33
royalists 42–53
Rutherford, Samuel 62
Rye House Plot 30, 42

Salkeld, John 51
Saltmarsh, John 16, 69–70, 122
Satan 14, 21, 122, 146, 149–51, 154–55, 159, 165n21
Saul 56
Scotland 7n4, 7n7; 31–2, 61, 63
Selden, John 49–50, 53–5
Shaftesbury, Anthony Ashley Cooper 1st Earl of, 30, 169
Shepherd, Thomas 113n2, 116n67
Sidney, Algernon 1, 26, 42–3, 172
sin 10–12, 111, 129, 134, 153, 176–79, 182–83
socinianism 172, 178
sola scriptura 15, 43, 48, 60
Solemn League and Covenant 63
South, Robert 48, 53
sovereignty 4, 22, 28, 43–6, 50, 57, 66, 71, 110, 185, 187, 199
Sparrow, John 69

Spinoza, Baruch 8, 84n179
Spirit 15–17, 19, 21, 36n34, 65, 121–22, 126, 132–33, 138
spiritualism 16–17, 120, 133
Stillingfleet, Edward 29
Suarez, Francesco 48–9, 55

Thorowgood, Thomas 72–3, 90, 102
Turretin, Francis 64–5, 73
Tyndale, William 13, 18
typology 18–20, 69, 105, 109, 122, 147, 157–58, 175–76; historical typology 19; spiritual typology 19–20, 99, 156–58
tyranny 132–34; resistance to tyranny 6, 14–15, 22, 27, 39n98, 44, 53, 62–3, 161, 169, 188, 192–93n10
Tyrell, James 26, 42–3, 46, 49, 59, 71, 169

Virginia Company 55–6, 116n70

Waban 88, 91–2
Warwick, Philip 45
Wequash 1, 89, 101, 116n72
Weld, Thomas 93, 96
Westminster Assembly 32, 61
Westminster Confession of Faith 61
Whaleley, William 51
Whitfield, Henry 97
Whittingham, William 13
Wildman, John 33
William III 5, 28, 30, 169–70, 200
Williams, Roger 4–5, 13, 24, 26, 29, 33, 62, 68, 71, 81n117, 85–119, 135, 138, 152, 176–77, 187, 197–203; *The Bloudy Tenent of Persecution* 20, 32, 87, 92, 100, 105, 110; *Christenings make not Christians* 87; *Examiner Defended* 100; *The Hireling Ministry None of Christ's* 15; *A Key into the Language of America* 2, 21, 58–9, 87–8; 90–3, 96, 98, 100–101, 111, 202
Winstanley, Gerrard 2, 4, 6, 13, 15–17, 20–22, 25, 27, 53, 63, 70, 73, 107, 120–138, 144, 163, 175, 182, 197–202; *Breaking of Day of God* 123, 125; *A Declaration to the Powers of England* 136; *Englands Spirit Unfoulded* 107;

Fire in the Bush 120, 134–35, 137; *The Law of Freedom in a Platform* 22, 120–21, 127–29, 133, 135–36, 138, 198–99, 201; *The Mysterie of God Concerning the Whole of Creation* 65, 120, 123–124; *The New Law of Righteousness* 120, 123–126, 130–31; *A New-yeers Gift for the Parliament and Armie* 120, 123–124, 126, 131–32; *Saints Paradice* 123, 125; *True Levellers Standard* 123, 128; *The Truth Lifting up its Head above Scandals* 120, 123, 125, 128–129, 137

Winthrop, John 26, 41n131, 67–8, 99, 102
Winthrop, John Jr 202
Wycliffe, John 67, 161